SACRED BOOKS OF THE EAST
Editor: F. Max Müller

These volumes of the Sacred Books of the East Series include translations of all the most important works of the seven non-Christian religions that have exercised a profound influence on the civilizations of the continent of Asia. The Vedic Brahmanic System claims 21 volumes, Buddhism 10, and Jainism 2; 8 volumes comprise Sacred Books of the Parsees; 2 volumes represent Islam; and 6 the two main indigenous systems of China. Translated by twenty leading authorities in the respective fields, the volumes have been edited by the late F. Max Müller. The inception, publication and the compilation of these books cover 34 years.

[ISBN: 81-208-0101-6] 50 Vols.

(Available in specially designed cartons)

VOLUMES

THE
SACRED BOOKS OF THE EAST

Translated by
VARIOUS ORIENTAL SCHOLARS

Edited by
F. MAX MÜLLER

Vol. 23

The Zend-Avesta

Translated by
JAMES DARMESTETER

PART II
The Sîrôzahs, Yasts and Nyâyis

MOTILAL BANARSIDASS PUBLISHERS
PRIVATE LIMITED • DELHI

First Published by the Oxford University Press, 1882
Reprint: Delhi, 1965, 1969, 1975, 1981, 1988, 1993, 2000

ISBN: 81-208-0124-5

Also available at:

MOTILAL BANARSIDASS

236, 9th Main III Block, Jayanagar, Bangalore 560 011
41 U.A. Bungalow Road, Jawahar Nagar, Delhi 110 007
8 Mahalaxmi Chamber, Warden Road, Mumbai 400 026
120 Royapettah High Road, Mylapore, Chennai 600 004
Sanas Plaza, 1302 Baji Rao Road, Pune 411 002
8 Camac Street, Calcutta 700 017
Ashok Rajpath, Patna 800 004
Chowk, Varanasi 221 001

UNESCO COLLECTION OF REPRESENTATIVE WORKS—Indian Series.
*This book has been accepted in the Indian Translation Series of the UNESCO
Collection of Representative Works, jointly sponsored by the United
Nations Educational, Scientific and Cultural Organization
(UNESCO) and the Government of India*

Printed in India
BY JAINENDRA PRAKASH JAIN AT SHRI JAINENDRA PRESS,
A-45 NARAINA, PHASE I, NEW DELHI 110 028
AND PUBLISHED BY NARENDRA PRAKASH JAIN FOR
MOTILAL BANARSIDASS PUBLISHERS PRIVATE LIMITED,
BUNGALOW ROAD, DELHI 110 007

RASHTRAPATI BHAVAN,
NEW DELHI-4
June 10, 1962

I am very glad to know that the Sacred Books of the East, published years ago by the Clarendon Press, Oxford, which have been out-of-print for a number of years, will now be available to all students of religion and philosophy. The enterprise of the publishers is commendable and I hope the books will be widely read.

S. RADHAKRISHNAN

PUBLISHER'S NOTE

First, the man distinguished between eternal and perishable. Later he discovered within himself the germ of the Eternal. This discovery was an epoch in the history of the human mind and the *East was the first to discover it.*

To watch in the Sacred Books of the East the dawn of this religious consciousness of man, must always remain one of the most inspiring and hallowing sights in the whole history of the world. In order to have a solid foundation for a comparative study of the Religions of the East, we must have before all things, complete and thoroughly faithful translation of their Sacred Books in which some of the ancient sayings were preserved because they were so true and so striking that they could not be forgotten. They contained eternal truths, expressed for the first time in human language.

With profoundest reverence for Dr. S. Radhakrishnan, President of India, who inspired us for the task; our deep sense of gratitude for Dr. C. D. Deshmukh & Dr. D. S. Kothari, for encouraging assistance; esteemed appreciation of UNESCO for the warm endorsement of the cause; and finally with indebtedness to Dr. H. Rau, Director, Max Müller Bhawan, New Delhi, in procuring us the texts of the Series for reprint, we humbly conclude.

PREFATORY NOTE TO THE NEW EDITION

Since 1948 the United Nations Educational, Scientific and Cultural Organisation (UNESCO), upon the recommendation of the General Assembly of the United Nations, has been concerned with facilitating the translation of the works most representative of the culture of certain of its Member States, and, in particular, those of Asia.

One of the major difficulties confronting this programme is the lack of translators having both the qualifications and the time to undertake translations of the many outstanding books meriting publication. To help overcome this difficulty in part, UNESCO's advisers in this field (a panel of experts convened every other year by the International Council for Philosophy and Humanistic Studies), have recommended that many worthwhile translations published during the 19th century, and now impossible to find except in a limited number of libraries, should be brought back into print in low-priced editions, for the use of students and of the general public. The experts also pointed out that in certain cases, even though there might be in existence more recent and more accurate translations endowed with a more modern apparatus of scholarship, a number of pioneer works of the greatest value and interest to students of Eastern religions also merited republication.

This point of view was warmly endorsed by the Indian National Academy of Letters (Sahitya Akademi), and the Indian National Commission for UNESCO.

It is in the spirit of these recommendations that this work from the famous series "Sacred Books of the East" is now once again being made available to the general public as part of the UNESCO Collection of Representative Works.

CONTENTS.

INTRODUCTION.

THE present volume contains a translation of the Sîrôzahs and Yasts, and of the Nyâyis. This part of the Avesta treats chiefly of the mythical and legendary lore of Zoroastrianism.

For a satisfactory translation of these texts, the etymological and comparative method is generally considered as the best or as the only possible one, on account of the entire absence of any traditional interpretation. I have tried, however, to reduce the sphere of etymological guesswork to its narrowest limits, with the help of different Pahlavi, Persian, and Sanskrit translations, which are as yet unpublished, and have been neglected by former translators. I found such translations for the Sîrôzahs, for Yasts I, VI, VII, XI, XXIII, XXIV, and for the Nyâyis[1] (besides the already published translations of Yasts XXI and XXII).

Of the remaining Yasts, which are mostly of an epical character, there is no direct translation available; but a close comparison of the legends in Firdausi's Shâh Nâmah seems to throw some light, even as regards philological points, on not a few obscure and important passages. This has enabled me, I believe, to restore a few myths to their original form, and to frame a more correct idea of others[2].

In this volume, as in the preceding one, I have to thank Mr. West for his kind assistance in making my translation more readable, as well as for valuable hints in the interpretation of several passages.

JAMES DARMESTETER.

PARIS,
13 December, 1882.

---

[1] These translations have been edited in our Études Iraniennes, II, 253 seq. (Paris, Vieweg, 1883).
[2] See ibidem, II, 206 seq.

YASTS AND SÎRÔZAHS.

YASTS AND SÎRÔZAHS.

THE word yast, in Zend yêsti, means properly 'the act of worshipping,' the performance of the yasna; and it is often used in Parsi tradition as synonymous with yasna. But it has also been particularly applied to a certain number of writings in which the several Izeds are praised and magnified. These writings are generally of a higher poetical and epical character than the rest of the Avesta, and are most valuable records of the old mythology and historical legends of Iran.

The Parsis believe that formerly every Amshaspand and every Ized had his particular Yast, but we now possess only twenty Yasts and fragments of another [1]. The writings known as Yast fragments, the Âfrîn Zartust, and Vîstâsp Yast (printed as Yasts XXI, XXII, XXIII, XXIV in Westergaard's edition), are not proper Yasts, and have no liturgical character; they are not devoted to the praise of any Ized.

The order in which the Yasts have been arranged by the Parsis follows exactly the order of the Sîrôzah, which is the proper introduction to the Yasts.

SÎRÔZAH.

Sîrôzah means 'thirty days:' it is the name of a prayer composed of thirty invocations addressed to the several Izeds who preside over the thirty days of the month.

There are two Sîrôzahs, but the only difference between them is that the formulas in the former are shorter [2], and there is also, occasionally, some difference in the epithets, which are fuller in the latter.

---

[1] The Bahman Yast (see Yt. I, §§ 24 and following).

[2] In the greater Sîrôzah the names of the gods invoked are introduced with the word yazamaidê, 'we sacrifice to;' in the lesser Sîrôzah there is no introductory word, the word khshnaothra, 'propitiation,' being understood, as can be seen from the introductory formulas to the several Yasts.

In India the Sîrôzah is recited in honour of the dead, on the thirtieth day after the death, on the thirtieth day of the sixth month, on the thirtieth day of the twelfth month, and then every year on the thirtieth day from the anniversary day (Anquetil, Zend-Avesta, II, 315).

The correspondence between the formulas of the Sîrôzah and the Ya*s*ts is as follows:

1.	Ormazd.	Ormazd Ya*s*t (I, 1–23).
2.	Bahman.	Bahman Ya*s*t (I, 24–33).
3.	Ardibehe*s*t.	Ardibehe*s*t Ya*s*t (III).
4.	Shahrêvar.	
5.	Sapendârmad.	
6.	Khordâd.	Khordâd Ya*s*t (IV).
7.	Murdâd.	
8.	Dai pa Âdar.	
9.	Âdar.	
10.	Âbân.	Âbân Yâ*s*t (V).
11.	Khorshêd.	Khorshêd Ya*s*t (VI).
12.	Mâh.	Mâh Ya*s*t (VII).
13.	Tîr.	Tîr Ya*s*t (VIII).
14.	Gô*s*.	Gô*s* Ya*s*t (IX).
15.	Dai pa Mihir.	
16.	Mihir.	Mihir Ya*s*t (X .
17.	Srôsh.	Srôsh Ya*s*t (XI).
18.	Rashn.	Rashn Ya*s*t (XII).
19.	Farvardîn.	Farvardîn Ya*s*t (XIII).
20.	Bahrâm.	Bahrâm Ya*s*t (XIV).
21.	Râm.	Râm Ya*s*t (XV).
22.	Bâd.	
23.	Dai pa Dîn.	
24.	Dîn.	Dîn Ya*s*t (XVI).
25.	Ard.	Ashi Ya*s*t (XVII).
26.	Â*s*tâd.	Â*s*tâd Ya*s*t (XVIII).
27.	Âsmân.	
28.	Zemyâd.	Zemyâd Ya*s*t (XIX).
29.	Mahraspand.	
30.	Anêrân.	

The Ya*s*ts that have been lost are, therefore, those of Khshathra-vairya, Spe*n*ta-Ârmaiti, Aminetâ*t*, Âtar, Vâta, Asman, Mãthra-Spe*n*ta, and Anaghra rao*k*au. The second Ya*s*t, or Ya*s*t of the seven Amshaspands, appears to have been no independent Ya*s*t: it was common to all the seven Ya*s*ts devoted to the several

Amshaspands, and, accordingly, it is recited on the first seven days of the month. One might suppose that it was originally a part of the Ormazd Ya*st*, as the Amesha-Spe*n*tas are invoked in company with Ahura Mazda (Sîrôzah 1, 8, 15, 23). There may, indeed, have been several Ya*st*s for one and the same formula of the Sîrôzah, as in all of these formulas more than one Ized are invoked: this would apply not only to the Ya*st* of the seven Amshaspands, but also to the Vana*nt* Ya*st* (Ya*st* XX), which, in that case, ought to follow the Tîr Ya*st* (see Sîrôzah 13).

Not every Ya*st*, however, is devoted to the Ized whose name it bears: thus the Ardibehe*st* Ya*st* is mostly devoted to Airyaman; the Râm-Ya*st* and the Zemyâd-Ya*st* are devoted to Vayu and to the *Hv*arenô: but Airyaman, Vayu, and the *Hv*arenô are invoked in the same Sîrôzah formulas as Ardibehe*st*, Râm, and Zemyâd, and a Ya*st* is named from the opening name in the correspondent Sîrôzah formula.

The systematic order so apparent in the Sîrôzah pervades the rest of the liturgy to a great extent: the enumeration of Izeds in Yasna XVII, 12–42 (XVI, 3–6) follows exactly the order of the Sîrôzah, except that it gives only the first name of each formula; and the question may be raised whether this passage in the Yasna is taken from the Sîrôzah, or whether the Sîrôzah is developed from the Yasna.

The very idea of the Sîrôzah, that is to say the attribution of each of the thirty days of the month to certain gods, seems to have been borrowed from the Semites: the tablets found in the library of Assurbanipal contain an Assyrian Sîrôzah, that is, a complete list of the Assyrian gods that preside over the thirty days of the month[1].

SÎRÔZAH I.

1. Ormazd.

To Ahura Mazda, bright and glorious[2], and to the Amesha-Spe*n*tas[3].

---

[1] J. Halévy, Revue des Études Juives, 1881, October, p. 188.
[2] See Yt. I, 1–23.
[3] See Yt. II.

2. Bahman.

To Vohu-Manô[1]; to Peace[2], whose breath is
friendly[3], and who is more powerful to destroy than
all other creatures[4]; to the heavenly Wisdom[5], made
by Mazda; and to the Wisdom acquired through the
ear[5], made by Mazda.

3. Ardibehe*s*t.

To Asha-Vahi*s*ta, the fairest[6]; to the much-
desired Airyaman, made by Mazda[7]; to the instrument made by Mazda[8]; and to the good Saoka[9],
with eyes of love[10], made by Mazda and holy.

---

[1] See Yt. I, 24–33.

[2] Âkh*s*ti does not so much mean Peace as the power that
secures peace; see note 4.

[3] Hãm-vai*n*ti, from hãm-vâ (Yt. X, 141); possibly from van,
to strike: 'Peace that smites.'

[4] Taradhâtem anyâi*s* dâmãn, interpreted: tarvînîtârtûm
min zakî ân dâmân pun anâshtîh akár kartan (Phl. Comm.),
'more destroying than other creatures, to make Non-peace (Anâ-
kh*s*ti) powerless.'

[5] Âsnya khratu, the inborn intellect, intuition, contrasted with
gaoshô-srûta khratu, the knowledge acquired by hearing and
learning. There is between the two nearly the same relation
as between the parâvidyâ and aparâvidyâ in Brahmanism, the
former reaching Brahma in se (parabrahma), the latter *s*abda-
brahma, the word-Brahma (Brahma as taught and revealed).
The Mobeds of later times interpreted their name Magû*s*, مغوش,
as meaning, 'men without ears,' ماگوش, 'pour insinuer que leur
Docteur avait puisé toute sa science dans le ciel et qu'il ne l'avait
pas apprise par l'ouïe comme les autres hommes' (Chardin,
III, 130; ed. Amsterdam).

[6] See Yt. III.   [7] See Vend. XXII.

[8] The 'golden instrument' mentioned in Nyâyi*s* I, 8.

[9] A personification of the Ormazdean weal; cf. Vend. XXII,
3 [8], and Yt. XIII, 42.

[10] Vouru-dôithra, kâmak dôisr; she is 'the genius of the good

4. Shahrêvar.

To Khshathra-vairya; to the metals[1]; to Mercy and Charity.

5. Sapendârmad.

To the good Spe*n*ta-Ârmaiti[2], and to the good Râta[3], with eyes of love, made by Mazda and holy.

6. Khordâd.

To Haurvatât[4], the master; to the prosperity of the seasons and to the years, the masters of holiness.

7. Murdâd.

To Ameretât[5], the master; to fatness and flocks; to the plenty of corn; and to the powerful Gaokerena[6], made by Mazda.

(At the gâh[7] Hâvan): to Mithra[8], the lord of wide pastures and to Râma *Hv*âstra[9].

(At the gâh Rapithwin): to Asha-Vahi*s*ta and to Âtar[10], the son of Ahura Mazda[11].

---

eye, mînôî hu*k*a*s*mîh' (Vend. XIX, 36 [123]), the reverse of the evil eye (Yasna LXVII, 62 [LXVIII, 22]; cf. Études Iraniennes, II, 182).

[1] Vend. Introd. IV, 33; Ormazd et Ahriman, §§ 202–206.

[2] Ibid.   [3] Vend. Introd. IV, 30.

[4] See Yt. IV.   [5] See Vend. Introd. IV, 34.

[6] The white Hôm, or plant of immortality; see Vend. Introd. IV, 28.

[7] See Gâhs.   [8] See Yt. X.

[9] See Yt. XV. Cf. Yasna I, 3 (7–9), where Mithra and Râma are invoked in company with the genius of the Hâvani period of the day.

[10] The Genius of Fire.

[11] Cf. Yasna I, 4 (10–12), where Asha-Vahi*s*ta and Âtar are invoked in company with the genius of the Rapithwin period of the day.

(At the gâh Uzîren): to Apâm Napâ*t* [1], the tall lord, and to the water made by Mazda [2].

(At the gâh Aiwisrûthrem): to the Fravashis [3] of the faithful, and to the females that bring forth flocks of males [4]; to the prosperity of the seasons; to the well-shapen and tall-formed Strength, to Verethraghna [5], made by Ahura, and to the crushing Ascendant [6].

(At the gâh Ushahin) : to the holy, devout, fiend-smiting Sraosha [7], who makes the world grow; to Rashnu Razi*s*ta [8], and to Ar*s*tâ*t* [9], who makes the world grow, who makes the world increase [10].

8. Dai pa Âdar [11].

To the Maker Ahura Mazda, bright and glorious, and to the Amesha-Spe*n*tas.

---

[1] Literally 'the Son of the Waters;' he was originally the Fire of lightning, as born in the clouds (like the Vedic Apâm napât); he still appears in that character, Yt. VIII, 34; he is for that reason 'the lord of the females' because the waters were considered as females (cf. Yasna XXXVIII, 1 [2]). But, as napâ*t* means also 'navel' (the same words having often the two meanings of 'navel' and 'offspring;' cf. nâbhi in the Vedas and the Zend nâfyô, 'offspring,' from nâfa 'navel'), Apâm Napâ*t* was interpreted as 'the spring of the waters, the navel of the waters,' which was supposed to be at the source of the Arvand (the Tigris; Neriosengh ad Yasna I, 5 [15]); cf. Yt. V, 72.

[2] Cf. Yasna I, 5 [13–15].   [3] See Yt. XIII.

[4] Perhaps better : 'to the flocks of Fravashis of the faithful, men and women.'

[5] The Genius of Victory; see Yt. XIV.

[6] Cf. Yasna I, 6 [16–19].

[7] See Yt. XI and Vend. Introd. IV, 31; Farg. XVIII, 14 seq.

[8] The Genius of Truth; see Yt. XII.

[9] Truth; see Yt. XVIII.   [10] Cf. Yasna I, 7 [20–23].

[11] The day before Âdar (Dai is the Persian دی, 'yesterday,' which is the same word as the Sanskrit hyas, Latin heri). The eighth, fifteenth, and twenty-third days of the month are under the

9. Âdar.

To Âtar, the son of Ahura Mazda; to the Glory and to the Weal, made by Mazda; to the Glory of the Aryas [1], made by Mazda; to the awful Glory of the Kavis [2], made by Mazda.

To Âtar, the son of Ahura Mazda; to king Husravah [3]; to the lake of Husravah [4]; to Mount Âsnava*nt* [5], made by Mazda; to Lake *K*aê*k*asta [6], made by Mazda; to the Glory of the Kavis, made by Mazda [7].

rule of Ahura and the Amesha-Spe*n*tas, like the first day; they have therefore no name of their own and are named from the day that follows. The month was divided into four weeks, the first two numbering seven days, the last two numbering eight.

[1] Or better 'the Glories of the Aryas' (Eramde*sa*srî*n*âm): the Glory or *Hv*arenô (Vend. Introd. IV, 11, p. lxiii, note 1) is threefold, according as it illuminates the priest, the warrior, or the husbandman. Ya*s*t XIX is devoted to the praise of the *Hv*arenô.

[2] Or 'the awful kingly glory:' Kavi means a king, but it is particularly used of the kings belonging to the second and most celebrated of the two mythical dynasties of Iran. The Kavis succeeded the Paradhâta or Pêshdâdians, and Darius Codomanes was supposed to be the last of them. For an enumeration of the principal Kavis, see Yt. XIII, 132 seq. The *Hv*arenô alluded to in this clause is the *Hv*arenô of the priest; 'it is the fire known as Âdaraprâ [Âdar Frobâ]; or better Âdar Farnbag: see Études Iraniennes, II, 84; its object is the science of the priests; by its help priests become learned and clever' (Sanskrit transl. to the Âtash Nyâyish).

[3] See Yt. V, 41, note.

[4] See Yt. XIX, 56.

[5] A mountain in Adarbaigân (Bundahi*s* XII, 26), where king Husravah settled the fire Gushasp.

[6] See Yt. V, 49.

[7] The glory of the warriors, the fire known as Âdar Gushasp or Gushnasp; with its help king Husravah destroyed the idol-temples near Lake *K*ê*k*ast, and he settled it on Mount Âsnava*nt* (Bund. XVII, 7).

To Âtar, the son of Ahura Mazda; to Mount
Raêva*nt* [1], made by Mazda; to the Glory of the
Kavis, made by Mazda [2].

To Âtar, the beneficent, the warrior; the God
who is a full source of Glory, the God who is a full
source of healing.

To Âtar, the son of Ahura Mazda, with all Âtars [3];
to the God Nairyô-Sangha [4], who dwells in the
navel of kings [5].

10. Âbân.

To the good Waters, made by Mazda; to the
holy water-spring Ardvi Anâhita [6]; to all waters
made by Mazda; to all plants made by Mazda.

11. Khorshêd.

To the undying, shining, swift-horsed Sun [7].

12. Mâh.

To the Moon that keeps in it the seed of the
Bull [8]; to the only-created Bull [9]; to the Bull of
many species [10].

---

[1] A mountain in Khorâsân on which the Burzîn fire is settled
(Bund. XII, 18).

[2] 'The fire known as Âdarabura*g*âmihira [Âdar Burzîn Mihir];
its object is the science of husbandry.' King Gu*s*tâsp established
it on Mount Raêva*nt* (Bund. XVII, 8).

[3] All sorts of fires. See another classification, Yasna XVII,
11 [63–67] and Bundahi*s* XVII, 1.

[4] See Vend. XXII, 7.

[5] The fire Nairyô-sangha, as the messenger of Ahura, burns
hereditarily in the bosom of his earthly representative, the king.

[6] See Yt. V.　　　　　　　　　　[7] See Yt. VI.

[8] See Yt. VII and Vend. XXI, 1, text and note.

[9] Aêvô-dâta gâu*s*; see Vend. l. l. and Bundahi*s* IV.

[10] Pouru-saredha gâu*s*: the couple born of the seed of the

13. Tîr.

To Tistrya [1], the bright and glorious star; to the powerful Satavaêsa [2], made by Mazda, who pushes waters forward ; to the stars, made by Mazda, that have in them the seed of the waters, the seed of the earth, the seed of the plants [3] ; to the star Vanant [4], made by Mazda; to those stars that are seven in number, the Haptôiringas [4], made by Mazda, glorious and healing.

14. Gôs.

To the body of the Cow, to the soul of the Cow, to the powerful Drvâspa [5], made by Mazda and holy.

15. Dai pa Mihir.

To the Maker Ahura Mazda, bright and glorious, and to the Amesha-Spentas.

16. Mihir.

To Mithra [6], the lord of wide pastures, who has a thousand ears and ten thousand eyes, a God invoked by his own name ; to Râma Hvâstra [7].

17. Srôsh.

To the holy, strong Sraosha [8], who is the incarnate Word, a mighty-speared and lordly God.

18. Rashn.

To Rashnu Razista [9] ; to Arstât [10], who makes the

---

only-created Bull, and from which arose two hundred and eighty species (Bund. XI, 3).

[1] See Yt. VIII.	[2] See Yt. VIII, 9.
[3] See Yt. XII, 29–31.	[4] See Yt. VIII, 12.
[5] See Yt. IX.	[6] See Yt. X.
[7] See Yt. XV.	[8] See Yt. XI.
[9] See Yt. XII.	[10] See Yt. XVIII.

world grow, who makes the world increase; to the
true-spoken speech, that makes the world grow.

19. Farvardîn.

To the awful, overpowering Fravashis of the
holy ones[1].

20. Bahrâm.

To the well-shapen, tall-formed Strength; to
Verethraghna[2], made by Ahura; to the crushing
Ascendant.

21. Râm.

To Râma *H*vâstra[3]; to Vayu[3], who works
highly[4] and is more powerful to destroy than all
other creatures: to that part of thee, O Vayu, that
belongs to Spe*n*ta-Mainyu[5]; to the sovereign Sky,
to the Boundless Time[6], to the sovereign Time of
the long Period[6].

22. Bâd.

To the bounteous Wind, that blows below, above,
before, and behind; to the manly Courage.

23. Dai pa Dîn.

To the Maker, Ahura Mazda, bright and glorious;
to the Amesha-Spe*n*tas.

24. Dîn.

To the most right *K*ista[7], made by Mazda and
holy; to the good Law[7] of the worshippers of
Mazda.

---

[1] See Yt. XIII.
[2] See Yt. XIV.
[3] See Yt. XV.
[4] Powerfully.
[5] See Yt. XV, 1.
[6] See Vend. Introd. IV, 39 and lxxxii, 1.
[7] See Yt. XVI.

25. Ard.

To Ashi Vanguhi[1]; to the good Kisti[2]; to the good Erethe[3]; to the good Rasãstât[4]; to the Weal and Glory, made by Mazda; to Pârendi[5], of the light chariot; to the Glory of the Aryas made by Mazda; to the kingly Glory made by Mazda; to that Glory that cannot be forcibly seized[6], made by Mazda; to the Glory of Zarathustra, made by Mazda.

26. Âstâd.

To Arstât[7], who makes the world grow; to Mount Ushi-darena[8], made by Mazda, the seat of holy happiness.

27. Âsmân.

To the high, powerful Heavens; to the bright, all-happy, blissful abode of the holy ones.

28. Zemyâd[9].

To the bounteous Earth; to these places, to these fields; to Mount Ushi-darena[8], made by Mazda, the seat of holy happiness; to all the mountains made by Mazda, that are seats of holy happiness, of full happiness; to the kingly Glory made by Mazda;

---

[1] See Yt. XVII.

[2] Religious knowledge, wisdom (fargânak; nirvânagnânam).

[3] Thought (kittam). [4] Thoughtfulness (kittasthiti).

[5] The keeper of treasures; cf. Vend. Introd. IV, 30.

[6] Ahvaretem hvarenô: 'the hvarenô of the priests: that it cannot be forcibly seized means that one must take possession of it through virtue and righteous exertion' (Neriosengh and Pahl. Comm. to Yasna I and IV, 14 [42]).

[7] See Yt. XVIII. [8] See Yt. I, 31, text and note.

[9] See Yt. XIX.

to that Glory that cannot be forcibly seized[1], made by Mazda.

29. Mahraspand.

To the holy, righteousness-performing Mãthra Speñta[2]; to the Law opposed to the Daêvas, the Law of Zarathustra; to the long-traditional teaching[3]; to the good Law of the worshippers of Mazda; to the Devotion to the Mãthra Speñta; to the understanding that keeps[4] the Law of the worshippers of Mazda; to the knowledge of the Mãthra Speñta; to the heavenly Wisdom made by Mazda; to the Wisdom acquired through the ear[5] and made by Mazda.

30. Anêrân.

To the eternal[6] and sovereign luminous space[7]; to the bright Garô-nmâna[8]; to the sovereign place of eternal Weal[9]; to the Kinvat-bridge[10], made by Mazda; to the tall lord Apãm Napât[11] and to the water made by Mazda; to Haoma[12], of holy birth; to the pious and good Blessing; to the awful cursing thought of the wise[13]; to all the holy Gods of the

---

[1] See p. 11, note 6.　　[2] The Holy Word.

[3] Daregha upayana: the Genius of Teaching (sixâm adrisya-rûpiñîm; Yasna I, 12 [40]).

[4] In memory.　　[5] See above, § 2.

[6] Or boundless (anaghra; the Parsi anêrân).

[7] Or Infinite Light; see Vend. Introd. p. lxxxii and Bund. I. 2.

[8] The abode of Ahura Mazda; see Vend. XIX, 32.

[9] See Vend. XIX, 36, note 1.

[10] See Vend. XIX, 29, note 3.

[11] See Sîrôzah II, 7, note.

[12] See Vend. Introd. IV, 28.

[13] 'The blessing (âfriti) is twofold: one by thought, one by words; the blessing by words is the more powerful; the curse

heavenly world and of the material one; to the awful, overpowering Fravashis of the faithful, to the Fravashis of the first men of the law, to the Fravashis of the next-of-kin [1]; to every God invoked by his own name [2].

SÎRÔZAH II.

1. Ormazd.

We sacrifice unto the bright and glorious Ahura Mazda; we sacrifice unto the Amesha-Spentas, the all-ruling, the all-beneficent.

2. Bahman.

We sacrifice unto Vohu-Manô, the Amesha-Spenta; we sacrifice unto Peace, whose breath is friendly, and who is more powerful to destroy than all other creatures. We sacrifice unto the heavenly Wisdom, made by Mazda; we sacrifice unto the Wisdom acquired through the ear, made by Mazda.

3. Ardibehest.

We sacrifice unto Asha-Vahista, the fairest, the Amesha-Spenta; we sacrifice unto the much-desired Airyaman; we sacrifice unto the instrument made by Mazda; we sacrifice unto the good Saoka, with eyes of love, made by Mazda and holy.

(upamana) in thought is the more powerful' (Neriosengh ad Yasna I, 15 [44]). Upamana is the same as the Vedic manyu.

[1] See Yt. XIII, o.

[2] In contradistinction to general invocations.

4. Shahrêvar.

We sacrifice unto Khshathra-Vairya, the Amesha-Spenta; we sacrifice unto the metals; we sacrifice unto Mercy and Charity.

5. Sapendârmad.

We sacrifice unto the good Spenta Ârmaiti; we sacrifice unto the good Râta, with eyes of love, made by Mazda and holy.

6. Khordâd.

We sacrifice unto Haurvatât, the Amesha-Spenta; we sacrifice unto the prosperity of the seasons. We sacrifice unto the years, the holy and masters of holiness.

7. Murdâd.

We sacrifice unto Ameretât, the Amesha-Spenta; we sacrifice unto fatness and flocks; we sacrifice unto the plenty of corn; we sacrifice unto the powerful Gaokerena, made by Mazda.

(At the gâh Hâvan): We sacrifice unto Mithra, the lord of wide pastures; we sacrifice unto Râma Hvâstra.

(At the gâh Rapithwin) : We sacrifice unto Asha-Vahista and unto Âtar, the son of Ahura Mazda.

(At the gâh Uzîren): We sacrifice unto Apãm Napât, the swift-horsed, the tall and shining lord, the lord of the females; we sacrifice unto the water made by Mazda and holy.

(At the gâh Aiwisrûthrem) : We sacrifice unto the good, powerful, beneficent Fravashis of the holy ones; we sacrifice unto the females that bring forth flocks of males; we sacrifice unto the thrift of the seasons; we sacrifice unto the well-shapen and tall-formed Strength; we sacrifice unto Verethraghna, made by Mazda; we sacrifice unto the crushing Ascendant.

(At the gâh Ushahin): We sacrifice unto the holy, tall-formed, fiend-smiting Sraosha, who makes the world grow, the holy and master of holiness; we sacrifice unto Rashnu Razi*s*ta; we sacrifice unto Ar*s*tâ*t*, who makes the world grow, who makes the world increase.

8. Dai pa Âdar.

We sacrifice unto the Maker Ahura Mazda, the bright and glorious; we sacrifice unto the Amesha-Spe*n*tas, the all-ruling, the all-beneficent.

9. Âdar.

We sacrifice unto Âtar, the son of Ahura Mazda; we sacrifice unto the Glory, made by Mazda; we sacrifice unto the Weal, made by Mazda; we sacrifice unto the Glory of the Aryas, made by Mazda; we sacrifice unto the awful Glory of the Kavis, made by Mazda.

We sacrifice unto Âtar, the son of Ahura Mazda; we sacrifice unto king Husravah; we sacrifice unto the lake of Husravah; we sacrifice unto Mount Âs-nava*nt*, made by Mazda; we sacrifice unto Lake *K*aê*k*asta, made by Mazda; we sacrifice unto the awful Glory of the Kavis, made by Mazda.

We sacrifice unto Âtar, the son of Ahura Mazda; we sacrifice unto Mount Raêva*nt*, made by Mazda; we sacrifice unto the awful Glory of the Kavis, made by Mazda.

We sacrifice unto Âtar, the son of Ahura Mazda; we sacrifice unto Âtar, the beneficent, the warrior.

We sacrifice unto that God, who is a full source of glory. We sacrifice unto that God, who is a full source of healing.

We sacrifice unto Âtar, the son of Ahura Mazda; we sacrifice unto all Fires; we sacrifice unto the God, Nairyô-Sangha, who dwells in the navel of kings.

10. Âbân.

We sacrifice unto the good Waters, made by Mazda and holy; we sacrifice unto the holy water-spring Ardvi Anâhita; we sacrifice unto all waters, made by Mazda and holy; we sacrifice unto all plants, made by Mazda and holy.

11. Khorshêd.

We sacrifice unto the bright, undying, shining, swift-horsed Sun.

12. Mâh.

We sacrifice unto the Moon that keeps in it the seed of the Bull. We sacrifice unto the Soul and Fravashi of the only-created Bull; we sacrifice unto the Soul and Fravashi of the Bull of many species.

13. Tîr.

We sacrifice unto Tistrya, the bright and glorious star; we sacrifice unto the powerful Satavaêsa, made by Mazda, who pushes waters forward; we sacrifice unto all the Stars that have in them the seed of the waters; we sacrifice unto all the Stars that have in them the seed of the earth; we sacrifice unto all the Stars that have in them the seeds of the plants; we sacrifice unto the Star Vanant, made by Mazda; we sacrifice unto those stars that are seven in number, the Haptôiringas, made by Mazda, glorious and healing; in order to oppose the Yâtus and Pairikas.

14. Gôs.

We sacrifice unto the soul of the bounteous Cow; we sacrifice unto the powerful Drvâspa, made by Mazda and holy.

15. Dai pa Mihir.

We sacrifice unto the Maker Ahura Mazda, the bright and glorious; we sacrifice unto the Amesha-Spentas, the all-ruling, the all-beneficent.

16. Mihir.

We sacrifice unto Mithra, the lord of wide pastures, who has a thousand ears and ten thousand eyes, a God invoked by his own name; we sacrifice unto Râma Hvâstra.

17. Srôsh.

We sacrifice unto the holy, tall-formed, fiend-smiting, world-increasing Sraosha, holy and master of holiness.

18. Rashn.

We sacrifice unto Rashnu Razista; we sacrifice unto Arstât, who makes the world grow, who makes the world increase; we sacrifice unto the true-spoken speech that makes the world grow.

19. Farvardîn.

We sacrifice unto the good, strong, beneficent Fravashis of the holy ones.

20. Bahrâm.

We sacrifice unto the well-shapen, tall-formed Strength; we sacrifice unto Verethraghna, made by Ahura; we sacrifice unto the crushing Ascendant.

21. Râm.

We sacrifice unto Râma *H*vâstra; we sacrifice unto the holy Vayu; we sacrifice unto Vayu, who works highly and is more powerful to destroy than all other creatures. Unto that part of thee do we sacrifice, O Vayu, that belongs to Spe*n*ta-Mainyu. We sacrifice unto the sovereign Sky; we sacrifice unto the Boundless Time; we sacrifice unto the sovereign Time of the long Period.

22. Bâd.

We sacrifice unto the beneficent, bounteous Wind; we sacrifice unto the wind that blows below; we sacrifice unto the wind that blows above; we sacrifice unto the wind that blows before; we sacrifice unto the wind that blows behind. We sacrifice unto the manly Courage.

23. Dai pa Dîn.

We sacrifice unto the Maker Ahura Mazda, the bright and glorious; we sacrifice unto the Amesha-Spe*n*tas.

24. Dîn.

We sacrifice unto the most right *K*ista, made by Mazda and holy; we sacrifice unto the good Law of the worshippers of Mazda.

25. Ard.

We sacrifice unto Ashi Vanguhi, the bright, high, strong, tall-formed, and merciful; we sacrifice unto the Glory made by Mazda; we sacrifice unto the Weal made by Mazda. We sacrifice unto Pâre*n*di, of the light chariot; we sacrifice unto the Glory of the Aryas, made by Mazda; we sacrifice unto the awful kingly Glory, made by Mazda; we sacrifice unto that awful Glory, that cannot be forcibly seized, made by Mazda; we sacrifice unto the Glory of Zarathustra, made by Mazda.

26. Âstâd.

We sacrifice unto Arstât, who makes the world grow; we sacrifice unto Mount Ushi-darena, made by Mazda, a God of holy happiness.

27. Âsmân.

We sacrifice unto the shining Heavens; we sacrifice unto the bright, all-happy, blissful abode of the holy ones.

28. Zemyâd.

We sacrifice unto the Earth, a beneficent God; we sacrifice unto these places, unto these fields; we sacrifice unto Mount Ushi-darena, made by Mazda, a God of holy happiness; we sacrifice unto all the mountains, that are seats of holy happiness, of full happiness, made by Mazda, the holy and masters of holiness; we sacrifice unto the awful kingly Glory, made by Mazda; we sacrifice unto the awful Glory that cannot be forcibly seized, made by Mazda.

29. Mahraspand.

We sacrifice unto the Mãthra Spenta, of high glory; we sacrifice unto the Law opposed to the Daêvas; we sacrifice unto the Law of Zarathustra; we sacrifice unto the long-traditional teaching; we sacrifice unto the good Law of the worshippers of Mazda; we sacrifice unto the Devotion to the Mãthra Spenta; we sacrifice unto the understanding that keeps the Law of the worshippers of Mazda; we sacrifice unto

the knowledge of the Mãthra Spe*n*ta; we sacrifice
unto the heavenly Wisdom, made by Mazda; we
sacrifice unto the Wisdom acquired through the
ear and made by Mazda.

30. Anêrân.

We sacrifice unto the eternal and sovereign luminous space; we sacrifice unto the bright Garô-
nmâna; we sacrifice unto the sovereign place of
eternal Weal; we sacrifice unto the *K*inva*t*-bridge,
made by Mazda; we sacrifice unto Apãm Napâ*t*, the
swift-horsed, the high and shining lord, who has
many wives; and we sacrifice unto the water, made
by Mazda and holy; we sacrifice unto the golden
and tall Haoma; we sacrifice unto the enlivening
Haoma, who makes the world grow; we sacrifice
unto Haoma, who keeps death far away; we sacrifice unto the pious and good Blessing; we sacrifice
unto the awful, powerful, cursing thought of the wise,
a God; we sacrifice unto all the holy Gods of the
heavenly world; we sacrifice unto all the holy Gods
of the material world.

I praise, I invoke, I meditate upon, and we sacrifice unto the good, strong, beneficent Fravashis of
the holy ones [1].

---

[1] Cf. Yasna XXVI, 1.

I. ORMAZD YAST.

The Ormazd Yast, properly so called, ends with § 23. The rest of the Yast, from § 24 to the end, is wanting in several manuscripts, and is supposed by the Parsis to be a fragment of the Bahman Yast.

The Ormazd Yast is exclusively devoted to an enumeration of the names of Ahura and to a laudation of their virtues and efficacy: the recitation of these names is the best defence against all dangers.

§§ 1–6. The names of Ahura Mazda are the most powerful part of the Holy Word.

§§ 7–8. The twenty names of Ahura Mazda are enumerated.

§§ 9–11. Efficacy of these names.

§§ 12–15. Another list of names.

§§ 16–19. Efficacy of Ahura's names.

§§ 20–23. Sundry formulas of invocation.

As may be seen from this summary, the subject has been treated twice over, first in §§ 1–11, and then in §§ 12–19; yet it does not appear that this Yast was formed out of two independent treatises, and it is more likely that the vague and indefinite enumeration in §§ 12–15, which interrupts so clumsily the train of ideas, is due either to an interpolation or simply to the literary deficiency of the writer himself.

The Ormazd Yast is recited every day at the Hâvan Gâh, after the morning prayer (Anquetil, Zend-Avesta, II, 143): it is well also to recite it when going to sleep and when changing one's residence (§ 17).

Speculations on the mystical powers of God's names have always been common among Orientals. The number of these names went on increasing: Dastûr Nôshîrvân wrote on the 101 names of God; Dastûr Marzbân on his 125 names. With the Musulmans, Allah had 1001 names. On the names of God among the Jews, see Zeitschrift der Deutschen Morgenländischen Gesellschaft, XXXV, pp. 162, 532.

We have three native translations of this Yast; one in Pahlavi (East India Office, XII, 39, and St. Petersburg, XCIX, 39; edited by Carl Salemann), one in Persian (East India Office, XXII, 43), and one in Sanskrit (Paris, fonds Burnouf, V, 66); the last two edited in our Études Iraniennes, II, 255).

The second part of the Ya*st*, the so-called Bahman Ya*st* frag-ment, is in a state of the utmost corruption. It is difficult to trace any connection in the ideas, yet §§ 28, 29, 30 seem to point rather clearly to the final struggle between Ormazd and Ahriman and to the annihilation of the Daêvas, and, thereby, some connection is established between this fragment and the Pahlavi Bahman Ya*st*[1], which deals with the same subject. If that correspondence be real, § 26 might refer to the beginning of the Pahlavi Bahman Ya*st*, in which Zarathu*st*ra is shown by Ahura the times to come and the end of the world.

Of this fragment we have only a bad Pahlavi translation in the St. Petersburg manuscript mentioned above.

0[2]. May Ahura Mazda be rejoiced! May Angra Mainyu be destroyed! by those who do truly what is the foremost wish (of God[3]).

I praise well-thought, well-spoken, and well-done thoughts, words, and deeds. I embrace all good thoughts, good words, and good deeds; I reject all evil thoughts, evil words, and evil deeds.

I give sacrifice and prayer unto you, O Amesha-Spe*n*tas! even with the fulness of my thoughts, of my words, of my deeds, and of my heart: I give unto you even my own life[4].

I recite the 'Praise of Holiness[5]:'

'Ashem Vohû: Holiness is the best of all good. Well is it for it, well is it for that holiness which is perfection of holiness!'

I confess myself a worshipper of Mazda, a follower of Zara-thu*st*ra, one who hates the Daêvas and obeys the laws of Ahura[6];

---

[1] Translated by West (Pahlavi Texts, I).

[2] The formulas of this section serve as an introduction to all Ya*st*s.

[3] The last clause of this sentence is imitated from Yasna XLVI [XLV], 19: 'he who does truly in holiness what was the foremost wish of Zarathu*st*ra' (that is, what he ordered most earnestly; Pahl. Comm.).

[4] 'If I must give up my life for the sake of my soul, I give it up' (Pahl. Comm.). The two sentences, 'I praise . . . ,' 'I give unto you . . . ,' are taken from Yasna XI, 17, 18 [XII].

[5] The Ashem Vohû, one of the holiest and most frequently recited prayers.

[6] The Fravarânê or profession of faith of the Zoroastrian (Yasna I, 23 [65–68]).

For sacrifice[1], prayer, propitiation, and glorification unto [Hâvani][2], the holy and master of holiness ;

For sacrifice, prayer, propitiation, and glorification unto [Sâvanghi and Vîsya][3], the holy and masters of holiness ;

For sacrifice, prayer, propitiation, and glorification unto the Masters of the days, of the periods of the day, of the months, of the seasons, and of the years[4] ;

Unto AHURA MAZDA, bright and glorious, be propitiation, with sacrifice, prayer, propitiation, and glorification.

Yathâ ahû vairyô: The will of the Lord is the law of holiness: the riches of Vohû-Manô shall be given to him who works in this world for Mazda, and wields according to the will of Ahura the power he gave him to relieve the poor.

1. Zarathustra asked Ahura Mazda : ' O Ahura Mazda, most beneficent Spirit, Maker of the material world, thou Holy One!

' What of the Holy Word is the strongest ? What is the most victorious ? What is the most glorious ? What is the most effective ?

2. ' What is the most fiend-smiting ? What is the best-healing ? What destroyeth best the malice of Daêvas and Men ? What maketh the material world best come to the fulfilment of its wishes[5] ? What freeth the material world best from the anxieties of the heart[6] ? '

---

[1] He shows himself a Zoroastrian by offering sacrifice . . . .

[2] The actual Gâh during which the Yast is being recited must be mentioned here. Hâvani is the first Gâh (see Gâhs).

[3] The Genii who co-operate with Hâvani, his hamkârs; for each Gâh the names of its proper hamkârs should be mentioned (see Gâhs).

[4] See Vendîdâd VIII, 19, text and notes.

[5] Pun mînishn ît barâ matârtûm, mandûm frârûn (Phl. tr.); manasas asti prâpakatarâ (Sansk. tr.) ; مراد رساننده (Pers. tr.).

[6] Pun akhû ît barâ mûshîtârtûm : pîm(î) u mandûm î apârûn

3. Ahura Mazda answered: 'Our Name, O Spitama Zarathu*s*tra! who are the Amesha-Spe*n*tas, that is the strongest part of the Holy Word; that is the most victorious; that is the most glorious; that is the most effective;

4. 'That is the most fiend-smiting; that is the best-healing; that destroyeth best the malice of Daêvas and Men; that maketh the material world best come to the fulfilment of its wishes; that freeth the material world best from the anxieties of the heart.'

5. Then Zarathu*s*tra said: 'Reveal unto me that name of thine, O Ahura Mazda! that is the greatest, the best, the fairest, the most effective, the most fiend-smiting, the best-healing, that destroyeth best the malice of Daêvas and Men;

6. 'That I may afflict all Daêvas and Men; that I may afflict all Yâtus and Pairikas[1]; that neither Daêvas nor Men may be able to afflict me; neither Yâtus nor Pairikas.'

7. Ahura Mazda replied unto him: 'My name is the One of whom questions are asked[2], O holy Zarathu*s*tra!

'My second name is the Herd-giver[3].

'My third name is the Strong One[4].

(Phl. tr.); vitarkâ*n*âm asti mûshakatarâ (Sansk. tr.); خيا لات
دفع كننده بيم چيزى اوارون (Pers. tr.).

[1] See Vendîdâd, Introd. IV, 20–21.

[2] As the revealer of the law, which is generally expounded by a process of questions from Zarathu*s*tra and answers from Ahura. The revelation itself is called spe*n*tô frasna, 'the holy questions' (Vendîdâd XXII, 19).

[3] 'That is, I give herds of men and cattle' (Phl. tr.).

[4] 'Strong, that is, I have strength for the works of the law' (Phl. tr.); the Sanskrit translation has, 'powerful, that is, I have power to create.'

'My fourth name is Perfect Holiness [1].

'My fifth name is All good things created by Mazda, the offspring of the holy principle.

'My sixth name is Understanding [2];

'My seventh name is the One with understanding.

'My eighth name is Knowledge;

'My ninth name is the One with Knowledge.

8. 'My tenth name is Weal;

'My eleventh name is He who produces weal.

'My twelfth name is AHURA (the Lord) [3].

'My thirteenth name is the most Beneficent.

'My fourteenth name is He in whom there is no harm [4].

'My fifteenth name is the unconquerable One.

'My sixteenth name is He who makes the true account [5].

'My seventeenth name is the All-seeing One.

'My eighteenth name is the healing One.

'My nineteenth name is the Creator.

'My twentieth name is MAZDA (the All-knowing One).

9. 'Worship me, O Zarathustra, by day and by

---

[1] Asha-Vahista, which is the name of the second Amesha-Spenta too. The commentary has : 'That is, my own being is all holiness.'

[2] Literally : 'My sixth name is that I am Understanding.' The same construction is used with regard to the eighth, the tenth, and the nineteenth names.

[3] 'It follows from this passage that a man is not fit to be a king, unless he possesses twelve virtues' (Phl. tr.).

[4] 'Some say : I keep harm from man' (Phl. tr.).

[5] 'That is, I make the account of good works and sins' (Phl. tr.); prakatam gananâkaras kila punyapâpayos sankhyâm aham karomi (Sansk. tr.). Cf. Yasna XXXII, 6, b.

night, with offerings of libations well accepted [1].
I will come unto thee for help and joy, I, Ahura
Mazda ; the good, holy Sraosha will come unto thee
for help and joy; the waters, the plants, and the
Fravashis of the holy ones will come unto thee for
help and joy.

10. ' If thou wantest, O Zarathustra, to destroy the
malice of Daêvas and Men, of the Yâtus and Pairikas, of the oppressors, of the blind and of the
deaf [2], of the two-legged ruffians [3], of the two-legged
Ashemaoghas [4], of the four-legged wolves ;

11. ' And of the hordes with the wide front, with
the many spears [5], with the straight spears, with the
spears uplifted, bearing the spear of havock; then,
recite thou these my names every day and every
night.

---

[1] Yasô-bereta : prâptena dânena; یافتهٔ ذهشن زور.

[2] The Kavis and the Karapans, the blind and the deaf, are
those ' who cannot see nor hear anything of God.' Those terms
were current in the theological language of the Sassanian times to
designate the unbelievers. An edict, promulgated by king Yazd-
gard III (fifth century A.C.) to make Zoroastrism the state religion
in Armenia, had the following words : 'You must know that any
man who does not follow the religion of Mazda is deaf, blind,
and deceived by Ahriman's devs' (Elisaeus, The War of Vartan).

[3] Or murderers (mairya); according to the Parsis highwaymen (راه زن).

[4] The heretics. Casuists distinguish three kinds of Ashemaogha:
the deceiver (frîftâr), the self-willed (khôt dôshak), and the
deceived (frîftak). The first and worst is one who knowingly
leads people astray, making forbidden what is lawful, and lawful
what is forbidden ; the second is one who follows his own will and
reason, instead of applying to a Dastûr (a spiritual guide) for
direction ; the third is one who has been led astray by another.

[5] Drafsa means also banner: the Persian درفش, derived from
drafsa, has preserved the two meanings. The Sanskrit translation
has sastra, the Persian has سلاح.

12. 'I am the Keeper[1]; I am the Creator and the Maintainer[2]; I am the Discerner[3]; I am the most beneficent Spirit.

'My name is the bestower of health; my name is the best bestower of health.

'My name is the Âthravan[4]; my name is the most Âthravan-like of all Âthravans.

'My name is Ahura (the Lord).

'My name is Mazdau (the all-knowing).

'My name is the Holy; my name is the most Holy.

'My name is the Glorious; my name is the most Glorious.

'My name is the Full-seeing; my name is the Fullest-seeing.

'My name is the Far-seeing; my name is the Farthest-seeing.

13. 'My name is the Protector; my name is the Well-wisher; my name is the Creator; my name is the Keeper; my name is the Maintainer.

'My name is the Discerner; my name is the Best Discerner.

'My name is the Prosperity-producer[5]; my name is the Word of Prosperity[6].

'My name is the King who rules at his will;

---

[1] 'I keep the creation' (Phl. tr.).

[2] 'I created the world and I maintain it' (ibid.).

[3] 'I can know what is useful and what is hurtful' (ibid.).

[4] 'The priest.'

[5] 'I impart increase to the righteous' (Phl. tr.).

[6] Doubtful. Fsûsô-mãthrô is used in several passages as the name of a part of the Avesta, Yasna LVIII [LVII], which appears to be called so from the presence in it of the words fsûsa, fsûmant, 'thriving, causing to thrive,' which aptly express its contents.

my name is the King who rules most at his will.

'My name is the liberal King[1]; my name is the most liberal King.

14. 'My name is He who does not deceive; my name is He who is not deceived.

'My name is the good Keeper; my name is He who destroys malice; my name is He who conquers at once; my name is He who conquers everything; my name is He who has shaped everything[2].

'My name is All weal; my name is Full weal; my name is the Master of weal.

15. 'My name is He who can benefit at his wish; my name is He who can best benefit at his wish.

'My name is the Beneficent One; my name is the Energetic One; my name is the most Beneficent.

'My name is Holiness; my name is the Great One; my name is the good Sovereign; my name is the Best of Sovereigns.

'My name is the Wise One; my name is the Wisest of the Wise; my name is He who does good for a long time.

16. 'These are my names.

'And he who in this material world, O Spitama Zarathustra! shall recite and pronounce those names of mine[3] either by day or by night;

---

[1] Nâma, translated âpât, and interpreted Khutâi rât. The Sanskrit translator has misread âzât for âpât, and translated svatantra, independent.

[2] The commentator observes orthodoxly, 'everything good.'

[3] That is to say, who will recite this Yast.

17. ' He who shall pronounce them, when he rises up or when he lays him down; when he lays him down or when he rises up; when he binds on the sacred girdle[1] or when he unbinds the sacred girdle; when he goes out of his dwelling-place, or when he goes out of his town, or when he goes out of his country and comes into another country;

18. ' That man, neither in that day nor in that night, shall be wounded by the weapons of the foe who rushes Aêshma-like[2] and is Dru*g*-minded; not the knife, not the cross-bow, not the arrow, not the sword, not the club, not the sling-stone[3] shall reach and wound him.

19. ' But those names shall come in to keep him from behind and to keep him in front[4], from the Dru*g* unseen, from the female Varenya fiend[5], from the evil-doer[6] bent on mischief[7], and from that fiend who is all death, Angra Mainyu. It will be as if there were a thousand men watching over one man[8].

20. ' " Who is he who will smite the fiend in order to maintain thy ordinances? Teach me clearly thy

---

[1] The aiwyâonghanem or kôsti (see Vendîdâd XVIII, p. 191, note 4).

[2] Or ' with anger.'

[3] Akavô, *k*akavô, ishavô, kareta, vazra, translated kartari, *k*akra, *s*ara, *s*astrikâ, va*g*ra.

[4] Min akhar u lûîn (Phl. tr.); pr*i*sh*th*a[ta]s purata*s*ka (Sansk. tr.).

[5] Interpreted as the demon of lust and envy. Cf. Vendîdâd, Introd. IV, 23.

[6] Kayadha, translated kâstâr (Phl.), 'the impairer;' kadar-thaka (Sansk.), 'he who holds for nothing, who makes slight of.'

[7] Doubtful. The Phl. tr. has ' who impairs living creatures,' etc.

[8] Cf. Yt. XIII, 71.

rules for this world and for the next, that Sraosha may come with Vohu-Manô and help whomsoever thou pleasest[1]."

21. 'Hail to the Glory of the Kavis[2]! Hail to the Airyanem Vaêgah[3]! Hail to the Saoka[4], made by Mazda! Hail to the waters of the Dâitya[5]! Hail to Ardvi[6], the undefiled well! Hail to the whole world of the holy Spirit!

'Yathâ ahû vairyô: The will of the Lord . . . .[7]

'Ashem Vohû: Holiness is the best of all good . . . .[8]

22. 'We worship the Ahuna Vairya[9]. We worship Asha-Vahista, most fair, undying, and beneficent[10]. We worship Strength and Prosperity and Might and Victory and Glory and Vigour[11]. We worship Ahura Mazda, bright and glorious.

'Yênghê hâtãm[12]: All those beings[13] of whom Ahura Mazda knows the goodness[14] for a sacrifice

---

[1] From Yasna XLIV, 16; cf. Vendîdâd VIII, 20.

[2] See Sîrôzah I, 9, p. 7, note 2.

[3] Irân Vêg; see Vendîdâd, p. 3.

[4] Saoka; see Sîrôzah I, 3.

[5] See Vendîdâd, p. 5, note 2.

[6] Ardvi Sûra Anâhita, the great goddess of the waters; see Yt. V.

[7] See above, p. 23.   [8] See above, p. 22.

[9] The prayer yathâ ahû vairyô, known as Ahuna vairya (Honover), from the first words in it: ahû vairyô. See above, p. 23.

[10] Or 'the fairest Amesha-Spenta;' cf. Vend. Introd. IV, 7.

[11] Impersonated as gods, to obtain from them the benefits of which they are the impersonations.

[12] A formula found at the end of most chapters of the Yasna and imitated from Yasna LI [L], 22.

[13] The Amesha-Spentas (Pahl. Comm. ad Yasna XXVII, fin.).

[14] The benefits of which they dispose, and which they impart as rewards to the righteous.

[performed] in holiness, all those beings, males [1] and females [2], do we worship.

23. 'Yathâ ahû vairyô: The will of the Lord is the law of holiness . . . .

'I bless the sacrifice and the prayer unto Ahura Mazda, bright and glorious, and his strength and vigour [3].'

(Bahman Yast [4].)

24. 'O Zarathustra! keep thou for ever that man who is friendly [to me] from the foe unfriendly [to me]! Do not give up that friend unto the stroke (of the foe), unto vexations to be borne; wish no harm unto that man who would offer me a sacrifice, be it ever so great or ever so small, if it has reached unto us, the Amesha-Spentas.

25. 'Here is Vohu-Manô, my creature, O Zara-thustra! here is Asha-Vahista, my creature, O Zara-thustra! here is Khsathra-Vairya, my creature, O Zarathustra! here is Spenta-Ârmaiti, my creature, O Zarathustra! here are Haurvatât and Ameretât, who are the reward of the holy ones [5], when freed from their bodies, my creatures, O Zarathustra!

26. 'Thou knowest this, and how it is, O holy Zarathustra! from my understanding and from my knowledge; namely, how the world first began [6], and how it will end [7].

---

[1] The first three.
[2] The last three, whose names are feminine.
[3] Which he will impart in return to his worshippers.
[4] See above, p. 21.
[5] As the Genii who preside over plants and waters, they are very likely entrusted with the care of feeding the righteous in Paradise. Cf. Yt. XXII, 18.
[6] From Yasna XXVIII, 12. [7] Cf. Yasna XXX, 4.

' A thousand remedies, ten thousand remedies [1]!
' A thousand remedies, ten thousand remedies!
' A thousand remedies, ten thousand remedies!

27. ' [We worship] the well-shapen, tall-formed Strength ; Verethraghna, made by Ahura ; the crushing Ascendant [2], and Spe*n*ta-Ârmaiti.

28. ' And with the help of Spe*n*ta-Ârmaiti, break ye [3] asunder their [4] malice, turn their minds astray, bind their hands, make their knees quake against one another, bind their tongues [5].

' When, O Mazda! shall the faithful smite the wicked [6]? When shall the faithful smite the Dru*g*? When shall the faithful smite the wicked ? '

29. Then Zarathu*s*tra said : ' I threw you back into the earth [7], and by the eyes of Spe*n*ta-Ârmaiti [8] the ruffian was made powerless [9].

30. ' We worship the powerful Gaokerena [10], made by Mazda ; the powerful Gaokerena, made by Mazda.

31. ' We worship the memory of Ahura Mazda, to keep the Holy Word.

' We worship the understanding of Ahura Mazda, to study the Holy Word.

' We worship the tongue of Ahura Mazda, to speak forth the Holy Word.

---

[1] Yasna LXVIII, 15 (LXVII, 50).   [2] See Sîrôzah I, 20.

[3] Refers probably to the Izeds mentioned in the preceding paragraph.

[4] Of the foes alluded to § 24.   [5] Derezvan ; see Yt. XI, 2.

[6] Cf. Yasna XLVIII [XLVII], 2.

[7] I follow the reading zamerena, which is followed by the Pahlavi translation too. In the Yasna IX, 15 (46) Zarathu*s*tra is said to have obliged the Daêvas to hide themselves in the earth.

[8] Cf. Yt. XIX, 94.   [9] Cf. Vend. IX, 12–13.

[10] See Sîrôzah I, 7.

'We worship the mountain that gives understanding, that preserves understanding[1]; [we worship
it] by day and by night, with offerings of libations
well-accepted[2].

32. 'We worship that creation [of Ahura's], Spe*n*ta-
Ârmaiti; and the holy creations of that creature and
of Asha [Vahi*s*ta], that are foremost in holiness[3].

'Here I take as lord and master[4] the greatest of
all, Ahura Mazda; to smite the fiend Angra Mainyu;
to smite Aê*s*ma of the wounding spear[5]; to smite
the Mâzainya fiends[6]; to smite all the Daêvas and
the Varenya fiends[6]; to increase Ahura Mazda,

---

[1] That mount is called in later literature Mount Ô*s*dâ*s*târ (the
Pahlavi translation of u s h i-d a r e n a, the keeper of understanding).
According to the Bundahi*s* (XII, 15), it stands in Seistan. High
mountains, being nearer heaven, are apt to become in the spirit of
mythology the seat of heavenly beings or treasures. It was on the
top of a mountain that Ahura revealed the law (see Vd. XXII, 19
[53]); the first man and king, Gayomarth, ruled on a mountain
and was called Gar-shâh, the king of the mountain. When the
Kayanian family failed, the Iranians went to Mount Alborz and
found there Kai Kobâd waiting for his fate.

[2] The order of the text differs in one series of manuscripts, in
which it begins with § 31; then comes § 29 with the following
additional words:
'A thousand remedies, ten thousand remedies! (three times;
    cf. above, § 26.)
We worship the Fravashi of the man whose name is Asmô-
    *hv*anva*nt*; then I will worship the Fravashis of the other
    holy ones who were strong of faith' (Yt. XXII, 37).
Asmô-*hv*anva*nt* was one of the first followers of Zarathu*s*tra, and with
his name begins the enumeration of the Fravashis (Yt. XIII, 96).
Then follows § 30, and then again § 31 with the Ashem Vohû;
and then the additional passage, 'We worship . . . . ,' is repeated
twice.

[3] Vispêrad XIX, 2.

[4] As a h u and r a t u, that is, as temporal chief and spiritual guide.

[5] See Vend. Introd. IV, 22.   [6] Ibid. 23.

bright and glorious ; to increase the Amesha-Spe*n*tas ;
to increase the star Ti*s*trya [1], the bright and glorious ;
to increase the faithful men ; to increase all the holy
creatures of the Beneficent Spirit.

'Ashem Vohû : Holiness is the best of all
good . . . .[2]

33. '[Give] unto that man [3] brightness and glory,
give him health of body, give him sturdiness of body,
give him victorious strength of body, give him full
welfare of wealth, give him a virtuous [4] offspring,
give him long, long life, give him the bright, all-
happy, blissful abode of the holy Ones [5].

' May it come according to my blessing [6] !

' A thousand remedies, ten thousand remedies [7] !
(three times.)

' Come to me for help, O Mazda !

' We worship the well-shapen, tall-formed Strength,
and Verethraghna, made by Mazda, and the crushing
Ascendant [8].

' We worship Râma *Hv*âstra, and Vayu who works
highly and is more powerful to destroy than all
other creatures. That part of thee do we worship,
O Vayu, that belongs to Spe*n*ta Mainyu. We worship the sovereign Sky, the boundless Time, and
the sovereign Time of the long Period [9].

'Ashem Vohû : Holiness is the best of all
good . . . .'

---

[1] See Ya*s*t VIII.   [2] As above, p. 22.

[3] Who shall offer thee a sacrifice. This paragraph is taken
from Yasna LXVIII, 11 (LXVII, 32), where it is addressed to the
Waters : ' Ye, good waters, give unto that man who will offer you
a sacrifice . . . .'

[4] Su*s*îla (Sansk. tr. ad Yasna LXI, 13).

[5] This clause serves as a conclusion to all Ya*s*ts.

[6] From Yasna LXVIII, 20 (LXVII, 52).

[7] Cf. above, § 26.   [8] Cf. Sîrôzah I, *7*0   [9] Ibid. 21.

II. HAPTÂN YAST.

The Yast of the seven Amshaspands is recited on the first seven days of the week, that is to say, on the days consecrated to the Amesha-Spentas. In fact it is nothing more than an extract from the Sîrôzahs, being composed of the first seven formulas in their two forms: §§ 1–5 = Sîrôzah I, 1–7; §§ 6–10 = Sîrôzah II, 1–7. Then come four sections which are the original part of the Yast (§§ 11–15).

---

0. May Ahura Mazda be rejoiced [1] ! . . . .

Ashem Vohû: Holiness is the best of all good [1] . . . .

I confess myself a worshipper of Mazda, a follower of Zarathustra, one who hates the Daêvas and obeys the laws of Ahura;

For sacrifice, prayer, propitiation, and glorification unto [Hâvani], the holy and master of holiness [1] . . . .

I.

1[2]. To Ahura Mazda, bright and glorious, and to the Amesha-Spentas;

To Vohu-Manô; to Peace, whose breath is friendly, and who is more powerful to destroy than all other creatures; to the heavenly Wisdom, made by Mazda, and to the Wisdom acquired through the ear, made by Mazda;

2[3]. To Asha-Vahista, the fairest; to the much-desired Airyaman; to the instrument made by Mazda; and to the good Saoka, with eyes of love, made by Mazda and holy;

---

[1] The rest as above, Yt. I, 0.   [2] Sîrôzah I, 1–2.

[3] Sîrôzah I, 3–4.

To Khshathra-Vairya; to the metals; to Mercy and Charity.

3 [1]. To the good Spenta-Ârmaiti, and to the good Râta, with eyes of love, made by Mazda and holy;

To Haurvatât, the master; to the prosperity of the seasons and to the years, the masters of holiness;

And to Ameretât, the master; to fatness and flocks; to the plenty of corn; and to the powerful Gaokerena, made by Mazda.

4 [2]. (At the Gâh Hâvan) : To Mithra, the lord of wide pastures and to Râma *Hvâstra*.

(At the Gâh Rapithwin) : To Asha-Vahista and to Âtar, the son of Ahura Mazda.

(At the Gâh Uzîren) : To Apãm Napât, the tall lord, and to water, made by Mazda.

5 [3]. (At the Gâh Aiwisrûthrem) : To the Fravashis of the faithful and to the females that bring forth flocks of males; to the prosperity of the seasons; to the well-shapen and tall-formed Strength; to Verethraghna, made by Ahura, and to the crushing Ascendant.

(At the Gâh Usahin) : To the holy, devout, fiend-smiting Sraosha, who makes the world grow; to Rashnu-Razista and to Arstât, who makes the world grow, who makes the world increase [3];

Be propitiation, with sacrifice, prayer, propitiation, and glorification!

Yathâ ahû vairyô : The will of the Lord is the law of holiness . . . .

---

[1] Sîrôzah I, 5–7. [2] Sîrôzah I, 7.

[3] Sîrôzah I, 7.

II.

6 [1]. We sacrifice unto Ahura Mazda, bright and glorious; we sacrifice unto the Amesha-Spentas, the all-ruling, the all-beneficent.

We sacrifice unto Vohu-Manô, the Amesha-Spenta; we sacrifice unto Peace, whose breath is friendly, and who is more powerful to destroy than all other creatures; we sacrifice unto the heavenly Wisdom, made by Mazda; we sacrifice unto the wisdom acquired through the ear, made by Mazda.

7 [2]. We sacrifice unto Asha-Vahista, the fairest, the Amesha-Spenta; we sacrifice unto the much-desired Airyaman; we sacrifice unto the instrument made by Mazda; we sacrifice unto the good Saoka, with eyes of love, made by Mazda and holy.

We sacrifice unto Khshathra-Vairya; we sacrifice unto the metals; we sacrifice unto Mercy and Charity.

8 [3]. We sacrifice unto the good Spenta-Ârmaiti; we sacrifice unto the good Râta, with eyes of love, made by Mazda and holy.

We sacrifice unto Haurvatât, the Amesha-Spenta; we sacrifice unto the prosperity of the seasons; we sacrifice unto the years, the holy and masters of holiness.

We sacrifice unto Ameretât, the Amesha-Spenta; we sacrifice unto fatness and flocks; we sacrifice unto the plenty of corn; we sacrifice unto the powerful Gaokerena, made by Mazda.

9 [4]. (At the Gâh Hâvan): We sacrifice unto

---

[1] Sîrôzah II, 1–2.   [2] Sîrôzah II, 3–4.
[3] Sîrôzah II, 5–7.   [4] Sîrôzah II, 7.

Mithra, the lord of wide pastures; we sacrifice unto
Râma *Hv*âstra.

(At the Gâh Rapithwin): We sacrifice unto Asha-
Vahi*s*ta and Âtar, the son of Ahura Mazda.

(At the Gâh Uzîren): We sacrifice unto Apãm
Napâ*t*, the swift-horsed, the tall and shining lord,
the lord of the females; we sacrifice unto the holy
waters, made by Mazda.

10 [1]. (At the Gâh Aiwisrûthrem): We sacrifice
unto the good, powerful, beneficent Fravashis of the
faithful; we sacrifice unto the females who bring
forth flocks of males; we sacrifice unto the prosperity
of the seasons; we sacrifice unto the well-shapen,
tall-formed Strength; we sacrifice unto Verethraghna,
made by Mazda; we sacrifice unto the crushing
Ascendant.

(At the Gâh U*s*ahin): We sacrifice unto the holy,
tall-formed, fiend-smiting Sraosha, who makes the
world grow, the holy and master of holiness; we
sacrifice unto Rashnu-Razi*s*ta; we sacrifice unto
Ar*s*tâ*t*, who makes the world grow, who makes the
world increase.

III.

11. Let the Yâtus be crushed, O Zarathu*s*tra [2]!
both Daêvas and men [3].

Who is he in whose house, O Spitama Zarathu*s*tra! every Dru*g* is destroyed, every Dru*g*
perishes, when he pronounces these words [4]:

12 [5]. . . . . ?

13. It is he who takes the seven Amesha-Spe*n*tas,

---

[1] Sîrôzah II, 7.   [2] Or: Let Zarathu*s*tra crush the Yâtus.
[3] The Yâtus are either demons or men: the man-Yâtu is the
sorcerer, the wizard. Cf. Yt. VIII, 44.
[4] Doubtful.   [5] I am unable to make anything of this section.

the all-ruling, the all-beneficent, as a shield [1] against his enemies.

We worship the Law of the worshippers of Mazda ; we worship the waters coming in the shape of a horse [2], made by Mazda.

14–15. He has renounced trespasses and faults, O Zarathustra! he has renounced all trespasses and faults [3], O Zarathustra! when he throws down [4] the destroyer of Vohu-Manô and his words [5], with a hundred times hundredfold, with a many times manifold preaching and smiting, and he takes away the Law of Mazda, that was carried away as a prisoner [6], from the hands of the [ungodly], who are destroyed by his strength.

Ashem Vohû: Holiness is the best of all good....

16. Yathâ ahû vairyô: The will of the Lord is the law of holiness....

I bless the sacrifice and the prayer, the strength and vigour

Of Ahura Mazda, bright and glorious, and of the Amesha-Spentas ;

Of Vohu-Manô; of Peace, whose breath is friendly [7]....

---

[1] Doubtful. [2] See Yt. VIII, 5, 42 ; cf. § 20.

[3] Âtare-vîtaremaibyâ.... vîmraoṭ; cf. âtarâish.... vî sarem mruyê (Yasna XII, 4 [XIII, 16]): âtareman seems to be a sin by commission, vîtareman a sin by omission.

[4] Doubtful (fraspâvares: fraspâ is generally translated ramî-tûntan).

[5] Doubtful.

[6] Cf. Yt. XIII, 100; XIX, 86; fravasnãm is the reverse of uzvazhaṭ (l.l.).

[7] The rest as above, § 1.

Of Asha-Vahista, the fairest; of the much-desired
Airyaman [1] ....

Of Khshathra-Vairya, of the metals [1] ....

Of the good Spenta-Ârmaiti and of the good
Râta [2] ....

Of Haurvatât, the master [2] ....

Of Ameretât, the master [2] ....

(At the Gâh Hâvan): Of Mithra [3] ....

(At the Gâh Rapithwin): Of Asha-Vahista [3] ....

(At the Gâh Uzíren): Of the high lord Apãm
Napât [3] ....

(At the Gâh Aiwisrûthrem): Of the Fravashis of
the faithful [4] ....

(At the Gâh Usahin): Of the holy, devout, fiend-
smiting Sraosha, who makes the world grow; of
Rashnu-Razista and of Arstât, who makes the world
grow, who makes the world increase.

Ashem Vohû: Holiness is the best of all good ....

Give unto that man [5] brightness and glory, give him health of
body, give him sturdiness of body, give him victorious strength of
body, give him full welfare of wealth, give him a virtuous offspring,
give him long, long life, give him the bright, all-happy, blissful
abode of the holy Ones.

---

[1] The rest as above, § 2.   [2] The rest as above, § 3.
[3] The rest as above, § 4.   [4] The rest as above, § 5.
[5] Who shall offer a sacrifice to the Amshaspands.

III. ARDIBEHIST [1] YAST.

This Yast is for a great part devoted to the praise of the Airyaman prayer, which is described as driving away all the diseases and plagues that have been brought upon the world by Angra Mainyu; and when the writer passes from the glorification of Airyaman to that of Asha-Vahista, which is put into the mouth of Angra Mainyu himself (§§ 13 seq.), he makes him speak of Asha-Vahista just in the same way, and ascribe him just the same powers, as he himself has done with regard to Airyaman. This is owing to the fact of Airyaman being invoked in company with Asha-Vahista in the second formula of the Sîrôzah [2].

The powers ascribed to Asha-Vahista have their origin in the twofold nature of that Amesha-Spenta, who being, in his abstract character, the impersonation of the highest element in Mazdeism, Divine Order and Holiness [3], and in his concrete character, the genius who presides over the mightiest of physical elements, Fire [4], is one of the most powerful and dreaded opponents of Angra Mainyu [5]. On the other hand, Airyaman is the genius to whom Ahura Mazda applied to heal the nine, and ninety, and nine hundred and nine thousand diseases created by Angra Mainyu [6].

This Yast is recited every day at the Gâhs Hâvan, Rapithwin, and Aiwisrûthrem (Anquetil).

---

0. May Ahura Mazda be rejoiced ! . . . .
Ashem Vohû: Holiness is the best of all good . . . .
I confess myself a worshipper of Mazda, a follower of Zarathustra, one who hates the Daêvas and obeys the laws of Ahura;
For sacrifice, prayer, propitiation, and glorification unto [Hâvani], the holy and master of holiness [7]. . . . .

---

[1] Ard-î-behist is the Parsi form for Asha vahista, ard being derived from arta, the Persian form corresponding to the Zend asha.

[2] See Sîrôzah I, 3, and below the introductory formula.

[3] See Vend. Introd. IV, 30.   [4] Ibid. 33.

[5] See Yt. XVII, 18.   [6] Fargard XXII and Introd.

[7] As above, Yt. I, 0.

Unto Asha-Vahi*s*ta, the fairest; unto the much-desired Airyaman, made by Mazda, and unto the good Saoka, with eyes of love, made by Mazda and holy [1];

Be propitiation, with sacrifice, prayer, propitiation, and glorification.

Yathâ ahû vairyô: The will of the Lord is the law of holiness [2] . . . .

I.

1. Ahura Mazda spake unto Spitama Zarathu*s*tra, saying: 'That thou mayest increase Asha-Vahi*s*ta, O Spitama Zarathu*s*tra! with hymns of praise, with performance of the office, with invocations, holy words, sacrifice, blessings, and adoration—once to abide in the shining luminous space, in the beautiful abodes [3]—for the sacrifice and invocation of us, the Amesha-Spe*n*tas [4]' . . . .

2. Zarathu*s*tra said: 'Say unto me the right words, such as they are, O Ahura Mazda! that I may increase Asha-Vahi*s*ta, with hymns of praise,

---

[1] Sîrôzah I, 3.

[2] Several manuscripts add here the full invocation of the greater Sîrôzah :

　'We sacrifice unto Asha-Vahi*s*ta, the fairest, the Amesha-Spe*n*ta;

　We sacrifice unto the much-desired Airyaman ;

　We sacrifice unto the instrument, made by Mazda ;

　We sacrifice unto the good Saoka, with eyes of love, made by Mazda and holy.'

[3] The Garô-nmânem or Paradise; see Yasna XVI, 7 [XVII, 42], Phl. tr.

[4] The principal clause appears to be wanting, unless Zarathu*s*tra is supposed to interrupt Ahura. One might also understand the sentence in an optative sense : 'Mayest thou increase . . . .'

with performance of the office, with invocations, holy words, sacrifice, blessings, and adoration,—once to abide in the shining luminous space, in the beautiful abodes,—for the sacrifice and invocation of you, the Amesha-Spentas.

3[1]. '. . . . I proclaim Asha-Vahista : if I proclaim Asha-Vahista, then easy is the way to the abode of the other Amesha-Spentas [2], which Ahura Mazda keeps with Good Thoughts, which Ahura Mazda keeps with Good Words, which Ahura Mazda keeps with Good Deeds [3];

4. '(Easy is the way to the Garô-nmâna of Ahura Mazda) : the Garô-nmâna is for the holy souls, and no one of the wicked can enter the Garô-nmâna and its bright, wide, holy ways ; (no one of them can go) to Ahura Mazda.

II.

5. 'The Airyaman prayer [4] smites down the strength of all the creatures of Angra Mainyu, of the Yâtus and Pairikas [5]. It is the greatest of spells, the best of spells, the very best of all spells ; the

---

[1] Here again it seems as if a paragraph had been lost : ' Ahura Mazda answered : Proclaim thou Asha-Vahista ; if thou proclaimest Asha-Vahista . . . .—Then Zarathustra replied : I proclaim Asha-Vahista . . . .'

[2] The Garôthmân.

[3] An allusion to the three Paradises of Humat, Hûkht, Hvarst, through which the souls of the blessed pass to Garôthmân (Yt. XXII, 15).

[4] The prayer known as Airyama-ishyô; see Vendîdâd XXI, 11–12.

[5] See Vend. Introd. IV, 20–21.

fairest of spells, the very fairest of all spells; the
fearful one amongst spells, the most fearful of all
spells; the firm one amongst spells, the firmest of
all spells; the victorious one amongst spells, the
most victorious of all spells; the healing one
amongst spells, the best-healing of all spells.

6. 'One may heal with Holiness, one may heal
with the Law, one may heal with the knife, one may
heal with herbs, one may heal with the Holy Word:
amongst all remedies this one is the healing one
that heals with the Holy Word; this one it is that
will best drive away sickness from the body of the
faithful: for this one is the best-healing of all
remedies [1].

7. 'Sickness fled away [before it], Death fled
away; the Daêva fled away, the Daêva's counter-
work [2] fled away; the unholy Ashemaogha [3] fled
away, the oppressor of men fled away.

8. ' The brood of the Snake fled away; the brood
of the Wolf fled away; the brood of the Two-legged [4]
fled away. Pride fled away; Scorn fled away; Hot
Fever fled away; Slander fled away; Discord fled
away; the Evil Eye fled away.

9. ' The most lying words of falsehood fled away;
the *G*ahi [5], addicted to the Yâtu, fled away; the

---

[1] Cf. Vendîdâd VII, 44 (118). That Airyaman made use of
the Holy Word (of spells) to cure diseases appears from Vend.
XXII, 6 seq.

[2] Paityâra: every work of Ahura was opposed and spoiled by
a counter-work of Angra Mainyu. Cf. Bundahi*s* I, 23 seq.;
III, 13 seq.; Vend. I; see Ormazd et Ahriman, §§ 195 seq.

[3] See Yt. I, 10 and note 4.

[4] The Ahrimanian creatures belonging to mankind, the Mair-
yas and Ashemaoghas (Yt. I, 10).

[5] The courtezan; cf. Vend. XXI, 17 (35), and Introd. IV, 25.

*G*ahi, who makes one pine [1], fled away; the wind that blows from the North [2] fled away; the wind that blows from the North vanished away.

10. 'He it is who smites me that brood of the Snake, and who might smite those Daêvas by thousands of thousands, by ten thousands of ten thousands; he smites sickness, he smites death, he smites the Daêvas, he smites the Daêva's counter-work, he smites the unholy Ashemaogha, he smites the oppressor of men.

11. 'He smites the brood of the Snake; he smites the brood of the Wolf; he smites the brood of the Two-legged. He smites Pride; he smites Scorn; he smites Hot Fever; he smites Slander; he smites Discord; he smites the Evil Eye.

12. 'He smites the most lying words of falsehood; he smites the *G*ahi, addicted to the Yâtu; he smites the *G*ahi, who makes one pine. He smites the wind that blows from the North; the wind that blows from the North vanished away.

13. 'He it is who smites me that brood of the Two-legged, and who might smite those Daêvas, by thousands of thousands, by ten thousands of ten thousands. Angra Mainyu, who is all death, the worst-lying of all Daêvas, rushed from before him:

14. 'He exclaimed, did Angra Mainyu: "Woe is me! Here is the god Asha-Vahista, who will smite the sickliest of all sicknesses, who will afflict the sickliest of all sicknesses;

---

[1] The Zend is Kahvaredhaini, a synonym of which, Kahvaredha, Yasna LXI, 2 [LX, 7], is translated impairer of Glory, which means very likely: he who makes one 'dwindle, peak, and pine' (cf. Vend. XVIII, 62–64).

[2] From the country of hell; cf. Vend. VII, 2; XIX, 1; Yt. XXII, 25.

' " He will smite the deadliest of all deaths, he will afflict the deadliest of all deaths;

' " He will smite the most fiendish of all fiends, he will afflict the most fiendish of all fiends;

' " He will smite the most counter-working of all counter-works, he will afflict the most counter-working of all counter-works;

' " He will smite the unholy Ashemaogha, he will afflict the unholy Ashemaogha;

' " He will smite the most oppressive of the oppressors of men, he will afflict the most oppressive of the oppressors of men.

15. ' " He will smite the snakiest of the Snake's brood, he will afflict the snakiest of the Snake's brood;

' " He will smite the most wolfish of the Wolf's brood, he will afflict the most wolfish of the Wolf's brood;

' " He will smite the worst of the two-legged brood, he will afflict the worst of the two-legged brood;

' " He will smite Pride, he will afflict Pride;

' " He will smite Scorn, he will afflict Scorn;

' " He will smite the hottest of hot fevers, he will afflict the hottest of hot fevers;

' " He will smite the most slanderous of slanders, he will afflict the most slanderous of slanders;

' " He will smite the most discordant of discords, he will afflict the most discordant of discords;

' " He will smite the worst of the Evil Eye, he will afflict the worst of the Evil Eye.

16. ' " He will smite the most lying words of falsehood, he will afflict the most lying words of falsehood;

'" He will smite the Gahi, addicted to the Yâtu,
he will afflict the Gahi, addicted to the Yâtu ;

'" He will smite the Gahi, who makes one pine,
he will afflict the Gahi, who makes one pine;

'" He will smite the wind that blows from the
North, he will afflict the wind that blows from the
North."

17 [1]. 'The Drug will perish away, the Drug will
perish ; the Drug will rush, the Drug will vanish.
Thou perishest away to the regions of the North,
never more to give unto death the living world of
the holy spirit [2].

18. 'For his brightness and glory I will offer unto him a sacrifice
worth being heard [3], namely, unto Asha-Vahista, the fairest,
the Amesha-Spenta. Unto Asha-Vahista, the fairest, the Amesha-
Spenta, we offer up the libations, the Haoma and meat [4], the
baresma [5], the wisdom of the tongue [6], the holy spells [7], the speech,
the deeds [8], the libations, and the rightly-spoken words.

'Yênhê hâtãm: All those beings of whom Ahura Mazda knows
the goodness [9] . . . .

19. 'Yathâ ahû vairyô: The will of the Lord is the law of
holiness . . . .

---

[1] One set of manuscripts insert: ' He will smite the wind that
blows against the North, he will afflict the wind that blows against
the North; the wind that blows against the North [will perish].'
This is most likely an interpolation, as the wind that blows against
the North (if this is the right meaning of aparô apâkhtara, as
opposed to pourvô apâkhtara) blows against Angra Mainyu.

[2] Cf. Vendîdâd VIII, 21.

[3] That is to say, worth being accepted: cf. Yt. X, 32 ; the Parsis
translate, 'a sacrifice heard [from the lips of the Dastûrs]' (به شنيده;
يزرشن از زبان دستوران; East India Office, XXV, 42).

[4] The Haoma and Myazda.   [5] See Vend. III, 1, note 2.

[6] Hizvô danghah: huzvân dânâkîh (Phl. tr.) means ' the
right formulas.'

[7] ' The Avestâ ' (Phl. tr.).

[8] The several operations of the sacrifice.

[9] As above, Yt. I, 22.

'I bless the sacrifice and prayer and the strength
and vigour of Asha-Vahi*s*ta, the fairest; of the much-
desired Airyaman, made by Mazda; and of the good
Saoka, with eyes of love, made by Mazda and
holy [1].

'A*s*hem Vohû: Holiness is the best of all good [2] . . . .
'[Give] unto that man [3] brightness and glory, give him health
of body; . . . . give him the bright, all-happy, blissful abode of the
holy Ones.'

IV. KHORDÂD YA*S*T.

Only the first two sections of this Ya*s*t refer to its nominal
object, Haurvatâ*t*, the Genius of Health and Waters (Vend. Introd.
IV, 7, 33). The rest of the Ya*s*t refers to the performance of the
Bareshnûm ceremony as being the test of the true Zoroastrian.
As the Bareshnûm purification was performed by Airyaman to
drive away the myriads of diseases created by Angra Mainyu [4], its
laudation is not quite unaptly inserted in a Ya*s*t devoted to the
Genius of Health.

The Khordâd Ya*s*t can be recited at any time. It is better to
recite it during the Gâh U*s*ahin, on the day Khordâd (Anquetil).
The text is corrupt.

o. May Ahura Mazda be rejoiced! . . . .
A*s*hem Vohû: Holiness is the best of all good . . . .
I confess myself a worshipper of Mazda, a follower of Zara-
thu*s*tra, one who hates the Daêvas and obeys the laws of Ahura;
For sacrifice, prayer, propitiation, and glorification unto [Hâvani],
the holy and master of holiness [5] . . . .

Unto Haurvatâ*t*, the master; unto the prosperity

---

[1] Cf. Sîrôzah I, 2.   [2] As above, p. 22.
[3] Who shall offer a sacrifice to Asha-Vahi*s*ta; cf. Yt. I, 33
and notes.
[4] Vend. XXII, 20 [54].
[5] As above, p. 22 and notes.

of the seasons and unto the years, the masters of holiness [1],

Be propitiation, with sacrifice, prayer, propitiation, and glorification.

Yathâ ahû vairyô: The will of the Lord is the law of holiness . . . .

We sacrifice unto Haurvatât, the Amesha-Spenta; we sacrifice unto the prosperity of the seasons; we sacrifice unto the years, the holy and masters of holiness [2].

1. Ahura Mazda spake unto Spitama Zarathustra, saying: 'I created for the faithful the help, the enjoyments, the comforts, and the pleasures of Haurvatât. We unite them with him who would come up to thee as one of the Amesha-Spentas, as he would come to any of the Amesha-Spentas, Vohu-Manô, Asha-Vahista, Khshathra-Vairya, Spenta-Ârmaiti, Haurvatât, and Ameretât.

2. 'He who against the thousands of thousands of those Daêvas, against their ten thousands of ten thousands, against their numberless myriads would invoke the name of Haurvatât, as one of the Amesha-Spentas, he would smite the Nasu, he would smite Hasi [3], he would smite Basi [3], he would smite Saêni [3], he would smite Bûgi [3].

3 [4]. 'I proclaim the faithful man as the first [of men]; if I proclaim the faithful man as the first

---

[1] Sîrôzah I, 6. [2] Sîrôzah II, 6.

[3] Names of Daêvas. According to the Parsi translator of the Dînkart (vol. ii, p. 65), Hasi is 'he who makes sceptical;' Basi is 'he who gives rise to the barking disease;' Saêni is 'he who causes harm;' Bûgi is 'he who preys upon.'

[4] The translation of this paragraph is quite conjectural.

[of men] [1], then Rashnu Razi*s*ta [2], then every heavenly Yazata of male nature in company with the Amesha-Spe*n*tas will free the faithful man [3]

4. 'From the Nasu, from Ha*s*i, from Ga*s*i [4], from Saêni, from Bû*g*i; from the hordes with the wide front, from the hordes with the many spears uplifted, from the evil man who oppresses, from the wilful sinner [5], from the oppressor of men, from the Yâtu, from the Pairika, from the straying way.

5. 'How does the way of the faithful turn and part from the way of the wicked [6]?'

Ahura Mazda answered: 'It is when a man pronouncing my spell, either reading [7] or reciting it by heart, draws the furrows [8] and hides [9] there himself, [saying]:

6. '"I will smite thee, O Dru*g*! whomsoever thou art, whomsoever thou art amongst the Dru*g*es that come in an open way, whomsoever thou art amongst the Dru*g*es that come by hidden ways, whomsoever thou art amongst the Dru*g*es that defile by contact; whatsoever Dru*g* thou art, I smite thee away from the Aryan countries; whatsoever Dru*g* thou art, I bind thee; I smite thee down, O Dru*g*! I throw thee down below, O Dru*g*!"

---

[1] If I am one of the faithful.
[2] The Genius of Truth, Yt. XII.
[3] Will free me as one of the faithful.
[4] Sic; cf. § 2.
[5] Starâi; cf. Études Iraniennes, II, 135.
[6] How is the wicked known from the faithful one?
[7] Marâo: Phl. ôsmôrît, Sansk. adhyeti; safarûnît, poshayati (pustakayati? Yasna XIX, 6 [9]).
[8] The furrows for the Bareshnûm purification (Vend. IX).
[9] Doubtful: gaozaiti; read yaozdâiti (? he cleanses).

7. 'He draws [then] three furrows[1]: I proclaim him one of the faithful; he draws six furrows[1]: I proclaim him one of the faithful; he draws nine furrows[1]: I proclaim him one of the faithful.

8. 'The names of those (Amesha-Spe*n*tas) smite the men turned to Nasus[2] by the Dru*g*es; the seed and kin of the deaf[3] are smitten, the scornful[4] are dead, as the Zaotar Zarathu*s*tra blows them away to woe[5], however fierce, at his will and wish, as many as he wishes.

9. 'From the time when the sun is down he smites them with bruising blows; from the time when the sun is no longer up, he deals deadly blows on the Nasu with his club struck down, for the propitiation and glorification of the heavenly gods.

10. 'O Zarathu*s*tra! let not that spell be shown to any one, except by the father to his son, or by the brother to his brother from the same womb, or by the Âthravan to his pupil[6] in black hair, devoted to the good law, who, devoted to the good law, holy[7] and brave, stills all the Dru*g*es[8].

11. 'For his brightness and glory, I will offer unto him a sacrifice worth being heard, namely, unto Haurvatâ*t*, the Amesha-Spe*n*ta. Unto Haurvatâ*t*, the Amesha-Spe*n*ta, we offer up the libations, the Haoma and meat, the baresma, the wisdom of the tongue, the

---

[1] To perform the Bareshnûm; cf. Vend. XXII, 20 [54].

[2] Reading nasûm kereta; cf. nasu-kereta (Vend. VII, 26 [67]).

[3] See above, p. 26, note 2.

[4] Sao*k*a; cf. Yt. XXII, 13.

[5] Du*z*avâ*t*: both the reading and the meaning are doubtful. Mr. West suggests, 'sends to hell' (reading du*z*anghvâ*t* or du*z*angha*t*).

[6] Doubtful.   [7] Reading ashava instead of asô ava.

[8] Cf. Yt. XIV, 46.

holy spells, the speech, the deeds, the libations, and the rightly-spoken words.

12. 'Yathâ ahû vairyô : The will of the Lord is the law of holiness . . . .
'I bless the sacrifice and prayer, and the strength and vigour of Haurvatâ*t*, the master; of the prosperity of the seasons and of the years, the masters of holiness.
'Ashem Vohû: Holiness is the best of all good . . . .
'[Give] unto that man [1] brightness and glory, ... give him the bright, all happy, blissful abode of the holy Ones.'

V. ÂBÂN YA*S*T.

The Âbân Ya*s*t (or Ya*s*t of the Waters) is devoted to the great goddess of the waters, the celebrated Ardvi Sûra Anâhita, the 'Αναῖτις of the Greeks. Ardvi Sûra Anâhita ('the high, powerful, undefiled') is the heavenly spring from which all waters on the earth flow down; her fountains are on the top of the mythical mountain, the Hukairya, in the star region. Her descent from the heavens is described in §§ 85 seq.; it reminds one of the Indian legend of the celestial Gaṅgâ.

This Ya*s*t contains much valuable information about the historical legends of Iran, as it enumerates the several heroes who worshipped Ardvi Sûra and asked for her help. First of all is Ahura himself (§ 16); then came Haoshyangha (§ 21), Yima (§ 25), Azi Dahâka (§ 29), Thraêtaona (§ 33), Keresáspa (§ 37), Franghrasyan (§ 41), Kava Usa (§ 45), Husravah (§ 49), Tusa (§ 53), Vaêsaka's sons (§ 57), Vafra Navâza (§ 61), *G*âmâspa (§ 68), Ashavazdah, the son of Pourudhâkh*s*ti, and Ashavazdah and Thrita, the sons of Sâyu*z*dri (§ 72), Vistauru (§ 76), Yôi*s*ta (§ 81); the Hvôvas and the Naotaras (§ 98), Zarathu*s*tra (§ 103), Kava Vî*s*tâspa (§ 107), Zairivairi (§ 112), Are*g*a*t*-aspa and Vandaremaini (§ 116).

This enumeration is interrupted by a description of the descent of Ardvi Sûra from the heavens (§§ 85-89), and of certain rules for her sacrifice given by herself to Zarathu*s*tra (§§ 90-97). This interruption may have been intentional, as it takes place just when

---

[1] Who shall have sacrificed to Haurvatâ*t*.

the course of the enumeration brings us to the times of Zarathustra
and of the institution of the new religion.

The Yast is opened with a laudation of the benefits bestowed by
Ardvi Sûra (§§ 1–16), and it closes with a description of her garments and apparel.

The first record of the worship of Ardvi Sûra is in a cuneiform
inscription by Artaxerxes Mnemon (404–361), in which her name
is corrupted into Anahata. Artaxerxes Mnemon appears to have
been an eager promoter of her worship, as he is said ' to have first
erected the statues of Venus-Anâhita ('Αφροδίτης, 'Αναίτιδος) in
Babylon, Suza, and Ecbatana, and to have taught her worship to
the Persians, the Bactrians, and the people of Damas and Sardes '
(Clemens Alexandrinus, Protrept. 5, on the authority of Berosus;
about 260 B.C.). My friend M. Halévy suggests to me that the
detailed and circumstantial description of Anâhita's appearance and
costume (in §§ 126–131) shows that the writer must have described
her from a consecrated type of statuary.

The principal data of the Greek writers on Anâhita will be
found in Windischmann's Essay (Die persische Anahita oder
Anaïtis, 1856). One must be cautious in the use of the Greek
sources, as the Greeks, with the eclectic turn of their mind, were
inclined to confound under the name of Anâhita all the great
female deities of Asia Minor, and her name became a common
appellation for the Aphrodites as well as for the Artemides of the
East.

---

0. May Ahura Mazda be rejoiced ! . . . .

Ashem Vohû : Holiness is the best of all good . . . .

I confess myself a worshipper of Mazda, a follower of Zarathustra, one who hates the Daêvas and obeys the laws of Ahura ;

For sacrifice, prayer, propitiation, and glorification unto [Hâvani].
the holy and master of holiness . . . .

Unto the good Waters, made by Mazda ; unto the
holy water-spring ARDVI ANÂHITA ; unto all waters,
made by Mazda ; unto all plants, made by Mazda [1],

Be propitiation, with sacrifice, prayer, propitiation,
and glorification.

Yathâ ahû vairyô : The will of the Lord is the law of holiness . . . .

---

[1] Sîrôzah I, 10

I.

1. Ahura Mazda spake unto Spitama Zarathu*s*tra, saying: ' Offer up a sacrifice, O Spitama Zarathu*s*tra! unto this spring of mine, Ardvi Sûra Anâhita, the wide-expanding[1] and health-giving, who hates the Daêvas and obeys the laws of Ahura, who is worthy of sacrifice in the material world, worthy of prayer in the material world ; the life-increasing[2] and holy, the herd-increasing and holy, the fold-increasing and holy, the wealth-increasing and holy, the country-increasing and holy;

2. 'Who makes the seed of all males pure[3], who makes the womb of all females pure for bringing forth[4], who makes all females bring forth in safety, who puts milk into the breasts of all females in the right measure and the right quality ;

3. ' The large river, known afar, that is as large as the whole of the waters that run along the earth ; that runs powerfully from the height Hukairya[5] down to the sea Vouru-Kasha[6].

4. 'All the shores of the sea Vouru-Kasha are

---

[1] ' As she comes down to all places' (Phl. tr. ad Yasna LXV, 1 [LXVI, 2]).

[2] Âdhu, translated *g*ân ; 'she makes life longer' (Aspendiârji). Perhaps âdhu will be better translated springs, rivers (reading *g*ûy instead of *g*ân ; cf. Yt. VIII, 29).

[3] ' Pure and sound, without blood and filth' (Phl. tr.).

[4] ' So that it may conceive again' (Phl. tr.).

[5] 'Hûgar the lofty is that from which the water of Arêdvîvsûr leaps down the height of a thousand men' (Bundahi*s* XII, 5, tr. West); cf. infra, §§ 96, 121, 126; Yt. XIII, 24. The Hukairya is mentioned again § 25 and Yt. IX, 8 ; Yt. X, 88 ; Yt. XV, 15 ; Yt. XVII, 28. It appears to be situated in the west (Bundahi*s* XXIV, 17 ; II, 7 ; Minokhired XLIV, 12).

[6] The earth-surrounding Ocean; cf. Vendîdâd V, 15 (49) seq., text and notes.

boiling over, all the middle of it is boiling over, when she runs down there, when she streams down there, she, Ardvi Sûra Anâhita, who has a thousand cells and a thousand channels[1]: the extent of each of those cells, of each of those channels is as much as a man can ride in forty days, riding on a good horse.

5. 'From this river of mine alone flow all the waters that spread all over the seven Karshvares; this river of mine alone goes on bringing waters, both in summer and in winter. This river of mine purifies the seed in males, the womb in females, the milk in females' breasts.

6. 'I, Ahura Mazda, brought it down with mighty vigour, for the increase of the house, of the borough, of the town, of the country, to keep them, to maintain them, to look over them, to keep and maintain them close.

7. 'Then Ardvi Sûra Anâhita, O Spitama Zarathustra! proceeded forth from the Maker Mazda. Beautiful were her white arms, thick as a horse's shoulder or still thicker; beautiful was her . . . .[2], and thus came she, strong, with thick arms, thinking thus in her heart:

8. '"Who will praise me? Who will offer me a sacrifice, with libations cleanly prepared and well-strained, together with the Haoma and meat? To whom shall I cleave, who cleaves unto me, and thinks with me, and bestows gifts upon me, and is of good will unto me?[3]"

9. 'For her brightness and glory, I will offer her

---

[1] See the description § 101 seq.

[2] Zaosa or zusa, an ἅπαξ λεγόμενον, seems to designate a part of the body; cf. § 126.

[3] Cf. §§ 11, 124.

a sacrifice worth being heard; I will offer up unto
the holy Ârdvi Sûra Anâhita a good sacrifice with
an offering of libations ;—thus mayest thou advise
us when thou art appealed to! Mayest thou be
most fully worshipped, O Ardvi Sûra Anâhita! with
the Haoma and meat, with the baresma, with the
wisdom of the tongue, with the holy spells, with the
words, with the deeds, with the libations, and with
the rightly-spoken words.

'Yê*n*hê hâtãm[1] : All those beings of whom
Ahura Mazda . . . .

II.

10. 'Offer up a sacrifice, O Spitama Zarathu*s*tra! unto this spring
of mine, Ardvi Sûra Anâhita, the wide-expanding and health-giving,
who hates the Daêvas and obeys the laws of Ahura, who is worthy
of sacrifice in the material world, worthy of prayer in the material world; the life-increasing and holy, the herd-increasing and
holy, the fold-increasing and holy, the wealth-increasing and holy,
the country-increasing and holy[2];

11. 'Who drives forwards on her chariot, holding
the reins of the chariot. She goes, driving, on this
chariot, longing for men[3] and thinking thus in her
heart: "Who will praise me? Who will offer me
a sacrifice, with libations cleanly prepared and well-
strained, together with the Haoma and meat? To
whom shall I cleave, who cleaves unto me, and
thinks with me, and bestows gifts upon me, and is of
good will unto me?"

'For her brightness and glory, I will offer her a sacrifice, worth
being heard[4] . . . .

---

[1] As above, p. 30; § 9 is repeated at the end of every chapter.

[2] § 10 = § 2.

[3] Viz. for their worshipping; cf. Yasna XXIII, 2 [5], paiti*s*mare*n*ti = Phl. hûmîtînît, they hope, they expect. Cf. § 123.

[4] As above, § 9.

III.

12. 'Offer up a sacrifice, O Spitama Zarathustra! unto this spring of mine, Ardvi Sûra' Anâhita [1]. . . .

13. 'Whom four horses carry, all white, of one and the same colour, of the same blood, tall, crushing down the hates of all haters, of the Daêvas and men, of the Yâtus and Pairikas, of the oppressors, of the blind and of the deaf [2].

'For her brightness and glory, I will offer her a sacrifice . . . .

IV.

14. 'Offer up a sacrifice, O Spitama Zarathustra! unto this spring of mine, Ardvi Sûra Anâhita . . . .

15. 'Strong and bright, tall and beautiful of form, who sends down by day and by night a flow of motherly [3] waters as large as the whole of the waters that run along the earth, and who runs powerfully [4].

'For her brightness and glory, I will offer her a sacrifice . . . .

V.

16. 'Offer up a sacrifice, O Spitama Zarathustra! unto this spring of mine, Ardvi Sûra Anâhita . . . .

17. 'To her did the Maker Ahura Mazda offer up a sacrifice [5] in the Airyana Vaêgah, by the good river Dâitya [6]; with the Haoma and meat, with the baresma, with the wisdom of the tongue, with the holy spells, with the words, with the deeds, with the libations, and with the rightly-spoken words [7].

---

[1] As above, § 10. [2] Cf. p. 26, note 2.
[3] Doubtful; cf. Yt. VIII, 47. [4] Cf. above, § 3.
[5] Cf. Vend. Introd. IV, 9, 40. This is the heavenly prototype of the Mazdean sacrifice as it was later shown to men by Zarathustra; cf. § 101.
[6] Cf. Yt. I, 4 and notes. [7] Cf. Yt. III, 18.

18. 'He begged of her a boon, saying : "Grant
me this, O good, most beneficent Ardvi Sûra Anâhita !
that I may bring the son of Pourushaspa, the holy
Zarathustra, to think after my law, to speak after my
law, to do after my law ! "

19. 'Ardvi Sûra Anâhita granted him that boon,
as he was offering libations, giving gifts, sacrificing,
and begging that she would grant him that boon.

'For her brightness and glory, I will offer her a sacrifice . . . .

VI.

20. 'Offer up a sacrifice, O Spitama Zarathustra! unto this spring
of mine, Ardvi Sûra Anâhita . . . .

21. 'To her did Haoshyangha, the Paradhâta [1],
offer up a sacrifice on the enclosure [2] of the Hara [3],
with a hundred male horses, a thousand oxen, and
ten thousand lambs.

22. 'He begged of her a boon, saying : "Grant
me this, O good, most beneficent Ardvi Sûra Anâhita ! that I may become the sovereign lord of
all countries, of the Daêvas and men, of the

---

[1] Haoshyangha was the first king of the Paradhâta (Pêsh-
dâdyan) dynasty (cf. above, p. 7, note 2, and Bundahis XXXI, 1).
It is related in Firdausi's Shâh Nâmah that he was the grandson of Gayomarth, the first man and king, and the son of Syâmak ;
that his father having been killed by the black Dîv, he encountered
him at the head of an army of lions, tigers, birds, and Paris, and
destroyed him ; he then succeeded his grandfather, and reigned
supreme over the seven Keshvars of the earth.

[2] Doubtful : upabda=upabanda, as thribda (Yt. VIII, 55)=
thribanda ; it appears from Yt. XV, 7 that the place meant here
is the Taêra which is said in the Bundahis (V, 7) to be surrounded
by the Albôrz (the Hara).

[3] The Hara berezaiti or Albôrz, in Mâzandarân, south of the
Caspian Sea, was supposed to surround the earth ; cf. Yt. X, 56.

Yâtus and Pairikas, of the oppressors, the blind and
the deaf; and that I may smite down two thirds [1]
of the Daêvas of Mâzana [2] and of the fiends of
Varena [3]."

23. 'Ardvi Sûra Anâhita granted him that boon,
as he was offering libations, giving gifts, sacrificing,
and entreating that she would grant him that boon.

'For her brightness and glory, I will offer her a sacrifice ....

VII.

24. 'Offer up a sacrifice, O Spitama Zarathu*s*tra! unto this
spring of mine, Ardvi Sûra Anâhita ....

25. 'To her did Yima Khshaêta [4], the good shepherd, offer up a sacrifice from the height Hukairya [5],
with a hundred male horses, a thousand oxen, ten
thousand lambs.

26. 'He begged of her a boon, saying: "Grant
me this, O good, most beneficent Ardvi Sûra Anâhita! that I may become the sovereign lord of all
countries, of the Daêvas and men, of the Yâtus
and Pairikas, of the oppressors, the blind and the
deaf; and that I may take from the Daêvas both

---

[1] A formula frequently used, not only in the Avesta, but also in
the Shâh Nâmah.

[2] The Daêvas in Mâzandarân. Mâzandarân was held a place
of resort for demons and sorcerers, and was in the Iranian legend
nearly the same as Ceylon is in the Râmâya*n*a. The Damâvand
mountain, to which Azi Dahâka was bound, is the sou*t*hern
boundary of Mâzandarân.

[3] See V*e*nd. Introd. IV, 23; cf. this Ya*s*t, § 33.

[4] Yima Khshaêta (*G*emshîd), as an earthly king, ruled over
the world for a thousand years, while he made immortality reign
in it (Yt. IX, 8; XV, 15; cf. Vendîdâd II, Introd.).

[5] See above, § 3.

riches and welfare, both fatness and flocks, both weal
and Glory [1]."

27. 'Ardvi Sûra Anâhita granted him that boon,
as he was offering libations, giving gifts, sacrificing,
and entreating that she would grant him that boon.
'For her brightness and glory, I will offer her a sacrifice . . . .

VIII.

28. 'Offer up a sacrifice, O Spitama Zarathustra! unto this
spring of mine, Ardvi Sûra Anâhita . . . .

29. 'To her did Azi Dahâka [2], the three-mouthed,
offer up a sacrifice in the land of Bawri [3], with a

---

[1] After his brother Takhma Urupa, who reigned before him, had
been killed and devoured by Angra Mainyu (Yt. IV, 11, note).

[2] When Yima began to sin and lost the Hvarenô (Glory), he was
overthrown by Azi Dahâka (Zohâk), who seized the power and
reigned in his place for a thousand years (cf. Yt. XIX, 33 seq.).
Azi Dahâka, literally 'the fiendish snake,' was first a mythical
personage ; he was the 'snake' of the storm-cloud, and a counterpart of the Vedic Ahi or Vritra. He appears still in that
character in Yast XIX seq., where he is described struggling
for the Hvarenô against Âtar (Fire), in the sea Vourukasha
(Vendîdâd, Introd. IV, 38 ; cf. this Yast, § 90). His struggle
with Yima Khshaêta bore at first the same mythological character,
'the shining Yima' being originally, like the Vedic Yama, a solar
hero : when Yima was turned into an earthly king, Azi underwent
the same fate.   In the Shâh Nâmah he is described as a man
with two snakes springing from his shoulders : they grew there
through a kiss of Ahriman's. For the myths referring to Azi, see
Ormazd et Ahriman, §§ 91–95.

[3] Babylon (cf. Yt. XV, 19). The usurper Azi, being a non-Aryan,
was identified with the hereditary foe, the Chaldæans : the name of
Babylon united in it, at the same time, a dim historical record of
the old Assyrian oppression, then shaken off and forgotten, and
an actual expression of the national antipathy of the Iranians
for their Semitic neighbours in Chaldæa. After the conquest of
Persia by the Musulmans, Azi was turned at last into an Arab.
The original seat of the Azi myths was on the southern coast
of the Caspian Sea (Études Iraniennes, II, 210).

hundred male horses, a thousand oxen, and ten thousand lambs.

30. ' He begged of her a boon, saying : " Grant me this boon, O good, most beneficent Ardvi Sûra Anâhita! that I may make all the seven Karshvares of the earth empty of men."

31. 'Ardvi Sûra Anâhita did not grant him that boon, although he was offering libations, giving gifts, sacrificing, and entreating her that she would grant him that boon.

' For her brightness and glory, I will offer her a sacrifice . . . .

IX.

32. 'Offer up a sacrifice, O Spitama Zarathustra! unto Ardvi Sûra Anâhita . . . .

33. ' To her did Thraêtaona[1], the heir[2] of the valiant Âthwya clan, offer up a sacrifice in the four-cornered Varena[3], with a hundred male horses, a thousand oxen, ten thousand lambs.

34. ' He begged of her a boon, saying : " Grant me this, O good, most beneficent Ardvi Sûra Anâhita! that I may overcome Azi Dahâka, the three-mouthed, the three-headed, the six-eyed, who has a thousand senses[4], that most powerful, fiendish Drug,

---

[1] Thraêtaona (Ferîdûn), son of Âthwya, conquered Azi and bound him to Mount Damâvand, where he is to stay till the end of the world, when he shall be let loose and then killed by Keresâspa (Vendîdâd, Introd. IV, 12, 18 ; Bahman Yast III, 55 seq. ; Bund. XXIX, 8 seq.).

[2] Vîsô-puthra=Pahlavi barbîtâ (see Études Iraniennes, II, 139).

[3] Cf. Vend. I, 18 and Introd. IV, 12. Modern tradition supposes Varena to have been the region of Ghilan (very likely on account of its proximity to Mâzandarân and Mount Damavand).

[4] See Yt. X, 82, note.

that demon, baleful to the world, the strongest
Drug that Angra Mainyu created against the material world, to destroy the world of the good principle [1]; and that I may deliver his two wives,
Savanghavâk and Erenavâk [2], who are the fairest
of body amongst women, and the most wonderful
creatures in the world [3]."

35. 'Ardvi Sûra Anâhita granted him that boon,
as he was offering libations, giving gifts, sacrificing,
and entreating that she would grant him that boon.

'For her brightness and glory, I will offer her a sacrifice . . . .

X.

36. 'Offer up a sacrifice, O Spitama Zarathustra! unto Ardvi
Sûra Anâhita . . . .

37. 'To her did Keresâspa [4], the manly-hearted,
offer up a sacrifice behind the Vairi Pisanah [5], with a

---

[1] Cf. Yt. XIX, 37.

[2] The two daughters of Yima, who had been ravished by Azi:
they are called in the Shâh Nâmah Shahrinâz and Arnavâz
(see Études Iraniennes, II, 213, Savanghavâk et Erenavâk).
Thraêtaona delivered them, and then married them; he had a son,
Airyu, from Arnavâz, and two sons from Shahrinâz, Tura and
Sairima; Airyu, Tura, and Sairima became the kings of Irân, Tûrân,
and Rûm.

[3] Cf. Yt. IX, 14; XV, 24; XVII, 34.

[4] Keresâspa (Garshâsp), one of the greatest heroes in the
Avestean romance, although Firdausi has all but passed him over
in silence. See his feats, Yt. XIX, 38 seq.; cf. Yt. V, 27 seq.;
Yasna IX, 10 (29); Vend. I, 10 (36).

[5] The Pisîn valley, south of Cabool. It was in the land of
Cabool that the Keresâspa legend had its rise, or at least it was
localised there. It is in the plain near the Pisîn valley that
Keresâspa lies asleep, till the end of the world comes (see Yt.
XIII, 61, note).

hundred male horses, a thousand oxen, ten thousand lambs.   *

38. ' He begged of her a boon, saying : " Grant me this, O good, most beneficent Ardvi Sûra Anâhita! that I may overcome the golden-heeled Ga*n*darewa [1], though all the shores of the sea Vouru-Kasha are boiling over; and that I may run up to the stronghold of the fiend on the wide, round earth, whose ends lie afar."

39. ' Ardvi Sûra Anâhita granted him that boon, as he was offering libations, giving gifts, sacrificing, and entreating that she would grant him that boon.

' For her brightness and glory, I will offer her a sacrifice . . . .

---

[1] A Parsi poem, of a very late date, gives further details about Ga*n*darewa. It was a monster who lived 'in the sea, on the mountain, and in the valley;' he was called Pâshnah zarah, because the sea did not go above his heel (a misinterpretation of his Avestean epithet zairi pâshna, golden-heeled, the Zend zairi being mistaken for the Persian zarah زه, sea); his head would rise to the sun and rub the sky; he could swallow up twelve men at once. Keresâspa fought him for nine days and nine nights together ; he drew him at last from the bottom of the sea and smashed his head with his club : when he fell on the ground, many countries were spoiled by his fall (Spiegel, Die traditionnelle Literatur der Parsen, p. 339, and West, Pahlavi Texts, II, pp. 369 seq.).

In the Vedic mythology the Gandharva is the keeper of Soma, and is described now as a god, now as a fiend, according as he is a heavenly Soma-priest or a jealous possessor who grudges it to man. What was the original form of the myth in Mazdeism is not clear. In the Shâh Nâmah he appears as the minister of Azi Dahâka. Cf. Yt. XV, 27 seq., and Ormazd et Ahriman, pp. 99, note 5 ; 215, note 1.

XI.

40. 'Offer up a sacrifice, O Spitama Zarathu*s*tra! unto this spring of mine, Ardvi Sûra Anâhita . . . .

41. 'To her did the Turanian murderer, Frangra-syan[1], offer up a sacrifice in his cave under the earth[2], with a hundred male horses, a thousand oxen, ten thousand lambs.

42. 'He begged of her a boon, saying: "Grant me this, O good, most beneficent Ardvi Sûra Anâhita! that I may seize hold of that Glory[3], that is waving in the middle of the sea Vouru-Kasha[3] and

---

[1] Frangrasyan (Afrâsyâb) was king of Tûrân for two hundred years. The perpetual struggle between Irân and Tûrân, which lasts to this day, was represented in the legend by the deadly and endless wars between Afrâsyâb and the Iranian kings from Mino-*k*ihr down to Kai Khosrav (Kavi Husravah). The chief cause of the feud was the murder of Syâvakhsh (Syâvarshâna) by Afrâsyâb; Syâvakhsh, son of Kai Kaus (Kava Usa), having been exiled by his father, at the instigation of his mother-in-law, took refuge with Afrâsyâb, who received him with honour, and gave him his daughter in marriage: but · the fortune of Syâvakhsh raised the jealousy of Afrâsyâb's brother, Karsîvaz (Keresavazda), who by means of calumnious accusations extorted from Afrâsyâb an order for putting him to death (see Yt. XIX, 77). Syâvakhsh was revenged by his son, Kai Khosrav, the grandson of Afrâsyâb (Yt. IX, 22).

[2] Ha*n*kanê: Firdausi speaks of a cave on the top of a mountain, near Barda (on the frontier of Adarbai*g*ân), where Afrâsyâb, when defeated, took refuge, and was discovered by Kai Khosrav; that cave was called 'the cave of Afrâsyâb' (hang i Afrâsiâb; Shâh Nâmah, IV, 196). In an older form of the legend, that cave was a palace built under-ground, with walls of iron and a hundred columns: its height was a thousand times a man's size (Aoge-maidê, § 61; cf. Bund. XII, 20: see Études Iraniennes, II, 225, Le Hang d'Afrâsyâb).

[3] Yt. XIX, 56 seq.

that belongs to the Aryan people, to those born and
to those not yet born, and to the holy Zarathustra."

43. 'Ardvi Sûra Anâhita did not grant him that
boon.

'For her brightness and glory, I will offer her a sacrifice . . . .

XII.

44. 'Offer up a sacrifice, O Spitama Zarathustra! unto this spring
of mine, Ardvi Sûra Anâhita . . . .

45. 'To her did the great, most wise Kavi Usa [1]
offer up a sacrifice from Mount Erezifya [2], with a
hundred male horses, a thousand oxen, ten thousand
lambs.

46. 'He begged of her a boon, saying: "Grant
me this, O good, most beneficent Ardvi Sûra Anâhita! that I may become the sovereign lord of all
countries, of the Daêvas and men, of the Yâtus and
Pairikas, of the oppressors, the blind and the deaf."

47. 'Ardvi Sûra Anâhita granted him that boon,
as he was offering libations, giving gifts, sacrificing,
and entreating that she would grant him that boon.

'For her brightness and glory, I will offer her a sacrifice . . . .

XIII.

48. 'Offer up a sacrifice, O Spitama Zarathustra! unto this spring
of mine, Ardvi Sûra Anâhita . . . .

49. 'To her did the gallant Husravah [3], he who

---

[1] Kavi Usa (Kai Kaus), the son of Kavi Kavâta (Kai Kobâd)
and the father of Syâvakhsh (see p. 64, note 1), was the second
king of the Kayanian dynasty.

[2] Mount Erezifya has been supposed to be the same as the
Sariphi Montes in Ptolemaeus, which stretch between Margiana
and Ariana (Burnouf, Commentaire sur le Yasna, p. 436).

[3] Kai Khosrav; cf. p. 64, notes 1 and 2.

[23]   F

united the Aryan nations into one kingdom [1], offer
up a sacrifice behind the *Ka͡ek*asta lake [2], the deep
lake, of salt waters [3], with a hundred male horses, a
thousand oxen, ten thousand lambs.

50. ' He begged of her a boon, saying : " Grant me
this, O good, most beneficent Ardvi Sûra Anâhita!
that I may become the sovereign lord of all countries, of Daêvas and men, of the Yâtus and Pairikas,
of the oppressors, the blind and the deaf; and that
I may have the lead in front of all the teams [4] and
that he may not pass through [5] the forest [6], he, the
murderer [7], who now is fiercely [8] striving against me [9]
on horseback [10]."

51. ' Ardvi Sûra Anâhita granted him that boon,
as he was offering libations, giving gifts, sacrificing,
and entreating that she would grant him that boon.

' For her brightness and glory, I will offer her a sacrifice . . . .

XIV.

52. 'Offer up a sacrifice, O Spitama Zarathuśtra! unto this spring
of mine, Ardvi Sûra Anâhita . . . .

53. ' To her did the valiant warrior Tusa [11] offer

---

[1] Doubtful.

[2] A lake in Adarbaig̃ân, with salt water : fish cannot live in it
(Bundahiś XXII, 2). It is the same as Lake Urumiah. Its name
is miswritten in Firdausi (Khang̃ast for *K*êg̃ast, خنگست for
جگست).

[3] Doubtful; see Études Iraniennes, II, uruyâpa, p. 179.

[4] In pursuing his adversary.   [5] Doubtful (cf. Yt. XV, 32).

[6] The White Forest (ibid.).   [7] Aurvasâra (ibid.).

[8] Doubtful.   [9] Trying to flee and escape.

[10] Possibly, 'vieing in horses' (for the swiftness of the race):
cf. Yt. XIX, 77.

[11] Tusa, in the Shâh Nâmah Tus; one of the most celebrated
Pahlavans of Kai Khosrav; he was the son of king Naotara
(Nôdar).

worship on the back of his horse [1], begging swiftness for his teams, health for his own body, and
that he might watch with full success [2] those who
hated him, smite down his foes, and destroy at one
stroke his adversaries, his enemies, and those who
hated him [3].

54. 'He begged of her a boon, saying: "Grant me
this, O good, most beneficent Ardvi Sûra Anâhita!
that I may overcome the gallant sons of Vaêsaka [4],
by the castle Khshathrô-saoka, that stands high up
on the lofty, holy Kangha [5]; that I may smite of the
Turanian people their fifties and their hundreds,
their hundreds and their thousands, their thousands
and their tens of thousands, their tens of thousands
and their myriads of myriads."

55. 'Ardvi Sûra Anâhita granted him that boon [6],
as he was offering libations, giving gifts, sacrificing,
and entreating that she would grant him that boon.

'For her brightness and glory, I will offer her a sacrifice . . . .

---

[1] He offers not a full sacrifice, being on horseback.

[2] Not to be taken by surprise.

[3] Cf. Yt. X, 11, 94, 114.

[4] Vaêsaka was the head of the Vîsah family, whose foremost
member was Pîrân Vîsah, the clever and upright minister of
Afrâsyâb, the Turanian Nestor; but his counsels were despised
for the common ruin, and himself perished with all his sons in the
war against Irân.

[5] Kangha was a town founded by Syâvarshâna, during his
exile, in a part of the land of Khvârizm, which is described as
an earthly paradise. This city was built on the top of a high
mountain (A*n*tare-Kangha, Yt. XIX, 4). The Khshathrô-saoka
castle is called in the Shâh Nâmah Kang de*z*, 'the fortress of
Kangha;' and, possibly, Khshathrô-saoka is a mere epithet of
dvarem, 'the castle of kingly welfare.'

[6] According to the Shâh Nâmah, Kang de*z* was stormed by
Kai Khosrav himself.

XV.

56. 'Offer up a sacrifice, O Spitama Zarathuſtra! unto this spring of mine, Ardvi Sûra Anâhita . . . .

57. ' To her did the gallant sons of Vaêsaka offer up a sacrifice in the castle Khshathrô-saoka, that stands high up on the lofty, holy Kangha, with a hundred male horses, a thousand oxen, ten thousand lambs.

58. ' They begged of her a boon, saying : " Grant us this, O good, most beneficent Ardvi Sûra Anâhita! that we may overcome the valiant warrior Tusa, and that we may smite of the Aryan people their fifties and their hundreds, their hundreds and their thousands, their thousands and their tens of thousands, their tens of thousands and their myriads of myriads [1]."

59. ' Ardvi Sûra Anâhita did not grant them that boon.

' For her brightness and glory, I will offer her a sacrifice . . . .

XVI.

60. 'Offer up a sacrifice, O Spitama Zarathuſtra! unto this spring of mine, Ardvi Sûra Anâhita . . . .

61. ' The old[2] Vafra Navâza worshipped her, when the strong fiend-smiter, Thraêtaona, flung him up in the air in the shape of a bird, of a vulture[3].

---

[1] Cf. §§ 53–54.

[2] Doubtful (pourvô); perhaps ' the man of the primitive faith' (the paoiryô-ʇkaêsha; cf. Yt. XIII, o, note): the sacrifice he offers is quite a Zoroastrian one (cf. §§ 17, 104, and note 2 to the latter).

[3] An allusion is made here to a myth, belonging to the Thraêtaona cyclus, of which no other trace is found in the Avesta (except in Yt. XXIII, 4). It referred most likely to the time when

62. 'He went on flying, for three days and three nights, towards his own house; but he could not, he could not turn down. At the end of the third night, when the beneficent dawn came dawning up, then he prayed unto Ardvi Sûra Anâhita, saying:

63. '"Ardvi Sûra Anâhita! do thou quickly hasten helpfully and bring me assistance at once. I will offer thee a thousand libations, cleanly prepared and well strained, along with Haomas and meat, by the brink of the river Rangha, if I reach alive the earth made by Ahura and my own house."

64. 'Ardvi Sûra Anâhita hastened unto him in the shape of a maid, fair of body, most strong, tall-formed, high-girded, pure, nobly born of a glorious race, wearing shoes up to the ankle, wearing a golden . . . . [1], and radiant [2].

65. 'She seized him by the arm: quickly was it done, nor was it long till, speeding, he arrived at the earth made by Mazda and at his own house, safe, unhurt, unwounded, just as he was before.

[66. 'Ardvi Sûra Anâhita granted him that boon, as he was offering up libations, giving gifts, sacrificing, entreating that she would grant him that boon [3].]

'For her brightness and glory, I will offer her a sacrifice . . . .

Thraêtaona, on his march to Bawri, the capital of Azi (cf. § 29), arrived at the Tigris (the Rangha); an angel then came and taught him magic to enable him to baffle the sortileges of Azi (Shâh Nâmah). We have in this passage an instance of his talents as a wizard, and one which helps us to understand why Thraêtaona is considered as the inventor of magic, and his name is invoked in spells and incantations (Hamzah Ispahanensis, p. 101; Anquetil, II, pp. 135 seq.). Cf. Yt. XIV, 40 and note

[1] Urvîkhsna, a word of doubtful meaning.

[2] Cf. Yt. V, 78, 126.

[3] This clause is no doubt spurious here.

XVII.

67. 'Offer up a sacrifice, O Spitama Zarathu*s*tra! unto this spring of mine, Ardvi Sûra Anâhita ....

68. 'To her did *G*âmâspa[1] offer up a sacrifice, with a hundred horses, a thousand oxen, ten thousand lambs, when he saw the army of the wicked, of the worshippers of the Daêvas, coming from afar in battle array.

69. 'He asked of her a boon, saying: "Grant me this, O good, most beneficent Ardvi Sûra Anâhita! that I may be as constantly victorious as any one of all the Aryans[2]."

70. 'Ardvi Sûra Anâhita granted him that boon, as he was offering up libations, giving gifts, sacrificing, and entreating that she would grant him that boon.

'For her brightness and glory, I will offer her a sacrifice ....

XVIII.

71. 'Offer up a sacrifice, O Spitama Zarathu*s*tra! unto this spring of mine, Ardvi Sûra Anâhita ....

72. 'To her did Ashavazdah, the son of Pouru-

---

[1] *G*âmâspa, the prime minister of Vîstâspa (Kai Gûstâsp), appears here in the character of a warrior, though generally he is described as a sage and a prophet (Yasna XLIX [XLVIII], 9; LI [L], 8; Zardûst Nâmah; yet cf. Yt. XXIII, 2). The Shâh Nâmah has an episode which recalls this one, although very different in its spirit, and more in accordance with the general character of *G*âmâspa. At the moment when the two armies meet together, Gûstâsp asks *G*âmâsp to reveal to him the issue of the encounter: *G*âmâsp obeys reluctantly, as the issue is to be fatal to the Iranians. *G*âmâsp belonged to the Hvôva family.

[2] Or, 'as all the rest of the Aryans together.'

dhâkhsti[1], and Ashavazdah and Thrita, the sons of
Sâyuzdri[2], offer up a sacrifice, with a hundred horses,
a thousand oxen, ten thousand lambs, by Apãm
Napât, the tall lord, the lord of the females, the
bright and swift-horsed[3].

73. 'They begged of her a boon, saying : "Grant
us this, O good, most beneficent Ardvi Sûra
Anâhita! that we may overcome the assemblers of
the Turanian Dânus[4], Kara Asabana[5], and Vara
Asabana, and the most mighty Dûraêkaêta, in the
battles of this world[6].

74. 'Ardvi Sûra Anâhita granted them that
boon, as they were offering up libations, giving gifts,
sacrificing, and entreating that she would grant
them that boon.

'For her brightness and glory, I will offer her a sacrifice . . . .

XIX.

75. 'Offer up a sacrifice, O Spitama Zarathustra! unto this spring
of mine, Ardvi Sûra Anâhita . . . .

76. 'Vistauru, the son of Naotara[7], worshipped

---

[1] Cf. Yt. XIII, 112. Ashavazdah, the son of Pourudhâkhsti,
is one of the immortals who will come forth to help Saoshyant in
the final struggle (Bundahis XXIX, 6; Yt. XIX, 95).

[2] Cf. Yt. XIII, 113.   [3] Cf. above, p. 6, note 1.

[4] A Turanian tribe, Yt. XIII, 37-38.

[5] Asabana is very likely an epithet; possibly, 'who kills with
a stone' (asan-ban); the sling was, as it seems, the favourite weapon
of the Dânus (Yt. XIII, 38).

[6] This section is the only fragment left of the legend of
Ashavazdah, which must have been an important one, since
Ashavazdah is one of the immortals (Yt. XIX, 95).

[7] Cf. Yt. XIII, 102. Vistauru, being the son of Naotara, is the
brother of Tusa, which identifies him with the Gustahm (كشتـم)
in the Shâh Nâmah: Nôdar had two sons, Tus and Gustahm.

her by the brink of the river Vîtanghuhaiti[1], with
well-spoken words, speaking thus:

77. '"This is true, this is truly spoken, that I
have smitten as many of the worshippers of the
Daêvas as the hairs I bear on my head. Do thou
then, O Ardvi Sûra Anâhita! leave me a dry passage, to pass over the good Vîtanghuhaiti."

78. 'Ardvi Sûra Anâhita hastened unto him in
the shape of a maid, fair of body, most strong, tall-
formed, high-girded, pure, nobly born of a glorious
race, wearing shoes up to the ankle, with all sorts of
ornaments and radiant[2]. A part of the waters she
made stand still, a part of the waters she made flow
forward, and she left him a dry passage to pass
over the good Vîtanghuhaiti[3].

[79. 'Ardvi Sûra Anâhita granted him that boon,
as he was offering up libations, giving gifts, sacrificing, and entreating that she would grant him that
boon[4].]

'For her brightness and glory, I will offer her a sacrifice . . . .

XX.

80. 'Offer up a sacrifice, O Spitama Zarathu*s*tra! unto this spring
of mine, Ardvi Sûra Anâhita . . . .

81. 'To her did Yôista, one of the Fryanas[5],

---

[1] A river not mentioned elsewhere.
[2] Cf. §§ 64, 126.
[3] Firdausi has no mention of this episode.
[4] Spurious.
[5] This legend is fully told in the Pahlavi tale of Gô*s*ti Fryân
(edited and translated by West): a sorcerer, named Akht, comes
with an immense army to the city of the enigma-expounders,
threatening to make it a beaten track for elephants, if his enigmas
are not solved. A Mazdayasnian, named Gô*s*ti Fryân, guesses the

offer up a sacrifice with a hundred horses, a thousand oxen, ten thousand lambs on the Pedvaêpa [1] of the Rangha.

82. 'He begged of her a boon, saying: "Grant me this, O good, most beneficent Ardvi Sûra Anâhita! that I may overcome the evil-doing Akhtya, the offspring of darkness, and that I may answer the ninety-nine hard riddles that he asks me maliciously, the evil-doing Akhtya, the offspring of darkness."

83. 'Ardvi Sûra Anâhita granted him that boon, as he was offering up libations, giving gifts, sacrificing, and entreating that she would grant him that boon.

'For her brightness and glory, I will offer her a sacrifice . . . .

XXI.

84. 'Offer up a sacrifice, O Spitama Zarathustra! unto this spring of mine, Ardvi Sûra Anâhita . . . .

85. 'Whom Ahura Mazda the merciful ordered thus, saying: "Come, O Ardvi Sûra Anâhita, come from those stars [2] down to the earth made by Ahura,

---

thirty-three riddles proposed by Akht; then, in his turn, he proposes him three riddles which the sorcerer is unable to guess, and, in the end, he destroys him by the strength of a Nîrang. Cf. Yt. XIII, 120. This tale, which belongs to the same widespread cycle as the myth of Oedipus and the Germanic legend of the Wartburg battle, is found in the Zarathustra legend too (Vendîdâd XIX, 4).

[1] Perhaps an affluent of the Rangha (cf. Yt. XIII, 19, 19; XV, 27).

[2] Between the earth and the region of infinite light there are three intermediate regions, the star region, the moon region, and the sun region. The star region is the nearest to the earth, and the sun region is the remotest from it. Ardvi Sûra has her seat in the star region (Yasna LXV [LXIV], 1; Phl. tr.); cf. Yt. V, 132.

that the great lords may worship thee, the masters of the countries, and their sons.

86. ' " The men of strength [1] will beg of thee swift horses and supremacy of Glory.

' " The Âthravans who read [2] and the pupils of the Âthravans will beg of thee knowledge and prosperity, the Victory made by Ahura, and the crushing Ascendant.

87. ' " The maids of barren womb [3], longing for a lord [3], will beg of thee a strong husband;

' " Women, on the point of bringing forth, will beg of thee a good delivery.

' " All this wilt thou grant unto them, as it lies in thy power, O Ardvi Sûra Anâhita ! "

88. ' Then Ardvi Sûra Anâhita came forth, O Zarathustra ! down from those stars to the earth made by Mazda; and Ardvi Sûra Anâhita spake thus :

89. ' " O pure, holy Zarathustra ! Ahura Mazda has established thee as the master of the material world : Ahura Mazda has established me to keep the whole of the holy creation.

' " Through my brightness and glory flocks and herds and two-legged men go on, upon the earth : I, forsooth, keep all good things, made by Mazda, the offspring of the holy principle, just as a shepherd keeps his flock."

90. ' Zarathustra asked Ardvi Sûra Anâhita : " O Ardvi Sûra Anâhita ! With what manner of sacrifice shall I worship thee ? With what manner of sacrifice shall I worship and forward thee ? So that Mazda may make thee run down (to the earth), that

---

[1] The warriors. [2] To teach. [3] Doubtful.

he may not make thee run up into the heavens, above the sun¹; and that the Serpent² may not injure thee with . . . .³, with . . . .⁴, with . . . .⁵, and . . . . poisons⁶."

91. 'Ardvi Sûra Anâhita answered: "O pure, holy Spitama! this is the sacrifice wherewith thou shalt worship me, this is the sacrifice wherewith thou shalt worship and forward me, from the time when the sun is rising to the time when the sun is setting.

'"Of this libation of mine thou shalt drink, thou who art an Âthravan, who hast asked and learnt the revealed law, who art wise, clever, and the Word incarnate.

92. '"Of this libation of mine let no foe drink, no man fever-sick, no liar, no coward, no jealous one, no woman, no faithful one who does not sing the Gâthas, no leper to be confined⁷.

93. '"I do not accept those libations that are drunk in my honour by the blind, by the deaf, by the wicked, by the destroyers, by the niggards, by the . . . .⁸, nor any of those stamped with those characters which have no strength for the holy Word⁹.

---

¹ When the beds of the rivers are dry, the cause is that Ardvi Sûra sends up her waters to the higher heavens (to the sun region) instead of sending them down to the earth (cf. p. 73, note 2).

² The serpent, Azi, is here Azi in his original naturalistic character, the storm-fiend (cf. Vend. Introd. IV, 38 and this Yast, § 29, note). The uncleanness and unhealthiness of the rivers are ascribed to his poison.

³ Arethna, an ἅπαξ λεγόμενον.   ⁴ Vawzaka, idem.
⁵ Varenva, idem.   ⁶ Varenva poisons.
⁷ Cf. Vend. II, 29.   ⁸ ? Ranghau.
⁹ Which incapacitate one for religious works.

' " Let no one drink of these my libations who is
hump-backed or bulged forward; no fiend with
decayed teeth [1]."

94. ' Then Zarathustra asked Ardvi Sûra Anâhita:
" O Ardvi Sûra Anâhita! What becomes of those
libations which the wicked worshippers of the
Daêvas bring unto thee after the sun has set [2]? "

95. ' Ardvi Sûra Anâhita answered: " O pure,
holy Spitama Zarathustra! howling, clapping, hop-
ping, and shouting [3], six hundred and a thousand
Daêvas, who ought not to receive that sacrifice [4],
receive those libations [5] that men bring unto me
after [the sun has set] [6]."

96. ' I will worship the height Hukairya, of the
deep precipices [7], made of gold, wherefrom this mine
Ardvi Sûra Anâhita leaps, from a hundred times the
height of a man [8], while she is possessed of as much
Glory as the whole of the waters that run along the
earth, and she runs powerfully [9].

' For her brightness and glory, I will offer her a sacrifice . . . .

XXII.

97. ' Offer up a sacrifice, O Spitama Zarathustra! unto this spring
of mine, Ardvi Sûra Anâhita . . . .

98. ' Before whom the worshippers of Mazda

---

[1] Cf. Vend. II, 29.

[2] Cf. Vend. VII, 79 and note 2; cf. above, § 91.

[3] For joy. The translations of those several words are not
certain.

[4] Doubtful.   [5] Perhaps, those cups (yam*au*).

[6] Filled up from § 94.

[7] The text here has vîspô-vahmem, ' worthy of all prayer;' the
reading vîspô-vaêmem from Yt. XII, 24 seems to be better.

[8] Cf. §§ 102, 121.   [9] Cf. §§ 4, 102, 121.

stand with baresma in their hands : the Hvôvas did worship her, the Naotaras did worship her[1]; the Hvôvas asked for riches, the Naotaras asked for swift horses. Quickly was Hvôva blessed with riches and full prosperity; quickly became Vîstâspa, the Naotaride, the lord of the swiftest horses in these countries[2].

99. ['Ardvi Sûra Anâhita granted them that boon, as they were offering up libations, giving gifts, sacrificing, and entreating that she would grant them that boon[3].]

'For her brightness and glory, I will offer her a sacrifice . . . .

XXIII.

100. 'Offer up a sacrifice, O Spitama Zarathu*s*tra! unto this spring of mine, Ardvi Sûra Anâhita . . . .

101. 'Who has a thousand cells and a thousand channels : the extent of each of those cells, of each of those channels, is as much as a man can ride in forty days, riding on a good horse[4]. In each channel there stands a palace, well-founded, shining with a hundred windows, with a thousand columns, well-built, with ten thousand balconies, and mighty.

102. 'In each of those palaces there lies a well-laid, well-scented bed, covered with pillows, and

---

[1] The Hvôva or Hvôgva family plays as great a part in the religious legend, as the Naotara family in the heroic one. Two of the Hvôvas, Frashao*s*tra and *G*âmâspa, were among the first disciples of Zarathu*s*tra and the prophet married Frashao*s*tra's daughter, Hvôgvi (cf. Yt. XIII, 139). For the Naotaras, see above, §§ 53, 76. According to the Bundahi*s*, Vîstâspa did not belong to the Naotara family (XXXI, 28) : perhaps he was considered a Naotaride on account of his wife Hutaosa, who was one (Yt. XV, 35).

[2] His very name means ' He who has many horses.'

[3] Spurious.   [4] Cf. § 4.

Ardvi Sûra Anâhita, O Zarathustra! runs down there
from a thousand times the height of a man, and she
is possessed of as much Glory as the whole of the
waters that run along the earth, and she runs
powerfully [1].

XXIV.

103. 'Offer up a sacrifice, O Spitama Zarathustra! unto this
spring of mine, Ardvi Sûra Anâhita . . . .

104. 'Unto her did the holy Zarathustra offer up
a sacrifice in the Airyana Vaêgah, by the good river
Dâitya; with the Haoma and meat, with the baresma,
with the wisdom of the tongue, with the holy spells,
with the speech, with the deeds, with the libations,
and with the rightly-spoken words [2].

105. 'He begged of her a boon, saying: "Grant
me this, O good, most beneficent Ardvi Sûra Anâhita! that I may bring the son of Aurvat-aspa [3], the
valiant Kavi Vîstâspa, to think according to the law,
to speak according to the law, to do according to
the law [4]."

106. 'Ardvi Sûra Anâhita granted him that
boon, as he was offering up libations, giving gifts,
sacrificing, and entreating that she would grant him
that boon.

'For her brightness and glory, I will offer her a sacrifice . . . .

---

[1] Cf. § 96.

[2] Cf. § 17. It is to be noticed that only Ahura and Zarathustra
(and perhaps Vafra Navâza; see p. 68, note 2) offer the pure
Zoroastrian sacrifice.

[3] Called Lôhrâsp in Parsi tradition.

[4] Cf. § 18. The conversion of Vîstâspa by Zarathustra is the
turning-point in the earthly history of Mazdeism, as the conversion
of Zarathustra by Ahura himself is in its heavenly history. Cf. Yt.
XXIV and IX, 26.

XXV.

107. 'Offer up a sacrifice, O Spitama Zarathustra! unto this spring of mine, Ardvi Sûra Anâhita . . . .

108. 'Unto her did the tall [1] Kavi Vîstâspa [2] offer up a sacrifice behind Lake Frazdânava [3], with a hundred male horses, a thousand oxen, ten thousand lambs.

109. 'He begged of her a boon, saying: "Grant me this, O good, most beneficent Ardvi Sûra Anâhita! that I may overcome Tãthravant, of the bad law, and Peshana, the worshipper of the Daêvas, and the wicked Aregat-aspa [4], in the battles of this world!"

110. 'Ardvi Sûra Anâhita granted him that boon, as he was offering up libations, giving gifts, sacrificing, and entreating that she would grant him that boon.

'For her brightness and glory, I will offer her a sacrifice . . . .

---

[1] Berezaidhi, translated buland (Yasna LVII, 11 [LVI, 5, 2]).

[2] See Yt. XIII, 99; V, 98, 105.

[3] A lake in Seistan (Bundahis XXII, 5); from that lake will rise Hôshêdar Bâmî (Ukhshyat-ereta), the first of the three sons of Zarathustra, not yet born (Bahman Yast III, 13; cf. Yt. XIII, 98).

[4] Of these three, Aregat-aspa alone is known to Firdausi; he is the celebrated Argâsp, who waged a deadly war against Gûstâsp to suppress the new religion: he stormed Balkh, slaughtered Lôhrâsp and Zartûst (Zarathustra), and was at last defeated and killed by Gûstâsp's son, Isfendyâr. He is the Afrâsyâb of the Zoroastrian period. In the Avesta he is not called a Turanian (Tura), but a Hvyaona; see Yt. IX, 30.

XXVI.

111. 'Offer up a sacrifice, O Spitama Zarathustra! unto this spring of mine, Ardvi Sûra Anâhita . . . .

112. 'Unto her did Zairi-vairi[1], who fought on horseback, offer up a sacrifice behind the river Dâitya[2], with a hundred male horses, a thousand oxen, ten thousand lambs.

113. 'He begged of her a boon, saying: "Grant me this, O good, most beneficent Ardvi Sûra Anâhita! that I may overcome Peshô-Kangha the corpse-burier[3], Humâyaka[4] the worshipper of the Daêvas, and the wicked Aregat-aspa[5], in the battles of this world.

114. 'Ardvi Sûra Anâhita granted him that boon[6], as he was offering up libations, giving gifts, sacrificing, and entreating that she would grant him that boon.

'For her brightness and glory, I will offer her a sacrifice . . . .

XXVII.

115. 'Offer up a sacrifice, O Spitama Zarathustra! unto this spring of mine, Ardvi Sûra Anâhita . . . .

116. 'Unto her did Aregat-aspa and Vandaremaini[7]

---

[1] Zarîr in Firdausi, the brother of Vîstâspa; cf. Yt. V, 117; XIII, 101.

[2] The Araxes (Vendîdâd I, 3).

[3] Doubtful (cf. Vend. III, 36 seq.).

[4] This is perhaps an epithet to Peshô-Kangha, 'the most malicious.'

[5] See p. 79, note 4.

[6] If we may trust the Shâh Nâmah, she did not grant her favour to the last, as Zarîr was killed by one of the generals of Argâsp, Bîdirafsh.

[7] A brother of Argâsp's: his name is slightly altered in Firdausi (Andarîmân miswritten for Vandarîmân, اندریمان for وندریمان; see Études Iraniennes, p. 228).

offer up a sacrifice by the sea Vouru-Kasha, with a hundred male horses, a thousand oxen, ten thousand lambs.

117. 'They[1] begged of her a boon, saying : " Grant us this, O good, most beneficent Ardvi Sura Anâhita! that we may conquer the valiant Kavi Vîstâspa and Zairivairi who fights on horseback, and that we may smite of the Aryan people their fifties and their hundreds, their hundreds and their thousands, their thousands and their tens of thousands, their tens of thousands and their myriads of myriads."

118. 'Ardvi Sûra Anâhita did not grant them [2] that favour, though they were offering up libations, giving gifts, sacrificing, and entreating that she should grant them that favour.

'For her brightness and glory, I will offer her a sacrifice . . . .

XXVIII.

119. 'Offer up a sacrifice, O Spitama Zarathustra! unto this spring of mine, Ardvi Sûra Anâhita . . . .

120. 'For whom Ahura Mazda has made four horses—the wind, the rain, the cloud, and the sleet—and thus ever [3] upon the earth it is raining, snowing, hailing, and sleeting; and whose armies are so many and numbered by nine-hundreds and thousands.

121. 'I will worship the height Hukairya, of the

---

[1] The text has the singular here and in the rest of the sentence : the names of the two brothers form a sort of singular dvandva; cf. Franghrasyanem Keresavazdem (Yt. XIX, 77); Ashavazdanghô Thritahê (Yt. XIII, 113; and same Yast, 115), and in the present passage Vîstâspô Zairivairis (see Études Iraniennes, II, 229).

[2] Both were killed by Isfendyâr (Shâh Nâmah).

[3] Mîsti translated hamêsak, sadâ (Yt. VII, 4).

[23]   G

deep precipices, made of gold, wherefrom this mine
Ardvi Sûra Anâhita leaps, from a hundred times the
height of a man, while she is possessed of as much
Glory as the whole of the waters that run along the
earth, and she runs powerfully [1].

'For her brightness and glory, I will offer her a sacrifice. . . .

XXIX.

122. 'Offer up a sacrifice, O Spitama Zarathu*s*tra! unto this
spring of mine, Ardvi Sûra Anâhita . . . .

123. 'She stands, the good Ardvi Sûra Anâhita,
wearing a golden mantle [2], waiting for a man who
shall offer her libations and prayers, and thinking
thus in her heart :

124. ' " Who will praise me ? Who will offer me a
sacrifice, with libations cleanly prepared and well-
strained, together with the Haoma and meat ? To
whom shall I cleave, who cleaves unto me, and
thinks with me, and bestows gifts upon me, and is
of good will unto me [3] ? "

'For her brightness and glory, I will offer her a sacrifice . . . .

XXX.

125. 'Offer up a sacrifice, O Spitama Zarathu*s*tra! unto this
spring of mine, Ardvi Sûra Anâhita . . . .

126. 'Ardvi Sûra Anâhita, who stands carried
forth in the shape of a maid, fair of body, most
strong, tall-formed, high-girded, pure, nobly born of

---

[1] § 121=§§ 96, 102.
[2] Paitidâna, a mantle, a tunic (Vend. XIV, 9 [28]).
[3] See §§ 8, 11.

a glorious race[1], wearing along her . . . . [2] a mantle fully embroidered with gold;

127. 'Ever holding the baresma in her hand, according to the rules, she wears square golden earrings on her ears bored[3], and a golden necklace around her beautiful neck, she, the nobly born Ardvi Sûra Anâhita; and she girded her waist tightly, so that her breasts may be well-shaped, that they may be tightly pressed[4].

128. 'Upon her head Ardvi Sûra Anâhita bound a golden crown, with a hundred stars[5], with eight rays, a fine . . . . [6], a well-made crown, in the shape of a . . . . [7], with fillets streaming down.

129. 'She is clothed with garments of beaver[8], Ardvi Sûra Anâhita; with the skin of thirty beavers of those that bear four young ones, that are the finest kind of beavers; for the skin of the beaver that lives in water is the finest-coloured of all skins, and when worked at the right time it shines to the eye with full sheen of silver and gold.

130. 'Here, O good, most beneficent Ardvi Sûra Anâhita! I beg of thee this favour: that I, fully blessed, may conquer large kingdoms, rich in horses[9], with high tributes, with snorting horses, sounding chariots, flashing swords, rich in aliments, with stores of food, with well-scented beds[10]; that I may have

---

[1] Cf. §§ 64, 78.   [2] Zaoṣa; cf. § 7, note 2.
[3] Doubtful (sispemna, from sif, سفتن).
[4] Doubtful.   [5] Gems.
[6] ? Anupôithwaitîm.
[7] ? Ratha; the usual meaning of ratha is 'a chariot;' perhaps the round shape of the chest of a chariot is meant.
[8] Possibly otter, Vend. XIV.   [9] Doubtful.
[10] Cf. Yt. XVII, 7.

at my wish the fulness of the good things of life and whatever makes a kingdom thrive[1].

131. 'Here, O good, most beneficent Ardvi Sûra Anâhita! I beg of thee two gallant companions, one two-legged and one four-legged[2]: one two-legged, who is swift, quickly rushing, and clever in turning a chariot round in battle; and one four-legged, who can quickly turn towards either wing of the host with a wide front, towards the right wing or the left, towards the left wing or the right.

132. 'Through the strength of this sacrifice, of this invocation, O Ardvi Sûra Anâhita! come down from those stars[3], towards the earth made by Ahura, towards the sacrificing priest, towards the full boiling [milk[4]]; come to help him who is offering up libations, giving gifts, sacrificing, and entreating that thou wouldst grant him thy favours; that all those gallant warriors may be strong, like king Vîstâspa.

'For her brightness and glory, I will offer her a sacrifice . . . .

133. 'Yathâ ahû vairyô: The will of the Lord is the law of holiness . . . .

'I bless the sacrifice and prayer, and the strength and vigour of the holy water-spring Anâhita.

'Ashem Vohû: Holiness is the best of all good . . . .

'[Give] unto that man brightness and glory, ... give him the bright, all-happy, blissful abode of the holy Ones!'

---

[1] The translation of the last clause is doubtful.
[2] A good horse and a good driver.
[3] Cf. §§ 85, 88. [4] Aspendiârji ad Vend. XIX, 40 [133].

VI. KHÔRSHÊ*D* YA*ST*.

(YA*ST* TO THE SUN.)

This Ya*st* is recited at any time, but particularly on the days consecrated to the sun and to Khshathra-Vairya (Shahrîvar), Mithra (Mihir), Asman (Âsmân), and Anaghra rao*kau* (Anîrân[1]): the last three, Mithra, Asman (the Heaven), Anaghra (the infinite Light), have a natural connection with the sun, but its connection with Khshathra-Vairya is not so clear.

Of this Ya*st* we have a Pahlavi (East India Office, XII), a Persian (ibid. XXIV), and a Sanskrit translation (Fonds Burnouf V ; all three edited in Études Iraniennes, II).

---

o. May Ahura Mazda be rejoiced ! . . . .
Ashem Vohû : Holiness is the best of all good . . . .
I confess myself a worshipper of Mazda, a follower of Zara-thu*st*ra, one who hates the Daêvas and obeys the laws of Ahura ;
For sacrifice, prayer, propitiation, and glorification unto [Hâvani], the holy and master of holiness[2] . . . .

Unto the undying, shining, swift-horsed Sun[3] ;

Be propitiation, with sacrifice, prayer, propitiation, and glorification.

Yathâ ahû vairyô : The will of the Lord is the law of holi-ness[2] . . . .

1. We sacrifice unto the undying, shining, swift-horsed Sun.

When the light of the sun waxes warmer[4], when the brightness of the sun waxes warmer, then up

---

[1] Or the 11th, 16th, 27th, and 30th days of the month (Anquetil, II, 184).
[2] As above, Yt. I, o.   [3] Sîrôzah I, 11.
[4] 'That is to say, rises up' (Phl. tr.).

stand the heavenly Yazatas, by hundreds and thousands : they gather together its Glory, they make its
Glory pass down, they pour its Glory upon the earth
made by Ahura, for the increase of the world of
holiness, for the increase of the creatures of holiness [1], for the increase of the undying, shining, swift-
horsed Sun.

2. And when the sun rises up, then the earth,
made by Ahura, becomes clean [2]; the running waters
become clean, the waters of the wells become clean,
the waters of the sea become clean, the standing
waters become clean ; all the holy creatures, the
creatures of the Good Spirit, become clean.

3. Should not the sun rise up, then the Daêvas
would destroy all the things that are in the seven
Karshvares, nor would the heavenly Yazatas find
any way of withstanding or repelling them in the
material world.

4. He who offers up a sacrifice unto the undying,
shining, swift-horsed Sun—to withstand darkness, to
withstand the Daêvas born of darkness, to withstand
the robbers and bandits, to withstand the Yâtus and
Pairikas, to withstand death that creeps in unseen—
offers it up to Ahura Mazda, offers it up to the
Amesha-Spe*n*tas, offers it up to his own soul [3]. He
rejoices all the heavenly and worldly Yazatas, who
offers up a sacrifice unto the undying, shining, swift-
horsed Sun.

5. I will sacrifice unto Mithra, the lord of wide

---

[1] Literally ' of the body of holiness,' that is to say, of the bodily
creatures that incorporate holiness.

[2] 'From the uncleanness that the Daêvas mix with the earth
during the night' (Phl. tr.).

[3] As he benefits them and himself thereby.

pastures, who has a thousand ears, ten thousand eyes.

I will sacrifice unto the club of Mithra, the lord of wide pastures, well struck down [1] upon the skulls of the Daêvas.

I will sacrifice unto that friendship, the best of all friendships, that reigns between the moon and the sun [2].

6. For his brightness and glory, I will offer unto him a sacrifice worth being heard, namely, unto the undying, shining, swift-horsed Sun. Unto the undying, shining, swift-horsed Sun we offer up the libations, the Haoma and meat, the baresma, the wisdom of the tongue, the holy spells, the speech, the deeds, the libations, and the rightly-spoken words [3].

Yênhê hâtãm: All those beings of whom Ahura Mazda ....

7. Yathâ ahû vairyô: The will of the Lord is the law of holiness ....

I bless the sacrifice and the invocation, and the strength and vigour of the undying, shining, swift-horsed Sun.

Ashem Vohû: Holiness is the best of all good ....

Give unto that man brightness and glory, give him health of body, ... give him the bright, all-happy, blissful abode of the holy Ones.

---

[1] Hunivikhtem: suniyuktam (Sansk. tr.); خوب نهادﮦ (Pers.tr.).
[2] As they succeed one another in regular order.
[3] Cf. Yt. III, 18.

VII. MÂH YAST.

This Yast to the Moon is recited on the day of the Moon, and on those of Bahman, Gôs, and Râm[1] (Anquetil, II, 185). Bahman and Gôs are so far connected with the Moon that all three are gaokithra: 'Bahman[2], the Moon, and Gôs[3], all three, are having in them the seed of the bull; Bahman can neither be seen nor seized with the hand; the Moon proceeded from Bahman[4] and can be seen, but cannot be seized with the hand; Gôs proceeded from the Moon[5] and can both be seen and seized with the hand[6].' Râm is referred to here as being hvâstra, 'lord of good pastures[7].'

Of this Yast we have translations in Pahlavi, Persian, and Sanskrit (edited in Études Iraniennes, II).

---

o. May Ahura Mazda be rejoiced ! . . . .

Ashem Vohû: Holiness is the best of all good . . . .

I confess myself a worshipper of Mazda, a follower of Zarathustra, one who hates the Daêvas and obeys the laws of Ahura;

For sacrifice, prayer, propitiation, and glorification unto [Hâvani], the holy and master of holiness . . . .

Unto the Moon that keeps in it the seed of the

---

[1] The 12th, 2nd, 14th, and 21st days of the month.

[2] The Amshaspand Bahman is entrusted with the care of cattle (Vend. XIX, 20, note 8).

[3] The Genius of Cattle; see Yt. IX.

[4] Bahman is 'good thought, good mind,' Vohu-Manô; in the Vedas the moon is said to have been made out of the mind (manas) of Purusa. For an explanation of that old mystical myth, see Ormazd et Ahriman, p. 74, note 3.

[5] See Vend. XXI, 9 [51], note 4.

[6] Pahlavi commentary to this Yast, I.

[7] Vend. Introd. IV, 16, and Études Iraniennes, II, 187 seq.

Bull ; unto the only-created Bull and unto the Bull[1] of many species ;

Be propitiation, with sacrifice, prayer, propitiation, and glorification.

Yathâ ahû vairyô : The will of the Lord is the law of holiness . . . .

1. Hail to Ahura Mazda! Hail to the Amesha-Spentas! Hail to the Moon that keeps in it the seed of the Bull[2]! Hail to thee when we look at thee! Hail to thee when thou lookest at us[3]!

2. How does the moon wax? How does the moon wane?

For fifteen days does the moon wax[4]; for fifteen days does the moon wane. As long as her waxing, so long is the waning[5]; as long as her waning, so long is the waxing.

'Who is there but thee[6] who makes the moon wax and wane[7]?'

---

[1] Sîrôzah I, 12.   [2] See Vend. XXI, 1, text and note.

[3] When the moon allows itself to be perceived.

[4] The Pahlavi translation has the following interesting details : 'For fifteen days they take good deeds from the earthly creatures and the rewards for virtue from the heavens; for fifteen days they make the rewards pass to the earth and the good deeds pass to the heavens.' The moon is thus a sort of moral clearing-house between earth and heaven.

[5] According to the Parsis this waning does not refer to the moon, but to the constellations that help it in the struggle against the planets, which are supposed to belong to the Ahrimanian world (see Ormazd et Ahriman, §§ 223–226): 'while it waxes—namely, the moon—they wane,—namely, those that are opposed to the planets, to the bad stars; for instance, Haftôiring, Vanand, Tistar, Satvês; . . . . while it wanes—namely, the moon—they wax, that is to say, they are strong for doing good.' Thus the moon and the stars relieve each other in the battle against Ahriman.

[6] Ahura.

[7] Quoted from Yasna XLIV [XLIII], 3.

3. We sacrifice unto the Moon that keeps in it
the seed of the Bull, the holy and master of
holiness.

Here I look at the moon, here I perceive the
moon ; here I look at the light of the moon, here
I perceive the light of the moon. The Amesha-
Spe*n*tas stand up [1], holding its glory ; the Amesha-
Spe*n*tas stand up, pouring its glory upon the earth,
made by Mazda [2].

4. And when the light of the moon waxes
warmer, golden-hued plants grow on [3] from the
earth during the spring [4].

We sacrifice unto the new moons, the full moons,
and the Vîshaptathas [5].

We sacrifice unto the new moon, the holy and
master of holiness ;

We sacrifice unto the full moon, the holy and
master of holiness ;

We sacrifice unto the Vîshaptatha, the holy and
master of holiness.

---

[1] As soon as the moon appears.   [2] Cf. Yt. VI, 2.

[3] Mi*s*ti, meaning sadâ, مسيشد; cf. mi-*s*â*k*i.

[4] Zaremaêm, meaning vasantamâse, بزمان بهار; it has the
same meaning in Vend. XVIII, 9 [23]; cf. Yt. XXII, 18.

[5] New moon and full moon are not used here in the English
meaning : the month was divided into six parts, of five days each
(the Norse fimt or five days' week; see Vigfusson, Icelandic
Dictionary, s. v.): the first five days (pan*k*ak fartûm) formed the
new moon or a*n*tare-ma*u*ngha, literally ' the moon within ; ' the next
five days (pan*k*ak datîgar) formed the pere nô-ma*u*ngha, literally
' the moon full,' which in fact partly answered to our first quarter ;
the next five days (pan*k*ak sitîgar), belonging to the full moon,
were called the Vîshaptatha; no mention is made of the last three
pan*k*ak, forming the second half of the month. It may be they
were not mentioned, as belonging to the waning period, when the
powers of the moon are suffering an eclipse. Cf. Neriosengh to
Yasna I, (23.)

5. I will sacrifice unto the Moon, that keeps in it the seed of the Bull, the liberal, bright, glorious, water-giving [1], warmth-giving, wisdom-giving [2], wealth-giving [3], riches-giving, thoughtfulness-giving [4], weal-giving, freshness-giving [5], prosperity-giving [6], the liberal, the healing.

6. For its brightness and glory, I will offer unto it a sacrifice worth being heard, namely, unto the Moon that keeps in it the seed of the Bull.

Unto the Moon that keeps in it the seed of the Bull, we offer up the libations, the Haoma and meat, the baresma, the wisdom of the tongue, the holy spells, the speech, the deeds, the libations, and the rightly-spoken words.

Yênhê hâtãm: All those beings of whom Ahura Mazda . . . .

7. Yathâ ahû vairyô: The will of the Lord is the law of holiness . . . .

I bless the sacrifice and prayer, and the strength and vigour of the Moon, that keeps in it the seed of the Bull, and of the only-created Bull, and of the Bull of many species.

Ashem Vohû: Holiness is the best of all good.

Give unto that man brightness and glory, give him health of body, ... give him the bright, all-happy, blissful abode of the holy Ones.

---

[1] Or possessing: giving may be replaced by possessing in this word as in the following.

[2] Varekanghantem: dânâk (Phl.); gñânitaram (Sansk.).

[3] Khstâvantem: lakshmîvantam (Sansk.).

[4] Yaokhstivantem, 'pondering on what good is to be done' (vikâryavantam kâryanyâyânâm; كار و عدل دارنده نيك انديشه).

[5] Zairimyâvantem: haritavarnavantam, kila prithivî(m) sârdratarâm karoti (Sansk.).

[6] Vohvâvantem : uttamasamriddhimantam (Sansk.).

VIII. TÎR YA*S*T.

Ti*s*trya is the leader of the stars against the planets, as stars and planets belong, respectively, to the worlds of Ahura Mazda and Angra Mainyu (Vend. Introd. IV, 36 ; Bund. II, 5 seq.). This Ya*s*t is a description of the production of the rain through the agency of the star Ti*s*trya. It has to struggle against the Daêva of Drought, Apaosha, is first overcome and conquers at last. This seems to be a refacimento of the old storm myths, which have been in so far renewed as the role of the hero in the original myth has been transferred to a star. It is to be noticed, however, that Apaosha is not described as a planet.

Ti*s*trya is Sirius [1]. It presides over the first month of summer (21 June–21 July). This Ya*s*t appears thus to have been written in a part of Iran where the dog-days must have fallen in July, and the rainy season began in the last days of July, unless the place of Ti*s*trya in the calendar has been changed at some later period.

This Ya*s*t is recited on the days of Ti*s*trya, Haurvatâ*t* (as the Genius of Waters), Farvardîn (as the Fravashis are his allies in the struggle ; § 34), and Bâd (the wind ; § 32).

The struggle between Ti*s*trya and Apaosha is described in the Bundahi*s* (VII), but it has there a cosmological character : it has not for its object the annual and regular return of the rains after the dog-days, but the production of the seas and lakes in the first ages of the world.

---

0. May Ahura Mazda be rejoiced ! . . . .

Ashem Vohû : Holiness is the best of all good . . . .

I confess myself a worshipper of Mazda, a follower of Zara-thu*s*tra, one who hates the Daêvas and obeys the laws of Ahura ;

For sacrifice, prayer, propitiation, and glorification unto [Hâvani], the holy and master of holiness . . . .

Unto Ti*s*trya, the bright and glorious star, and unto the powerful Satavaêsa, made by Mazda, who pushes waters forward [2],

---

[1] Ἕνα δ' ἀστέρα πρὸ πάντων, οἷον φύλακα καὶ πρόοπτην ἐγκατέστησε, τὸν Σείριον (Plutarchus, de Iside et Osiride, § 47 ; cf. infra, § 48).

[2] Sîrôzah I, 13.

Be propitiation, with sacrifice, prayer, propitiation, and glorification.

Yathâ ahû vairyô: The will of the Lord is the law of holiness . . . .

I.

1. Ahura Mazda spake unto Spitama Zarathustra, saying: 'We worship the lordship and mastership [of Tistrya], whereby he protects [1] the Moon, the dwelling, the food, when my glorious stars come along and impart their gifts [2] to men. I will sacrifice unto the star Tistrya, that gives the fields their share [of waters].

2. 'We offer up libations unto Tistrya, the bright and glorious star, that gives happy dwelling and good dwelling; the white, shining, seen afar, and piercing; the health-bringing, loud-snorting [3], and high, piercing from afar with its shining, undefiled rays; and unto the waters of the wide sea, the Vanguhi of wide renown [4], and the species [5] of the Bull, made by Mazda, the awful kingly Glory, and the Fravashi of the holy Spitama Zarathustra.

3. 'For his brightness and glory, I will offer unto him a sacrifice worth being heard, namely, unto the star Tistrya.

'Unto Tistrya, the bright and glorious star, we offer up the libations, the Haoma and meat, the baresma, the wisdom of the tongue, the holy spells, the speech, the deeds, the libations, and the rightly-spoken words [6].

---

[1] Doubtful.
[2] The rain.
[3] In his disguise as a horse; § 18.
[4] See Vend., pp. 3, 5, note 2.
[5] Nãma; see Études Iraniennes, II, 124.
[6] Cf. p. 47.

'Yê*n*hê hâtãm: All those beings of whom
Ahura Mazda . . . .

II.

4: 'We sacrifice unto Ti*s*trya, the bright and
glorious star, who is the seed of the waters,
powerful, tall, and strong, whose light goes afar;
powerful and highly[1] working, through whom the
brightness and the seed of the waters come from
the high Apãm Napâ*t*[2].

'For his brightness and glory, I will offer him a sacrifice worth
being heard . . . .

III.

5. 'We sacrifice unto Ti*s*trya, the bright and glorious star; for whom long[3] flocks and herds and
men, looking forward for him and deceived in their
hope[4]: "When shall we see him rise up, the bright
and glorious star Ti*s*trya? When will the springs
run with waves as thick as a horse's size and still
thicker? Or will they never come?"

'For his brightness and glory, I will offer him a sacrifice worth
being heard . . . .

IV.

6. 'We sacrifice unto Ti*s*trya, the bright and glorious star; who flies, towards the sea Vouru-Kasha[5],
as swiftly as the arrow darted through the heavenly

---

[1] Powerfully.

[2] Or, 'through whom the beauty of the waters comes from
Bereza, and their seed from Apãm Napâ*t*.' Bereza, the high, the
tall, an epithet of Apãm Napâ*t*, became one of his names (Ized
Bôr*g*; cf. § 34); for Apãm Napâ*t*, see above, p. 6, note 1.

[3] Paiti*s*mare*n*ti; cf. Yt. V, 123.

[4] Or better, 'in their looking.'

[5] See above, p. 54, note 6.

space [1], which Erekhsha [2], the swift archer, the Arya amongst the Aryas whose arrow was the swiftest, shot from Mount Khshaotha to Mount *Hvanvant* [3].

7. 'For Ahura Mazda gave him assistance; so did the waters and the plants ; and Mithra, the lord of wide pastures, opened a wide way unto him.

'For his brightness and glory, I will offer him a sacrifice worth being heard . . . .

V.

8. 'We sacrifice unto Ti*s*trya, the bright and glorious star, that afflicts the Pairikas, that vexes the Pairikas, who, in the shape of worm-stars [4], fly

---

[1] Mainivas*au*=mainyu-as*au* (meaning pun mînôî *g*îvâkîh, svargasthânam, Yasna LVII, 27 [LVI, 11, 3]).

[2] Erekhsha khshviwi-ishu*s*, in Pahlavi Ari*s* Shîvâtîr (see Études Iraniennes, II, 220), or 'Ari*s* of the swift arrow,' was the best archer in the Iranian army. When Mino*k*ihr and Afrâsyab determined to make peace and to fix the boundary between Irân and Tûrân, 'it was stipulated that Ari*s* should ascend Mount Damâvand, and from thence discharge an arrow towards the east ; and that the place in which the arrow fell should form the boundary between the two kingdoms. Ari*s* thereupon ascended the mountain, and discharged towards the east an arrow, the flight of which continued from the dawn of day until noon, when it fell on the banks of the *G*ihûn (the Oxus),' (Mirkhond, History of the Early Kings of Persia, trans. by David Shea, p. 175 ; cf. Noeldeke, Zeitschrift der Deutschen Morgenländischen Gesellschaft, 1881, p. 445.)

[3] Mount Khshaotha seems to be the same as Mount Damâvand (see preceding note); Mount *Hv*anvan*t* may be the same as Mount Bâmîân, from which the Balkh river springs, as according to Tabari (trans. by Noeldeke, l. l.), Ari*s*' arrow stopped at the Balkh river (an affluent of the Oxus). But it may be that the limits given refer to the course of Ti*s*trya ; cf. § 38, text and note.

[4] Doubtful. Shooting stars are alluded to. Mr. Geiger remarks that there is a swarm of shooting stars falling every year just at the time when Ti*s*trya, in the European climate, is supposed to be most active, on the 10th of August.

between the earth and the heavens, in the sea
Vouru-Kasha, the powerful sea, the large-sized, deep
sea of salt [1] waters. He goes to its lake in the shape
of a horse, in a holy shape; and down there he
makes the waters boil over, and the winds flow
above powerfully all around.

9. 'Then Satavaêsa [2] makes those waters flow
down to the seven Karshvares of the earth [3], and
when he has arrived down there, he stands, beautiful, spreading ease and joy on the fertile countries
(thinking in himself): "How shall the countries of
the Aryas grow fertile?"

'For his brightness and glory, I will offer him a sacrifice worth
being heard . . . .

VI.

10. 'We sacrifice unto Ti*s*trya, the bright and
glorious star, who spake unto Ahura Mazda, saying:
"Ahura Mazda, most beneficent Spirit, Maker of the
material world, thou Holy One!

11. '"If men would worship me with a sacrifice in
which I were invoked by my own name, as they
worship the other Yazatas with sacrifices in which
they are invoked by their own names, then I should
have come to the faithful at the appointed time [4];
I should have come in the appointed time of my

---

[1] See above, p. 66, note 3.

[2] Satavaêsa is said to be the leader of the western stars (to be
read southern stars, Bund. II, 7), and has in its protection the
seas of the southern quarter (ibid. XIII, 12); the Satavaêsa sea is
the Persian gulf.

[3] This seems to be an allusion to the tide in the Arabian sea
(the sea Vouru-Kasha) and in the gulf of Oman, which, being a
southern sea, is under the control of Satavaêsa (cf. preceding note
and Vend. V, 18, note 1).

[4] At the right time of the year when rain is expected.

beautiful, immortal life [1], should it be one night, or two nights, or fifty, or a hundred nights."

12. 'We sacrifice unto Tistrya;

'We sacrifice unto the rains of Tistrya [2].

'We sacrifice unto the first star [3]; we sacrifice unto the rains of the first star.

'I will sacrifice unto the stars Haptôiri*n*ga [4], to oppose the Yâtus and Pairikas.

'We sacrifice unto Vana*nt* [5], the star made by Mazda; for [6] the well-shapen strength, for the Victory, made by Ahura, for the crushing Ascendant, for the destruction of what distresses us, for the destruction of what persecutes us.

'We sacrifice unto Tistrya, whose eye-sight is sound [7].

13. 'For ten nights, O Spitama Zarathustra! Tistrya, the bright and glorious star, mingles his shape

---

[1] Cf. §§ 23–24 and Yt. X, 54–55, 74.

[2] As Tistrya is the producer of the rain : Tistryênyas*k*a = Tistaratârakasya vri*sh*/im|(Khorshê*d* Nyâyi*s* 8, Sansk. tr.).

[3] Tistrya; cf. p. 105, note 3.

[4] Haptôiri*n*ga (Ursa Major) is the leader of the stars in the north (Bund. II, 7). It is 'entrusted with the gate and passage of hell, to keep back those of the nine, and ninety, and nine hundred, and nine thousand and nine myriad demons, and demonesses, and fairies (Pairikas) and sorcerers (Yâtus) who are in opposition to the celestial sphere and constellations' (Minokhired XLIX, 15; tr. by West).

[5] Vana*nt* is the leader of the stars in the south (read west; Bund. II, 7). Cf. Yt. XX.

[6] To obtain . . . . This invocation is brought about by the very name of Vana*nt*, which means ' who smites, who overcomes.' The peculiar office of Vana*nt* is to keep the passes and gates of Mount Albôrz, around which the sun, the moon, and the stars revolve, and to prevent the Paris and Daêvas from cutting off and breaking the road of the sun (Minokhired XLIX, 12).

[7] 'I sacrifice to Ti*s*tar for (= to obtain) the soundness of the sight' (Khorshê*d* Nyâyi*s* 8, Pahl. tr.).

with light, moving in the shape of a man of fifteen years of age[1], bright, with clear eyes, tall, full of strength, strong, and clever.

14. 'He is active as the first man[2] was; he goes on with the strength of the first man; he has the virility[3] of the first man.

15[4]. 'Here he calls for people to assemble, here he asks, saying: "Who now will offer me the libations with the Haoma and the holy meat? To whom shall I give wealth of male children, a troop of male children, and the purification of his own soul? Now I ought to receive sacrifice and prayer in the material world, by the law of excellent holiness."

16. 'The next ten nights, O Spitama Zarathustra! the bright and glorious Tistrya mingles his shape with light, moving in the shape of a golden-horned bull[5].

17. 'Here he calls for people to assemble, here he asks, saying: "Who now will offer me the libations with the Haoma and the holy meat? To whom shall I give wealth of oxen, a herd of oxen, and the purification of his own soul? Now I ought to receive sacrifice and prayer in the material world, by the law of excellent holiness."

18. 'The next ten nights, O Spitama Zarathustra! the bright and glorious Tistrya mingles his shape with light, moving in the shape of a white, beautiful horse, with golden ears and a golden caparison.

---

[1] The age of fifteen is the paradisiacal age in the Avesta (Yasna IX, 5 [18]).

[2] Gayô maratan. But the translation is doubtful; possibly 'as a first-rate man is.'

[3] Doubtful; cf. erezi, Yt. XIV, 29.   [4] Cf. Yt. V, 8.

[5] Cf. Vend. XIX, 37 (123).

19. 'Here he calls for people to assemble, here he asks, saying : "Who now will offer me the libations with the Haoma and the holy meat? To whom shall I give wealth of horses, a troop of horses, and the purification of his own soul? Now I ought to receive sacrifice and prayer in the material world, by the law of excellent holiness."

20. 'Then, O Spitama Zarathustra! the bright and glorious Tistrya goes down to the sea Vouru-Kasha in the shape of a white, beautiful horse, with golden ears and a golden caparison [1].

21. 'But there rushes down to meet him the Daêva Apaosha, in the shape of a dark horse, black with black ears, black with a black back, black with a black tail, stamped with brands of terror.

22. 'They meet together, hoof against hoof, O Spitama Zarathustra! the bright and glorious Tistrya and the Daêva Apaosha. They fight together, O Spitama Zarathustra! for three days and three nights. And then the Daêva Apaosha proves stronger than the bright and glorious Tistrya, he overcomes him.

23. 'And Tistrya flees from the sea Vouru-Kasha, as far as a Hâthra's [2] length. He cries out in woe and distress, the bright and glorious Tistrya : "Woe is me, O Ahura Mazda! I am in distress, O Waters and Plants! O Fate and thou, Law of the worshippers of Mazda! Men do not worship me with a

---

[1] 'Tistar was converted into three forms, the form of a man and the form of a horse and the form of a bull . . . . as the astrologers say that every constellation has three forms' (Bund. VII, 4; tr. West). Tistrya promises his worshippers children (§ 15), oxen (§ 17), or horses (§ 19), according as he appears in the form of a man (§ 13), of a bull (§ 16), or of a horse (§ 18).

[2] A mile (Bundahis XXVI, 1; tr. West, note 1).

sacrifice in which I am invoked by my own name, as they worship the other Yazatas with sacrifices in which they are invoked by their own names [1].

24. '" If men had worshipped me with a sacrifice in which I had been invoked by my own name, as they worship the other Yazatas with sacrifices in which they are invoked by their own names, I should have taken to me the strength of ten horses, the strength of ten camels, the strength of ten bulls, the strength of ten mountains, the strength of ten rivers [2]."

25. 'Then I, Ahura Mazda, offer up to the bright and glorious Tistrya a sacrifice in which he is invoked by his own name, and I bring him the strength of ten horses, the strength of ten camels, the strength of ten bulls, the strength of ten mountains, the strength of ten rivers.

26 [3]. 'Then, O Spitama Zarathustra! the bright and glorious Tistrya goes down to the sea Vouru-Kasha in the shape of a white, beautiful horse, with golden ears and golden caparison.

27. 'But there rushes down to meet him the Daêva Apaosha in the shape of a dark horse, black with black ears, black with a black back, black with a black tail, stamped with brands of terror.

28. 'They meet together, hoof against hoof, O Spitama Zarathustra! the bright and glorious Tistrya, and the Daêva Apaosha; they fight together, O Zarathustra! till the time of noon. Then the bright and glorious Tistrya proves stronger than the Daêva Apaosha, he overcomes him.

29. 'Then he goes from the sea Vouru-Kasha as far as a Hâthra's length: "Hail!" cries the

---

[1] Cf. § 10 and Yt. X, 54 seq., 74.
[2] Cf. Vend. Introd. IV, 27.   [3] §§ 26-27 = §§ 20-21.

bright and glorious Ti*s*trya. "Hail unto me, O Ahura Mazda! Hail ˌunto you, O waters and plants! Hail, O Law of the worshippers of Mazda! Hail will it be unto you, O lands! The life [1] of the waters will flow down unrestrained to the big-seeded [2] corn-fields, to the small-seeded [3] pasture-fields, and to the whole of the material world!"

30. 'Then the bright and glorious Ti*s*trya goes back down to the sea Vouru-Kasha, in the shape of a white, beautiful horse, with golden ears and a golden caparison [4].

31. 'He makes the sea boil up and down; he makes the sea stream this and that way; he makes the sea flow this and that way: all the shores of the sea Vouru-Kasha are boiling over, all the middle of it is boiling over.

32. 'And the bright and glorious Ti*s*trya rises up from the sea Vouru-Kasha, O Spitama Zarathu*s*tra! the bright and glorious Satavaêsa rises up from the sea Vouru-Kasha; and vapours rise up above Mount Us-hindu, that stands in the middle of the sea Vouru-Kasha [5].

---

[1] Adhavô; possibly 'the streams;' cf. Yt. V, 1, note 2. A month in the ancient Persian calendar, supposed to correspond to September–October, was called âdukani, which might, on that hypothesis, mean '(the month) that makes streams spring up.'

[2] Of which the representative is wheat (Bundahi*s* XXIV, 19).

[3] Of which the representative is the summer vetch (ibid. 21).

[4] Cf. § 18.

[5] 'The Aûsindôm mountain is that which, being of ruby, of the substance of the sky, is in the midst of the wide-formed ocean (the sea Vouru-Kasha),' (Bund. XII, 6; tr. West). Mount Aûsindôm receives its waters through a golden channel from the height Hukairya (cf. Yt. V, 3); 'from there one portion flows forth to the ocean for the purification of the sea, and one portion drizzles in moisture upon the whole of this earth, and all the creations of

33. 'Then the vapours push forward, in the regular shape of clouds [1]; they go following the wind, along the ways which Haoma traverses, the increaser of the world [2]. Behind him travels the mighty wind, made by Mazda, and the rain, and the cloud, and the sleet, down to the several places, down to the fields, down to the seven Karshvares of the earth.

34. 'Apãm Napât [3], O Spitama Zarathustra! divides the waters amongst the countries in the material world, in company with the mighty wind, the Glory, made by the waters [4], and the Fravashis of the faithful [5].

'For his brightness and glory, I will offer him a sacrifice worth being heard . . . .

VII.

35. 'We sacrifice unto Tistrya, the bright and glorious star, who from the shining east, moves along his long winding course, along the path made by the gods, along the way appointed for him the

---

Aûharmazd acquire health from it, and it dispels the dryness of the atmosphere' (ibid. XIII, 5).

[1] Doubtful.

[2] Haoma opens the way for the waters from heaven, as being the foremost element in sacrifice (cf. § 24). For the same reason the Bundahis numbers Vohu-Manô, 'Good Mind,' amongst the co-operators of Tistrya.

[3] See p. 6, note 1.

[4] Or better, 'seated in the waters;' see Yt. XIX, 56 seq. and Yt. XIII, 65.

[5] The Fravashis are active in the world struggle; cf. Yt. XIII, 43. 'Co-operators with Tîstar were Vohûman and the angel Hôm, with the assistance of the angel Bûrg (the same as Apãm Napât; see p. 94, note 2) and the righteous guardian spirits in orderly arrangement' (Bundahis VII, 3, tr. West).

watery way, at the will of Ahura Mazda, at the will
of the Amesha-Spentas.

'For his brightness and glory, I will offer him a sacrifice worth
being heard . . . .

VIII.

36. 'We sacrifice unto Tistrya, the bright and
glorious star, whose rising is watched by men who
live on the fruits of the year, by the chiefs of deep [1]
understanding[2]; by the wild beasts in the mountains,
by the tame beasts that run in the plains; they
watch him, as he comes up to the country for a
bad year, or for a good year[3], (thinking in themselves): "How shall the Aryan countries be
fertile?"

'For his brightness and glory, I will offer him a sacrifice worth
being heard . . . .

IX.

37[4]. 'We sacrifice unto Tistrya, the bright and
glorious star, swift-flying and swift-moving, who flies
towards the sea Vouru-Kasha, as swiftly as the
arrow darted through the heavenly space, which
Erekhsha, the swift archer, the Arya amongst the
Aryas whose arrow was the swiftest, shot from
Mount Khshaotha to Mount Hvanvant.

38. 'Ahura Mazda gave him assistance, and the
Amesha-Spentas and Mithra, the lord of wide pastures, pointed him the way: behind him went the

---

[1] Doubtful.   [2] The chiefs of the state.
[3] For good or bad harvest.   [4] § 37 = § 6.

tall Ashi*s* Vanguhi[1] and Pâre*n*di[2] on her light
chariot: always till, in his course, he reached Mount
*Hv*anva*nt* on the shining waters[3].

'For his brightness and glory, I will offer him a sacrifice worth
being heard . . . .

X.

39. 'We sacrifice unto Ti*s*trya, the bright and
glorious star, who afflicts the Pairikas, who destroys
the Pairikas, that Angra Mainyus flung to stop all
the stars that have in them the seed of the waters[4].

40. 'Ti*s*trya afflicts them, he blows them away
from the sea Vouru-Kasha; then the wind blows the
clouds forward, bearing the waters of fertility, so
that the friendly showers spread wide over, they
spread helpingly and friendly over the seven
Karshvares.

'For his brightness and glory, I will offer him a sacrifice worth
being heard . . . .

XI.

41. 'We sacrifice unto Ti*s*trya, the bright and
glorious star, for whom long the standing waters,
and the running spring-waters, the stream-waters,
and the rain-waters:

42. '"When will the bright and glorious Ti*s*trya
rise up for us? When will the springs with a flow
and overflow of waters, thick as a horse's shoulder,
run to the beautiful places and fields, and to the

---

[1] See Yt. XVII.   [2] See above, p. 11, note 5.

[3] Doubtful. Mount *Hv*anva*nt*, being situated in the sea Vouru-
Kasha (as appears from Ti*s*trya travelling towards that sea, § 38),
seems to be the same with Mount Aûsindôm (§ 32).

[4] Cf. above, § 8.

pastures, even to the roots of the plants, that they
may grow with a powerful growth ?"

'For his brightness and glory, I will offer him a sacrifice worth
being heard . . . .

XII.

43. 'We sacrifice unto Tistrya, the bright and
glorious star, who washes away all things of fear [1],
who stunts the growth of all . . . . [2], and brings health
to all these creations, being most beneficent, when
he has been worshipped with a sacrifice and propitiated, rejoiced, and satisfied.

'For his brightness and glory, I will offer him a sacrifice worth
being heard . . . .

XIII.

44. 'I will sacrifice unto Tistrya, the bright and
glorious star, whom Ahura Mazda has established
as a lord and overseer above all stars [3], in the same
way as he has established Zarathustra above men;
whom neither Angra Mainyu, nor the Yâtus and
the Pairikas, nor the men Yâtus [4] can deliver unto
death, nor can all the Daêvas together prevail for
his death.

'For his brightness and glory, I will offer him a sacrifice worth
being heard . . . .

---

[1] Sim_au_, meaning sahmgûn, bhayamkara (Yasna IX, 38
[93]).

[2] ? Vazdris.

[3] In the Bundahis it is especially the leader of the eastern stars;
but the Minokhired calls it the first star (XLIX, 5; cf. above, § 12).

[4] See above, p. 38, note 3.

XIV.

45. 'We sacrifice unto Ti*s*trya, the bright and glorious star, to whom Ahura Mazda has given a thousand senses[1], and who is the most beneficent amongst the stars that have in them the seed of the waters :

46. 'Who moves in light with the stars that have in them the seed of the waters : he, from the sea Vouru-Kasha, the powerful sea, the large-sized, deep, and salt of waters, goes to all the lakes, and to all the beautiful caves, and to all the beautiful channels[2], in the shape of a white, beautiful horse, with golden ears and a golden caparison.

47. 'Then, O Spitama Zarathu*s*tra! the waters flow down from the sea Vouru-Kasha, mother-like[3], friendly, and healing : he divides them amongst these countries, being most beneficent, when he has been worshipped with a sacrifice and propitiated, rejoiced, and satisfied[4].

'For his brightness and glory, I will offer him a sacrifice worth being heard . . . .

XV.

48. 'We sacrifice unto Ti*s*trya, the bright and glorious star, for whom long all the creatures of Spe*n*ta-Mainyu, those that live under the ground, and those that live above the ground; those that live in the waters, and those that live on dry land; those that fly, and those that run in the plains[5]; and all those

---

[1] See Yt. X, 82, note.

[2] Those of Ardvi Sûra Anâhita; cf. Yt. V, 4, 101.

[3] Cf. Yt. V, 15.　　　　　　　　　　[4] Cf. § 43.

[5] See Yt. XIII, 10, note; cf. Vispêrad I, 1, and Bundahi*s* XXIV, tr. West, note 1.

that live within this boundless and endless world of the holy Spirit.

'For his brightness and glory, I will offer him a sacrifice worth being heard . . . .

XVI.

49. 'We sacrifice unto Tistrya, the bright and glorious star, the healthful, wise, happy, and powerful, who is the lord of a thousand boons, and grants many boons to that man who has pleased him, whether begging or not begging for them.

50. 'I, O Spitama Zarathustra! have created that star Tistrya as worthy of sacrifice, as worthy of prayer, as worthy of propitiation, as worthy of glorification as myself, Ahura Mazda[1];

51. 'In order to withstand, to break asunder, to afflict, to drive back the malice of that Pairika Duz-yâirya[2], whom evil-speaking[3] people call Huyâirya[4].

52. 'Had I not created that star Tistrya as worthy of sacrifice, as worthy of prayer, as worthy of propitiation, as worthy of glorification as myself, Ahura Mazda;

53. 'In order to withstand, to break asunder, to afflict, to drive back the malice of that Pairika Duz-yâirya, whom evil-speaking people call Huyâirya;

---

[1] Cf. Yt. X, 1.

[2] Bad year, that is to say, sterility, drought. Darius, the son of Hystaspes, also deprecates Duzyâirya in one of his inscriptions: 'May Ahura Mazda keep this country from the hostile host, from sterility (dusiyâra), from lying (disloyalty): may never the foreigner enter this country, nor the hostile host, nor sterility, nor lying' (Persepolis, H, 15).

[3] People who object to rain and are fond of fine weather (?).

[4] Good year.

54. 'Then all day long, all night long, that Pairika
Duzyâirya would wage war against this material
world of mine, wanting to extinguish its life[1], and
she goes on, rushing upon and around it.

55. 'But the bright and glorious Tistrya keeps
that Pairika in bonds, with twofold bonds, with
threefold bonds, that cannot be overcome, with
bonds all over the body: it is as if there were a
thousand men keeping one man in bonds, a thousand men of those who are the strongest in
strength.

56. 'If the Aryan countries, O Spitama Zarathustra! would perform in honour of the bright and
glorious Tistrya the due sacrifice and invocation,
just as that sacrifice and invocation ought to be performed in the perfection of holiness; never should a
hostile horde enter these Aryan countries, nor any
plague, nor leprosy, nor venomous plants[2], nor the
chariot of a foe, nor the uplifted spear of a foe.'

57[3]. Zarathustra asked: 'What is then, O Ahura
Mazda! the sacrifice and invocation in honour of the
bright and glorious Tistrya, as it ought to be performed in the perfection of holiness?'

58. Ahura Mazda answered: 'Let the Aryan
nations bring libations unto him; let the Aryan
nations tie bundles of baresma for him; let the
Aryan nations cook for him a head of cattle, either
white, or black, or of any other colour, but all of
one and the same colour.

---

[1] Reading ava[-derenãm]; cf. Vend. XVIII, 18 [45].
[2] Kapasti is properly the colocynthis or bitter-apple:
      'Occidet et serpens, et fallax herba veneni
        Occidet.'   (Ecl. IV, 24, 25.)
[3] §§ 57-61 = Yt. XIV, 49-53; cf. Yt. V, 89 seq.

59. 'Let not a murderer take of these offerings, nor a whore, nor a . . . .[1] who does not sing the Gâthâs, who spreads death in the world and withstands the law of Mazda, the law of Zarathustra.

60. 'If a murderer take of these offerings, or a whore, or a . . . . who does not sing the Gâthâs, who spreads death in the world and withstands the law of Mazda, the law of Zarathustra, then the bright and glorious Tistrya takes back his healing virtues.

61. 'Plagues will ever pour upon the Aryan nations; hostile hordes will ever fall upon the Aryan nations; the Aryans will be smitten, by their fifties and their hundreds, by their hundreds and their thousands, by their thousands and their tens of thousands, by their tens of thousands and their myriads of myriads.

62. 'Yathâ ahû vairyô: The will of the Lord is the law of holiness . . . .

'I bless the sacrifice and prayer, and the strength and vigour of Tistrya, the bright and glorious star, and of the powerful Satavaêsa, made by Mazda, who pushes waters forward.

'Ashem Vohû: Holiness is the best of all good . . . .

'[Give] unto that man brightness and glory, ... give him the bright, all-happy, blissful abode of the holy Ones[2].'

---

[1] ? Ashaovô.   [2] Cf. Yt. I, 33.

IX. GÔS YAST.

Gôs, 'the cow,' κατ' ἐξοχήν, is a personation of the animal kingdom which she maintains and protects. She is also called Drvâspa and Gosûrûn: Drvâspa means 'she who keeps horses in health,' and is nothing more than an epithet of Gôs: Gôsûrûn (from the Zend Geus urvan) means 'the Soul of the Bull' (the primeval Bull). Although urvan is a masculine noun in Zend, yet Gôsûrûn is considered a female angel, as this name is only a substitute for Gôs.

Gôs is the angel of the 14th day (Sîrôzah I, 14), and her Yast is recited during the Gâh Usahin, on the days of Gôs, Bahman, Mâh, and Râm (the same days as those on which the Mâh Yast is recited; see above, p. 88).

Gôs is hardly described in this Yast (§§ 1-2); the greater part of it being filled with the several prayers addressed to her by the Iranian heroes, Haoshyangha (§ 3), Yima (§ 8), Thraêtaona (§ 13), Haoma (§ 17), Husravah (§ 21), Zarathustra, and Vîstâspa. Her worshippers and their prayers to her are the same as in the case of Ashi Vanguhi (see Yt. XVII).

o. May Ahura Mazda be rejoiced! May Angra Mainyu be afflicted! . . . .

Ashem Vohû: Holiness is the best of all good . . . .

I confess myself a worshipper of Mazda, a follower of Zarathustra, one who hates the Daêvas and obeys the laws of Ahura;

For sacrifice, prayer, satisfaction, and glorification unto Hâvani, the holy and master of holiness.

Unto the powerful Drvâspa, made by Mazda and holy [1],

Be propitiation, with sacrifice, prayer, propitiation, and glorification.

Yathâ ahû vairyô: The will of the Lord is the law of holiness . . . .

---

[1] Sîrôzah I, 14.

I.

1. We sacrifice unto the powerful Drvâspa, made by Mazda and holy, who keeps the flocks in health, the herds in health, the grown-up [1] (cattle) in health, the young ones in health; who watches well from afar, with a wide-spread and long-continued welfare-giving friendship;

2. Who yokes teams of horses, who makes her chariot turn and its wheels sound, fat and glistening [2], strong, tall-formed, weal-possessing, health-giving, powerful to stand and powerful to turn for assistance to the faithful.

3. To her did Haoshyangha, the Paradhâta [3], offer up a sacrifice on the enclosure of the Hara, the beautiful height, made by Mazda, with a hundred male horses, a thousand oxen, and ten thousand lambs, and with an offering of libations:

4. 'Grant me this boon, O good, most beneficent Drvâspa! that I may overcome all the Daêvas of Mâzana [4]; that I may never fear and bow through terror before the Daêvas, but that all the Daêvas may fear and bow in spite of themselves before me, that they may fear and flee down to darkness [5].'

5. The powerful Drvâspa, made by Mazda, the holy Drvâspa, the maintainer, granted him that boon, as he was offering libations, giving gifts, sacrificing, and entreating that she would grant him that boon.

6. For her brightness and glory, I will offer her a sacrifice worth being heard; I will offer her a sacrifice well performed, namely, unto the powerful

---

[1] Doubtful; possibly 'the friend in health, the child in health.'
[2] Doubtful.
[3] Cf. p. 58, note 1.
[4] Cf. p. 59, note 2.
[5] To hell.

Drvâspa, made by Mazda and holy. We offer up
libations to the powerful Drvâspa, made by Mazda
and holy; we offer her the Haoma and meat, the
baresma, the wisdom of the tongue, the holy spells,
the speech, the deeds, the libations, and the rightly-
spoken words.

Yê*n*hê hâtãm: All those beings of whom
Ahura Mazda . . . .[1]

II.

7. We offer up a sacrifice unto the powerful Drvâspa, made by
Mazda and holy, who keeps the flocks in health . . . .
Who yokes teams of horses . . . . for assistance to the faithful[2].

8. To her did Yima Khshaêta, the good shepherd,
offer up a sacrifice from the height Hukairya, with a
hundred male horses, a thousand oxen, ten thousand
lambs, and with an offering of libations :

9. 'Grant me this boon, O good, most beneficent
Drvâspa! that I may bring fatness and flocks down
to the world created by Mazda; that I may bring
immortality down to the world created by Mazda;

10. 'That I may take away both hunger and thirst,
from the world created by Mazda; that I may take
away both old age and death, from the world created
by Mazda; that I may take away both hot wind and
cold wind, from the world created by Mazda, for a
thousand years[3].'

11. The powerful Drvâspa, made by Mazda, the
holy Drvâspa, the maintainer, granted him that boon,

---

[1] As above, p. 30.   [2] § 7 = §§ 1–2.
[3] §§ 8–10 = Yt. XVII, 28–30; cf. Yasna IX, 4–5 [11–20]; Yt.
V, 25–27.

as he was offering up libations, giving gifts, sacrificing, and entreating that she would grant him that boon.

For her brightness and glory, I will offer her a sacrifice worth being heard . . . .

III.

12. We offer up a sacrifice unto the powerful Drvâspa, made by Mazda and holy, who keeps the flocks in health . . . .
Who yokes teams of horses . . . . for assistance to the faithful.

13[1]. To her did Thraêtaona, the heir of the valiant Âthwya clan, offer up a sacrifice in the four-cornered Varena, with a hundred male horses, a thousand oxen, ten thousand lambs, and with an offering of libations :

14. 'Grant me this boon, O good, most beneficent Drvâspa ! that I may overcome Azi Dahâka, the three-mouthed, the three-headed, the six-eyed, who has a thousand senses, that most powerful, fiendish Drug, that demon, baleful to the world, the strongest Drug that Angra Mainyu created against the material world, to destroy the world of the good principle ; and that I may deliver his two wives, Savanghavâk and Erenavâk, who are the fairest of body amongst women, and the most wonderful creatures in the world[1].'

15. The powerful Drvâspa, made by Mazda, the holy Drvâspa, the maintainer, granted him that boon, as he was offering up libations, giving gifts, sacrificing, and entreating that she would grant him that boon.

For her brightness and glory, I will offer her a sacrifice worth being heard . . . .

---

[1] Yt. V, 34 ; XV, 24 ; XVII, 34.

IV.

16. We offer up a sacrifice unto the powerful Drvâspa, made by Mazda and holy, who keeps flocks in health . . . . Who yokes teams of horses . . . . for assistance to the faithful.

17 [1]. To her did Haoma [2] offer up a sacrifice, Haoma, the enlivening, the healing, the beautiful, the lordly, with golden eyes, upon the highest height of the Haraiti Bareza. He begged of her a boon, saying:

18. 'Grant me this boon, O good, most beneficent Drvâspa! that I may bind the Turanian murderer, Franghrasyan [3] that I may drag him bound, that I may bring him bound unto king Husravah, that king Husravah may kill him, behind the Kaêkasta lake [4], the deep lake of salt [5] waters, to avenge the murder of his father Syâvarshâna [6], a man, and of Aghraêratha, a semi-man [7].'

---

[1] §§ 17–19 = Yt. XVII, 37–38.

[2] Cf. Yasna XI, 7 [20–21]. The destruction of the fiends, being one of the principal effects of sacrifice, is ascribed to Haoma as the most powerful element in the sacrifice. In the Shâh Nâmah, the god Haoma has been turned into a hermit who, living near the cave in which Afrâsyâb had taken refuge (see above, Yt. V, 41), overhears his lamentations, takes him by surprise, binds him, and delivers him into the hands of Khosrav (Études Iraniennes, II, 227).

[3] See p. 64, note 1.   [4] See above, p. 66, note 2.

[5] See p. 66, note 3.   [6] See p. 64, note 1.

[7] Doubtful (narava, as opposed to nara). Aghraêratha (Aghrêrath) was a brother of Afrâsyâb's; he was a righteous man, and Afrâsyâb killed him for his having saved the Iranian king Minokihr with his army, when captive in the Padashkhvâr mountains (Bundahis XXXI, 21). Yet he is still living as an immortal in the land of Saukavastân, under the name of Gôpatshâh (the king of the bulls); 'from foot to mid-body he is a bull, and from mid-body to

19. The powerful Drvâspa, made by Mazda, the holy Drvâspa, the maintainer, granted him that boon, as he was offering up libations, giving gifts, sacrificing, and entreating that she would give him that boon.

For her brightness and glory, I will offer her a sacrifice worth being heard . . . .

V.

20. We offer up a sacrifice unto the powerful Drvâspa, made by Mazda and holy, who keeps the flocks in health . . . . Who yokes teams of horses . . . . for assistance to the faithful.

21 [1]. To her did the gallant Husravah, he who united the Arya nations into one kingdom, offer up a sacrifice, behind the *Ka*ê*k*asta lake, the deep lake of salt waters, with a hundred male horses, a thousand oxen, ten thousand lambs, and an offering of libations :

22. 'Grant me this boon, O good, most beneficent Drvâspa! that I may kill the Turanian murderer, Franghrasyan, behind the *Ka*ê*k*asta lake, the deep lake of salt waters, to avenge the murder of my father Syâvarshâna, a man, and of Aghraêratha, a semi-man [2].'

23. The powerful Drvâspa, made by Mazda, the holy Drvâspa, the maintainer, granted him that boon, as he was offering up libations, giving gifts, sacri-

---

the top he is a man ; at all times he stays on the sea-shore, and always performs the worship of God, and always pours holy-water into the sea' (Minokhired LXII, 31 seq., tr. West; Bund. XXIX, 5); according to Bund. XXXI, 20, Aghrêrath was not Gôpatshâh, he was his father. Cf. Yt. XIX, 93.

[1] §§ 21–22 = Yt. XVII, 41–42.
[2] See p. 114, note 7.

I 2

ficing, and entreating that she would grant him that boon.

For her brightness and glory, I will offer her a sacrifice worth being heard . . . .

VI.

24. We offer up a sacrifice unto the powerful Drvâspa, made by Mazda and holy, who keeps the flocks in health . . . .
Who yokes teams of horses . . . . for assistance to the faithful.

25 [1]. To her did the holy Zarathu*s*tra offer up a sacrifice in the Airyana Vaê*g*ah, by the good river Dâitya, with the Haoma and meat, with the baresma, with the wisdom of the tongue, with the holy spells, with the speech, with the deeds, with the libations, and with the rightly-spoken words. He begged of her a boon, saying:

26. 'O good, most beneficent Drvâspa! grant me this boon, that I may bring the good and noble Hutaosa [2] to think according to the law, to speak according to the law, to do according to the law, that she may spread my Mazdean law and make it known, and that she may bestow beautiful praises upon my deeds.'

27. The strong Drvâspa, made by Mazda, the holy Drvâspa, the maintainer, granted him that boon, as he was offering up libations, giving gifts, sacrificing, and entreating that she would grant him that boon.

For her brightness and glory, I will offer her a sacrifice worth being heard . . . .

---

[1] §§ 25–26=XVII, 44–45; cf. Yt. V, 104.
[2] Hutaosa was the wife of king Vî*s*tâspa; cf. Yt. XV, 37.

VII.

28. We offer up a sacrifice unto the powerful Drvâspa, made by Mazda and holy, who keeps the flocks in health . . . . Who yokes teams of horses . . . . for assistance to the faithful.

29 [1]. To her did the tall Kavi Vîstâspa offer up a sacrifice behind the waters of the river Dâitya, with a hundred male horses, a thousand oxen, ten thousand lambs, and with an offering of libations :

30. 'Grant me this boon, O good, most beneficent Drvâspa! that I may put to flight Asta-aurva*nt*, the son of Vîspa-thaurvô-asti, the all-afflicting, of the brazen helmet, of the brazen armour, of the thick neck, behind whom seven hundred camels . . . .[2]; that I may put to flight the *Hv*yaona murderer, Are*gat*-aspa[3]; that I may put to flight Dar*s*inika[4], the wor-shipper of the Daêvas ;

31. And that I may smite Tãthrava*nt*[5] of the bad law; that I may smite Spin*g*auru*s*ka[4], the wor-shipper of the Daêvas ; and that I may bring unto the good law the nations of the Varedhakas and of the *Hv*yaonas[6]; and that I may smite of the *Hv*yaona nations their fifties and their hundreds, their hun-dreds and their thousands, their thousands and their

---

[1] §§ 29–31 = Yt. XVII, 49–51.

[2] ? Gainyâvara*t*.

[3] See above, p. 79, note 4.

[4] Ἄπαξ λεγόμενος.

[5] Mentioned Yt. V, 109 and XIX, 87.

[6] The *Hv*yaonas seem to have been the Chionitae, a bellicose tribe, near the land of Gilan, often at war with the first Sassanides (Amm. Marcellinus XVII, 5). The name of the Varedhakas re-minds one of the Vertae who are mentioned once in company with the Chionitae (ibid. XIX, 1); but their geographical situation is not ascertained. In any case the proximity of the Dâitya (§ 29) shows that both people must have inhabited the western coast of the Caspian sea.

tens of thousands, their tens of thousands and their myriads of myriads.

32. The strong Drvâspa, made by Mazda, the holy Drvâspa, the maintainer, granted him that boon, as he was offering up libations, giving gifts, sacrificing, and entreating that she would grant him that boon.

For her brightness and glory, I will offer her a sacrifice worth being heard; I will offer her a sacrifice well performed, namely, unto the powerful Drvâspa, made by Mazda and holy. We offer up libations to the powerful Drvâspa, made by Mazda and holy; we offer her the Haoma and meat, the baresma, the wisdom of the tongue, the holy spells, the speech, the deeds, the libations, and the rightly-spoken words.

Yathâ ahû vairyô: The will of the Lord is the law of holiness . . . .

I bless the sacrifice and prayer, and the strength and vigour of the powerful Drvâspa, made by Mazda and holy.

Ashem Vohû: Holiness is the best of all good . . . .

[Give] unto that man brightness and glory, give him health of body, ... give him the bright, all-happy, blissful abode of the holy Ones.

X. MIHIR YAST.

This Yast, one of the longest of the Avesta and one of the most interesting in a literary point of view, is not very instructive for mythology. It consists of long descriptive pieces, sometimes rather spirited, and of fervent prayers and invocations for mercy or protection. Originally Mithra was the god of the heavenly light (§§ 12, 50, 67, 104, 124 seq., 136 seq., &c.); and in that character he knows the truth, as he sees everything; he is therefore taken as a witness of truth, he is the preserver of oaths and good faith (§§ 2, 44 seq., 79 seq., 81 seq., &c.); he chastises those who break their promises and lie to Mithra, destroys their houses and smites them in battle (§§ 17 seq., 28 seq., 35 seq., 47 seq., 99 seq., 105 seq., 112 seq., 128 seq., &c.).

Particularly interesting are §§ 115–118, as giving a sketch of moral hierarchy in Iran, and §§ 121–122, as being perhaps the source of the trials in the later Roman Mithriacism. Cf. Vend. Introd. IV, 8 and Ormazd et Ahriman, §§ 59–61.

0. May Ahura Mazda be rejoiced ! . . . .
Ashem Vohû: Holiness is the best of all good . . . .
I confess myself a worshipper of Mazda, a follower of Zara-thustra, one who hates the Daêvas, and obeys the laws of Ahura ;
For sacrifice, prayer, propitiation, and glorification unto [Hâvani], the holy and master of holiness . . . .

Unto Mithra, the lord of wide pastures, who has a thousand ears, ten thousand eyes, a Yazata invoked by his own name, and unto Râma *Hv*âstra [1],

Be propitiation, with sacrifice, prayer, propitiation, and glorification.

Yathâ ahû vairyô: The will of the Lord is the law of holi-ness . . . .

I.

1. Ahura Mazda spake unto Spitama Zarathustra, saying: 'Verily, when I created Mithra, the lord of

---

[1] Sîrôzah I, 16.

wide pastures, O Spitama! I created him as worthy
of sacrifice, as worthy of prayer as myself, Ahura
Mazda[1].

2. 'The ruffian who lies unto Mithra[2] brings death
unto the whole country, injuring as much the faithful
world as a hundred evil-doers[3] could do. Break not
the contract, O Spitama! neither the one that thou
hadst entered into with one of the unfaithful, nor the
one that thou hadst entered into with one of the
faithful who is one of thy own faith[4]. For Mithra
stands for both the faithful and the unfaithful.

3. 'Mithra, the lord of wide pastures, gives swiftness to the horses of those who lie not unto
Mithra.

'Fire, the son of Ahura Mazda, gives the straight-
est way to those who lie not unto Mithra.

'The good, strong, beneficent Fravashis of the
faithful give a virtuous offspring to those who lie
not unto Mithra.

4. 'For his brightness and glory, I will offer unto
him a sacrifice worth being heard, namely, unto
Mithra, the lord of wide pastures.

'We offer up libations unto Mithra, the lord of
wide pastures, who gives a happy dwelling and a
good dwelling to the Aryan nations.

5. 'May he come to us for help! May he come
to us for ease! May he come to us for joy! May
he come to us for mercy! May he come to us for
health! May he come to us for victory! May he

---

[1] Cf. Yt. VIII, 50.

[2] The Mithradrug: one might also translate 'who breaks the
contract,' as mithra, as a common noun, means 'a contract.'

[3] Kayadhas; cf. Yt. I, 19.   [4] Cf. Ardâ Viraf, chap. lii.

come to us for good conscience[1]! May he come to us for bliss[2]! he, the awful and overpowering, worthy of sacrifice and prayer, not to be deceived anywhere in the whole of the material world, Mithra, the lord of wide pastures.

6. 'I will offer up libations unto him, the strong Yazata, the powerful Mithra, most beneficent to the creatures: I will apply unto him with charity[3] and prayers: I will offer up a sacrifice worth being heard unto him, Mithra, the lord of wide pastures, with the Haoma and meat, with the baresma, with the wisdom of the tongue, with the holy spells, with the speech, with the deeds, with the libations, and with the rightly-spoken words.

'Yê*n*hê hâtãm: All those beings of whom Ahura Mazda[4] . . . .

II.

7. 'We sacrifice unto Mithra, the lord of wide pastures, who is truth-speaking, a chief in assemblies, with a thousand ears, well-shapen, with ten thousand eyes, high, with full knowledge[5], strong, sleepless, and ever awake[6];

---

[1] Cheerfulness at the head of the *K*inva*t* bridge (Yasna LXII, 6 [LXI, 17]; cf. Vend. XVIII, 6).

[2] The condition of the blessed in the next world.

[3] Va*n*ta, 'assistance, that is, making *g*âdangôi' (Yasna LXII [LXI], 1; *g*âdangôi is making a collection for the poor (Études Iraniennes, II, 155).

[4] As p. 30.

[5] Perethu-vaêdhayana: sampûr*n*avittâram kâryanyâyânam (Khorshê*d* Nyâyi*s* 6).

[6] *G*aghâurva*un*ghem: this word, strangely enough, is generally translated 'who has most strong arms' (balish*th*abhu*g*am); *g*agâuru is translated in the same way.

8. 'To whom the chiefs of nations offer up sacrifices, as they go to the field, against havocking hosts, against enemies coming in battle array, in the strife of conflicting nations.

9. 'On whichever side he has been worshipped first in the fulness of faith of a devoted heart, to that side turns Mithra, the lord of wide pastures, with the fiend-smiting wind, with the cursing thought of the wise [1].

'For his brightness and glory, I will offer him a sacrifice worth being heard . . . .

III.

10. 'We sacrifice unto Mithra, the lord of wide pastures, ... sleepless, and ever awake.

11. 'Whom the horsemen worship on the back of their horses, begging swiftness for their teams, health for their own bodies, and that they may watch with full success those who hate them, smite down their foes, and destroy at one stroke their adversaries, their enemies, and those who hate them [2].

'For his brightness and glory, I will offer him a sacrifice worth being heard . . . .

IV.

12. 'We sacrifice unto Mithra, the lord of wide pastures, ... sleepless, and ever awake;

13. 'Who first of the heavenly gods reaches over the Hara [3], before the undying, swift-horsed sun [4];

---

[1] See p. 12, note 13.   [2] Cf. Yt. V, 53; X, 94.

[3] Mount Albôrz, whence the sun rises; see § 50.

[4] Mithra is closely connected with the sun, but not yet identical with it, as he became in later times (ﻣﻬﺮ, the sun; Deo invicto Soli Mithrae).

who, foremost in a golden array, takes hold of the beautiful summits, and from thence looks over the abode of the Aryans with a beneficent eye.

14. 'Where the valiant chiefs draw up their many troops in array [1]; where the high mountains, rich in pastures and waters, yield plenty to the cattle [2]; where the deep lakes, with salt waters, stand [3]; where wide-flowing rivers swell and hurry towards Iskata and Pouruta, Mouru and Harôyu, the Gava-Sughdha and *Hv*âirizem [4];

15. 'On Arezahi and Savahi, on Fradadhafshu and Vîdadhafshu, on Vourubaresti and Vourugaresti, on this bright Karshvare of *Hv*aniratha [5], the abode of cattle, the dwelling of cattle, the powerful Mithra looks with a health-bringing eye;

16. 'He who moves along all the Karshvares, a Yazata unseen, and brings glory; he who moves along all the Karshvares, a Yazata unseen, and brings sovereignty; and increases [6] strength for

---

[1] In the flat countries.

[2] In the mountainous parts of Iran.

[3] In the lake regions (Seistan, Farsistan, Âdarbaigân).

[4] In the country of the large rivers in the East. Mouru is Marv (Margiana), with the Murghâb river (the Margus); Harôyu is the Herat country, with the Harêrûd; Gava-Sughdha and *Hv*ârizm are Sogdiana and Khvârizm, with the Oxus. The situation of Iskata and Pouruta is not clear: one might think of Alexander eschata on the Iaxartes and the Paretacene country between the Oxus and the Iaxartes.

[5] The earth is divided into seven Karshvares, separated from one another by seas and mountains impassable to men. Arezahi and Savahi are the western and the eastern Karshvare; Fradadhafshu and Vîdadhafshu are in the south; Vourubaresti and Vourugaresti are in the north; *Hv*aniratha is the central Karshvare. *Hv*aniratha is the only Karshvare inhabited by man (Bundahis XI, 3).

[6] Doubtful.

victory to those who, with a pious intent, holily offer him libations.

'For his brightness and glory, I will offer him a sacrifice worth being heard . . . .

V.

17. 'We sacrifice unto Mithra, the lord of wide pastures, ... sleepless, and ever awake ;

'Unto whom nobody must lie, neither the master of a house, nor the lord of a borough, nor the lord of a town, nor the lord of a province.

18. 'If the master of a house lies unto him, or the lord of a borough, or the lord of a town, or the lord of a province, then comes Mithra, angry and offended, and he breaks asunder the house, the borough, the town, the province; and the masters of the houses, the lords of the boroughs, the lords of the towns, the lords of the provinces, and the foremost men of the provinces.

19. 'On whatever side there is one who has lied unto Mithra, on that side Mithra stands forth, angry and offended, and his wrath [1] is slow to relent [2].

20. 'Those who lie unto Mithra, however swift they may be running, cannot overtake [3]; riding, cannot . . . . [3]; driving, cannot . . . . [3]. The spear that the foe of Mithra flings, darts backwards, for the

---

[1] Mainyu, in the meaning of the Sanskrit manyu (?).

[2] Doubtful; aspakat: cf. سوختن, to be late.

[3] Apayêinti, frastanvainti, framanyêintê: these are three technical words for the movements of the three classes of soldiers, footmen, horsemen, and chariot-men; the last two words are probably synonymous with the first, but the exact shades of meaning are not known. Mr. West suggests, cannot outrun, outride, outdrive him.

number of the evil spells that the foe of Mithra works out[1].

21. 'And even though the spear be flung well, even though it reach the body, it makes no wound, for the number of the evil spells that the foe of Mithra works out[1]. The wind drives away the spear that the foe of Mithra flings, for the number of the evil spells that the foe of Mithra works out.

'For his brightness and glory, I will offer him a sacrifice worth being heard . . . .

VI.

22. 'We sacrifice unto Mithra, the lord of wide pastures, ... sleepless, and ever awake ;

'Who takes out of distress the man who has not lied unto him, who takes him out of death.

23. 'Take us out of distress, take us out of distresses, O Mithra! as we have not lied unto thee. Thou bringest down terror upon the bodies of the men who lie unto Mithra; thou takest away the strength from their arms, being angry and all-powerful; thou takest the swiftness from their feet, the eye-sight from their eyes, the hearing from their ears.

24. 'Not the wound[2] of the well-sharpened spear or of the flying arrow reaches that man to whom Mithra comes for help with all the strength of his soul, he, of the ten thousand spies, the powerful, all-seeing, undeceivable Mithra.

'For his brightness and glory, I will offer him a sacrifice worth being heard . . . .

---

[1] The sacramental words of the contract, by their not being kept, turn to evil spells against the contract-breaker.

[2] Doubtful: *sanamayô, or *sanamaoyô; read shanmaoyô (?), from shan, Sansk. kshan.

VII.

25. 'We sacrifice unto. Mithra, the lord of wide pastures, ...
sleepless, and ever awake;

'Who is lordly, deep, strong, and weal-giving;
a chief in assemblies, pleased with prayers[1], high,
holily clever, the incarnate Word, a warrior with
strong arms;

26. 'Who breaks the skulls of the Daêvas, and is
most cruel in exacting pains; the punisher of the
men who lie unto Mithra, the withstander of the
Pairikas; who, when not deceived, establisheth
nations in supreme strength; who, when not deceived, establisheth nations in supreme victory;

27. 'Who confounds the ways of the nation that
delights in havoc, who turns away their Glory[2], takes
away their strength for victory, blows them away
helpless[3], and delivers them unto ten thousand
strokes; he, of the ten thousand spies, the powerful,
all-seeing, undeceivable Mithra.

'For his brightness and glory, I will offer him a sacrifice worth
being heard . . . .

VIII.

28. 'We sacrifice unto Mithra, the lord of wide pastures, ...
sleepless, and ever awake;

'Who upholds the columns of the lofty house and
makes its pillars[4] solid; who gives herds of oxen
and male children to that house in which he has
been satisfied; he breaks to pieces those in which
he has been offended.

29. 'Thou, O Mithra! art both bad and good to

---

[1] Vahmô-sendah; cf. Vispêrad VIII (IX, 1), Phl. tr.
[2] Their *Hvareñô*.   [3] Doubtful.
[4] Āithya; cf. Lat. antae (Brugmann).

nations; thou, O Mithra! art both bad and good
to men; thou, O Mithra! keepest in thy hands both
peace and trouble for nations.

30. 'Thou makest houses large, beautiful with
women, beautiful with chariots, with well-laid foundations [1], and high above their groundwork [2]; thou
makest that house lofty, beautiful with women,
beautiful with chariots, with well-laid foundations,
and high above its groundwork, of which the master,
pious and holding libations in his hand, offers thee
a sacrifice, in which thou art invoked by thy own
name and with the proper words.

31. 'With a sacrifice, in which thou art invoked
by thy own name, with the proper words will I offer
thee libations, O powerful Mithra!

'With a sacrifice, in which thou art invoked by
thy own name, with the proper words will I offer
thee libations, O most beneficent Mithra!

'With a sacrifice, in which thou art invoked by
thy own name, with the proper words will I offer
thee libations, O thou undeceivable Mithra!

32. 'Listen unto our sacrifice [3], O Mithra! Be
thou pleased with our sacrifice, O Mithra! Come
and sit at our sacrifice! Accept our libations!
Accept them as they have been consecrated [4]!
Gather them together with love and lay them in
the Garô-nmâna!

33. 'Grant us these boons which we beg of thee,
O powerful god! in accordance [5] with the words of
revelation, namely, riches, strength, and victory,
good conscience and bliss [6], good fame and a good

---

[1] Doubtful.   [2] Doubtful.   [3] Cf. Yt. III, 18.
[4] By the proper prayers (yastau).   [5] Doubtful.
[6] Cf. § 5.

soul; wisdom and the knowledge that gives happiness [1], the victorious strength given by Ahura, the crushing Ascendant of Asha Vahista, and conversation (with God) on the Holy Word [2].

34. ' Grant that we, in a good spirit and high spirit, exalted in joy and a good spirit, may smite all our foes ; that we, in a good spirit and high spirit, exalted in joy and a good spirit, may smite all our enemies ; that we, in a good spirit and high spirit, exalted in joy and a good spirit, may smite all the malice of Daêvas and Men, of the Yâtus and Pairikas, of the oppressors, the blind, and the deaf [3].

'For his brightness and glory, I will offer him a sacrifice worth being heard . . . .

IX.

35. 'We sacrifice unto Mithra, the lord of wide pastures, ... sleepless, and ever awake;

'Victory-making [4], army-governing, endowed with a thousand senses [5]; power-wielding, power-possessing, and all-knowing ;

36. 'Who sets the battle a going, who stands against (armies) in battle, who, standing against (armies) in battle, breaks asunder the lines arrayed. The wings of the columns gone to battle shake, and he throws terror upon the centre of the havocking host.

37. 'He can bring and does bring down upon them distress and fear ; he throws down the heads of those who lie unto Mithra, he takes off the heads of those who lie unto Mithra.

---

[1] Spiritual happiness, bliss.   [2] Vend. XVIII, 51 [111].

[3] See above, p. 26, note 2.   §§ 30–34=§§ 56–59.

[4] Doubtful (reading arenat-gaêsha?).

[5] See § 82, note.

38. 'Sad is the abode, unpeopled with children, where abide men who lie unto Mithra, and, verily, the fiendish killer of faithful men. The grazing cow goes a sad straying way, driven along the vales [1] of the Mithradruges: they [2] stand on the road, letting tears run over their chins [3].

39. 'Their falcon-feathered arrows, shot from the string of the well-bent bow, fly towards the mark, and hit it not, as Mithra, the lord of wide pastures, angry, offended, and unsatisfied, comes and meets them.

'Their spears, well whetted and sharp, their long spears fly from their hands towards the mark, and hit it not, as Mithra, the lord of wide pastures, angry, offended, and unsatisfied, comes and meets them.

40. 'Their swords, well thrust and striking at the heads of men, hit not the mark, as Mithra, the lord of wide pastures, angry, offended, and unsatisfied, comes and meets them.

'Their clubs, well falling and striking at the heads of men, hit not the mark, as Mithra, the lord of wide pastures, angry, offended, and unsatisfied, comes and meets them.

41. 'Mithra strikes fear into them; Rashnu [4] strikes a counter-fear into them [5]; the holy Sraosha blows them away from every side towards the two Yazatas, the maintainers of the world [6]. They make the ranks of the army melt away, as Mithra, the lord

---

[1] Doubtful.   [2] The cattle.

[3] The meaning is, that the cattle of the Mithradruges do not thrive, and that their pasture-fields are waste.

[4] See Yt. XII.

[5] As they flee from Mithra, they fall into the hands of Rashnu.

[6] Thrâtâra; one might feel inclined to read thrâstâra, 'the fear-striking;' cf. § 36.

of wide pastures, angry, offended, and unsatisfied, comes and meets them[1].

42. 'They cry unto Mithra, the lord of wide pastures, saying: " O Mithra, thou lord of wide pastures! here are our fiery horses taking us away, as they flee from Mithra; here are our sturdy arms cut to pieces by the sword, O Mithra!"

43. 'And then Mithra, the lord of wide pastures, throws them to the ground, killing their fifties and their hundreds, their hundreds and their thousands, their thousands and their tens of thousands, their tens of thousands and their myriads of myriads; as Mithra, the lord of wide pastures, is angry and offended.

'For his brightness and glory, I will offer him a sacrifice worth being heard . . . .

X.

44. 'We sacrifice unto Mithra, the lord of wide pastures, ... sleepless, and ever awake;

'Whose dwelling, wide as the earth, extends over the material world, large[2], unconfined[2], and bright, a far-and-wide-extending abode.

45. 'Whose eight friends[3] sit as spies for Mithra, on all the heights, at all the watching-places, observing the man who lies unto Mithra, looking at those, remembering those who have lied unto Mithra, but guarding the ways of those whose life is sought by

---

[1] Cf. §§ 99–101.

[2] Doubtful. The text is corrupt.

[3] Doubtful. The number eight has probably an astronomical signification, each of the eight râtis of Mithra occupying one of the eight points of the compass.

men who lie unto Mithra, and, verily, by the fiendish killers of faithful men.

46. 'Helping and guarding, guarding behind and guarding. in front, Mithra, the lord of wide pastures, proves an undeceivable spy and watcher for the man to whom he comes to help with all the strength of his soul, he of the ten thousand spies, the powerful, all-knowing, undeceivable god.

'For his brightness and glory, I will offer him a sacrifice worth being heard . . . .

XI.

47. 'We sacrifice unto Mithra, the lord of wide pastures, ... sleepless, and ever awake;

'A god of high renown and old age [1], whom wide-hoofed horses carry against havocking hosts, against enemies coming in battle array, in the strife of conflicting nations [2].

48. 'And when Mithra drives along towards the havocking hosts, towards the enemies coming in battle array, in the strife of the conflicting nations, then he binds the hands of those who have lied unto Mithra, he confounds their eye-sight, he takes the hearing from their ears; they can no longer move their feet; they can no longer withstand those people, those foes, when Mithra, the lord of wide pastures, bears them ill-will.

'For his brightness and glory, I will offer him a sacrifice worth being heard . . . .

XII.

49. 'We sacrifice unto Mithra, the lord of wide pastures, ... sleepless, and ever awake;

50. 'For whom the Maker, Ahura Mazda, has

---

[1] Doubtful.   [2] Cf. § 8.

built up a dwelling on the Hara Berezaiti, the bright mountain around which the many (stars) revolve [1], where come neither night nor darkness, no cold wind and no hot wind, no deathful sickness, no uncleanness made by the Daêvas, and the clouds cannot reach up unto the Haraiti Bareza [2];

51. 'A dwelling that all the Amesha-Spentas, in one accord with the sun, made for him in the fulness of faith of a devoted heart, and he surveys the whole of the material world from the Haraiti Bareza.

52. 'And when there rushes a wicked worker of evil, swiftly, with a swift step, Mithra, the lord of wide pastures, goes and yokes his horses to his chariot, along with the holy, powerful Sraosha and Nairyô-sangha [3], who strikes a blow that smites the army, that smites the strength of the malicious [4].

'For his brightness and glory, I will offer him a sacrifice worth being heard . . . .

XIII.

53. 'We sacrifice unto Mithra, the lord of wide pastures, ... sleepless, and ever awake;

54. 'Who, with hands lifted up, ever cries unto Ahura Mazda, saying : " I am the kind keeper of all creatures, I am the kind maintainer of all creatures; yet men worship me not with a sacrifice in which I am invoked by my own name, as they worship the other gods with sacrifices in which they are invoked by their own names.

55 [5]. ' " If men would worship me with a sacrifice

---

[1] Bundahis V, 3 seq.; cf. Yt. XII, 13, and Yt. X, 13.
[2] The Haraiti Bareza is the same as Hara Berezaiti.
[3] Sîrôzah I, 9, notes 4 and 5.   [4] Doubtful (mâyaos).
[5] Cf. Yt. VIII, 11, 24, and Yt. X, 74.

in which I were invoked by my own name, as they
worship the other Yazatas with sacrifices in which
they are invoked by their own names, then I would
come to the faithful at the appointed time ; I would
come in the appointed time of my beautiful, immortal
life."

56 [1]. 'But the pious man, holding libations in his
hands, does worship thee with a sacrifice, in which
thou art invoked by thy own name, and with the
proper words.

' With a sacrifice, in which thou art invoked by thy
own name, with the proper words will I offer thee
libations, O powerful Mithra !

' With a sacrifice, in which thou art invoked by thy
own name, with the proper words will I offer thee
libations, O most beneficent Mithra !

' With a sacrifice, in which thou art invoked by thy
own name, with the proper words will I offer thee
libations, O thou undeceivable Mithra !

57. ' Listen unto our sacrifice, O Mithra ! Be thou
pleased with our sacrifice, O Mithra ! Come and sit
at our sacrifice ! Accept our libations ! Accept them
as they have been consecrated ! Gather them together with love and lay them in the Garô-nmâna !

58. ' Grant us these boons which we beg of thee,
O powerful god ! in accordance with the words of
revelation, namely, riches, strength, and victory,
good conscience and bliss, good fame and a good
soul; wisdom and the knowledge that gives happiness, the victorious strength given by Ahura, the
crushing Ascendant of Asha-Vahista, and conversation (with God) on the Holy Word.

---

[1] §§ 56–59 = §§ 30–34.

59. 'Grant that we, in a good spirit and high
spirit, exalted in joy and a good spirit, may smite all
our foes; that we, in a good spirit and high spirit,
exalted in joy and a good spirit, may smite all our
enemies; that we, in a good spirit and high spirit,
exalted in joy and a good spirit, may smite all the
malice of Daêvas and Men, of the Yâtus and
Pairikas, of the oppressors, the blind, and the deaf.

'For his brightness and glory, I will offer him a sacrifice worth
being heard . . . .

XIV.

60. 'We sacrifice unto Mithra, the lord of wide pastures, ...
sleepless, and ever awake;

'Whose renown is good, whose shape is good,
whose glory is good; who has boons to give at his
will, who has pasture-fields to give at his will;
harmless to the tiller of the ground, ... [1], beneficent; he, of the ten thousand spies, the powerful,
all-knowing, undeceivable god.

'For his brightness and glory, I will offer him a sacrifice worth
being heard . . . .

XV.

61. 'We sacrifice unto Mithra, the lord of wide pastures, ...
sleepless, and ever awake;

'Firm-legged [2], a watcher fully awake; valiant, a
chief in assemblies; making the waters flow forward; listening to appeals; making the waters run
and the plants grow up; ruling over the Karsh-

---

[1] The text is corrupt (vasô-yaonâi inatăm?).

[2] Eredhwô-zangem: sudridhagaṅghatâ, kila kârye yad pâdâ-
bhyâm yugyate kartum vyavasâyî saktaska (Yasna LXII, 5 [LXI,
13]).

vares[1]; delivering[2]; happy[3]; undeceivable; endowed with many senses [4]; a creature of wisdom ;

62. 'Who gives neither strength nor vigour to him who has lied unto Mithra; who gives neither glory nor any boon to him who has lied unto Mithra.

63. 'Thou takest away the strength from their arms, being angry and all-powerful ; thou takest the swiftness from their feet, the eye-sight from their eyes, the hearing from their ears.

'Not the wound of the well-sharpened spear or of the flying arrow reaches that man to whom Mithra comes for help with all the strength of his soul, he, of the ten thousand spies, the powerful, all-knowing, undeceivable god [5].

'For his brightness and glory, I will offer him a sacrifice worth being heard . . . .

XVI.

64. 'We sacrifice unto Mithra, the lord of wide pastures, ... sleepless, and ever awake;

'Who takes possession [6] of the beautiful, wide-expanding law, greatly and powerfully, and whose face looks over all the seven Karshvares of the earth ;

65. 'Who is swift amongst the swift, liberal amongst the liberal, strong amongst the strong, a chief of assembly amongst the chiefs of assemblies ; increase-giving, fatness-giving, cattle-giving, sovereignty-giving, son-giving, cheerfulness [7]-giving, and bliss [7]-giving.

---

[1] Karsô-râzanghem : kêsvar vîrâi (Pahl. tr. ibid.).

[2] From Ahriman; cf. Yasna XXIX, 6 (vyâna = vikârisn, visuddhatâ.)

[3] Yaokhstivant: kâmakômand (possessing whatever he wishes for, Vend. XX, 1 [3]).

[4] See Yt. X, 82, note.   [5] From Yt. X, 23–24.

[6] Cf. Yasna XLIII, 7 : vyânayâ : amat vandînît, yat grihnâti.

[7] Cf. Yt. X, 5, p. 121, notes 1 and 2.

66. 'With whom proceed Ashi Vanguhi, and Pâ-
re*n*di on her light chariot [1], the awful Manly Courage,
the awful kingly Glory, the awful sovereign Sky, the
awful cursing thought [2] of the wise, the awful Fravashis of the faithful, and he who keeps united together the many faithful worshippers of Mazda [3].

'For his brightness and glory, I will offer him a sacrifice worth
being heard . . . .

XVII.

67. 'We sacrifice unto Mithra, the lord of wide pastures, ...
sleepless, and ever awake;

'Who drives along on his high-wheeled chariot,
made of a heavenly [4] substance, from the Karshvare
of Arezahi [5] to the Karshvare of *Hv*aniratha, the
bright one; accompanied by [6] the wheel of sovereignty [7], the Glory made by Mazda, and the Victory
made by Ahura;

68. 'Whose chariot is embraced [8] by the great
Ashi Vanguhi; to whom the Law of Mazda opens a
way, that he may go easily; whom four heavenly
steeds, white, shining, seen afar, beneficent, endowed
with knowledge, swiftly [9] carry along the heavenly
space [10], while the cursing thought of the wise pushes
it forward;

69. 'From whom all the Daêvas unseen and the
Varenya fiends [11] flee away in fear. Oh! may we

---

[1] Cf. Yt. VIII, 38.   [2] See above, p. 12, note 13.

[3] Mithra himself (?).   [4] Or 'invisible.'

[5] The western Karshvare (see above, p. 123, note 5); this seems
to refer to the career of Mithra during the night; cf. § 95.

[6] And rolling upon it.   [7] Cf. Yt. XIII, 89, note.

[8] And uplifted.   [9] Doubtful.

[10] See above, p. 95, note 1.   [11] See Vend. Introd. IV, 23.

never fall across the rush of the angry lord[1], who goes and rushes from a thousand sides against his foe, he, of the ten thousand spies, the powerful, all-knowing, undeceivable god.

' For his brightness and glory, I will offer him a sacrifice worth being heard . . . .

XVIII.

70. ' We sacrifice unto Mithra, the lord of wide pastures, ... sleepless, and ever awake ;

' Before whom Verethraghna, made by Ahura, runs opposing the foes in the shape of a boar[2], a sharp-toothed he-boar, a sharp-jawed boar, that kills at one stroke, pursuing[3], wrathful, with a dripping face; strong, with iron feet, iron fore-paws[4], iron weapons, an iron tail, and iron jaws ;

71. ' Who, eagerly clinging to the fleeing foe, along with Manly Courage, smites the foe in battle, and does not think he has smitten him, nor does he consider it a blow till he has smitten away the marrow[5] and the column of life[6], the marrow[5] and the spring of existence.

72. ' He cuts all the limbs to pieces, and mingles, together with the earth, the bones, hair, brains, and blood of the men who have lied unto Mithra[7].

' For his brightness and glory, we offer him a sacrifice worth being heard . . . .

---

[1] Cf. § 98.
[2] See Yt. XIV, 15; cf. Yt. X, 127.
[3] Anupôithwa; cf. pôithwa (Vend. XIV [114])=rânînisn.
[4] Literally, hands.   [5] Doubtful.
[6] The spine.   [7] Cf. § 80.

XIX.

73. 'We sacrifice unto Mithra, the lord of wide pastures, ... sleepless, and ever awake ;

'Who, with hands lifted up, rejoicing, cries out, speaking thus :

74. '"O Ahura Mazda, most beneficent spirit! Maker of the material world, thou Holy One!

'"If men would worship me [1] with a sacrifice in which I were invoked by my own name, as they worship the other gods with sacrifices in which they are invoked by their own names, then I should come to the faithful at the appointed time; I should come in the appointed time of my beautiful, immortal life [2]."

75. 'May we keep our field; may we never be exiles [3] from our field, exiles from our house, exiles from our borough, exiles from our town, exiles from our country.

76. 'Thou dashest in pieces the malice of the malicious, the malice of the men of malice : dash thou in pieces the killers of faithful men!

'Thou hast good horses, thou hast a good chariot : thou art bringing help at every appeal, and art powerful.

77. 'I will pray unto thee for help, with many consecrations, with good consecrations of libations ; with many offerings, with good offerings of libations, that we, abiding in thee, may long inhabit a good abode, full of all the riches that can be wished for.

---

[1] They have worshipped him and he has consequently overcome the Mithradruges ; this accounts for the word rejoicing.

[2] Cf. Yt. X, 55.   [3] Iric ; cf. linquo.

78. 'Thou keepest those nations that tender a good worship to Mithra, the lord of wide pastures; thou dashest in pieces those that delight in havoc. Unto thee will I pray for help: may he come to us for help, the awful, most powerful Mithra, the worshipful and praiseworthy, the glorious lord of nations.

'For his brightness and glory, I will offer him a sacrifice worth being heard . . . .

XX.

79. 'We sacrifice unto Mithra, the lord of wide pastures, ... sleepless, and ever awake;

'Who made a dwelling for Rashnu [1], and to whom Rashnu gave all his soul for long friendship;

80. 'Thou art a keeper and protector of the dwelling of those who lie not: thou art the maintainer of those who lie not. With thee hath Verethraghna, made by Ahura, contracted the best of all friendships [2], and thus it is how so many men who have lied unto Mithra, even privily [3], lie smitten down on the ground.

'For his brightness and glory, I will offer him a sacrifice worth being heard . . . .

XXI.

81. 'We sacrifice unto Mithra, the lord of wide pastures, ... sleepless, and ever awake;

'Who made a dwelling for Rashnu, and to whom Rashnu gave all his soul for long friendship;

82. 'To whom Ahura Mazda gave a thousand

---

[1] The Genius of Truth (Yt. XII); Mithra gives a dwelling to the truthful man in the same way as he destroys the dwelling of the liar (§ 80).

[2] Cf. § 70.

[3] Aipi vithisi; Vedic api vyathis (VIII, 45, 19).

senses [1] and ten thousand eyes to see. With those
eyes and those senses, he watches the man who
injures Mithra, the man who lies unto Mithra.
Through those eyes and those senses, he is undeceivable, he, of the ten thousand spies, the powerful,
all-knowing, undeceivable god.

'For his brightness and glory, I will offer him a sacrifice worth
being heard . . . .

XXII.

83. 'We sacrifice unto Mithra, the lord of wide pastures, ...
sleepless, and ever awake;

'Whom the lord of the country invokes for help,
with hands uplifted;

'Whom the lord of the town invokes for help,
with hands uplifted;

84. 'Whom the lord of the borough invokes for
help, with hands uplifted;

'Whom the master of the house invokes for help,
with hands uplifted;

'Whom the . . . .[2] in danger of death [3] invokes for
help, with hands uplifted;

'Whom the poor man, who follows the good law,
when wronged and deprived of his rights, invokes
for help, with hands uplifted.

85. 'The voice of his wailing reaches up to the
sky, it goes over the earth all around, it goes over

---

[1] Yaokhsti, the root of Persian nyôsîdan, Pahlavi niyôkh-
sîtan, to hear; one might be inclined to translate 'a thousand
ears,' or 'a thousand hearings;' but the meaning of the word must
have been rather more general, as Neriosengh translates it
(pranidhi, IX, 8 [25]).

[2] Dvâkina?

[3] Pithê: mrityu (Yasna LIII [LII], 6).

the seven Karshvares, whether he utters his prayer in a low tone of voice [1] or aloud.

86. 'The cow driven astray invokes him for help [2], longing for the stables:

'"When will that bull, Mithra, the lord of wide pastures, bring us back, and make us reach the stables? when will he turn us back to the right way from the den of the Dru*g* where we were driven [3]?"

87. 'And to him with whom Mithra, the lord of wide pastures, has been satisfied, he comes with help; and of him with whom Mithra, the lord of wide pastures, has been offended, he crushes down the house, the borough, the town, the province, the country.

'For his brightness and glory, I will offer him a sacrifice worth being heard . . . .

XXIII.

88. 'We sacrifice unto Mithra, the lord of wide pastures, ... sleepless, and ever awake;

'To whom the enlivening, healing, fair, lordly, golden-eyed Haoma offered up a sacrifice on the highest of the heights, on the Haraiti Bareza [4], he

---

[1] Vâ*k*em, the so-called vâ*g*.

[2] Most manuscripts have added here, from the preceding clauses, 'with hands uplifted!'

[3] An allusion to a myth in which Mithra was described as an Indra delivering the cows carried away by a V*ri*tra: Firmicus Maternus called him abactorem boum (De Errore Profan. Relig. V); Commodianus compares him with Cacus:

'Vrtebatque boves alienos semper in antris
Sicut et Cacus Vulcani filius ille.'

(Apud Windischmann, Mithra, p. 64.)

[4] See above, p. 132, note 2.

the undefiled to one undefiled, with undefiled baresma, undefiled libations, and undefiled words ;

89. 'Whom [1] the holy Ahura Mazda has established as a priest, quick in performing the sacrifice and loud in song. He performed the sacrifice with a loud voice, as a priest quick in sacrifice and loud in song, a priest to Ahura Mazda, a priest to the Amesha-Spentas. His voice reached up to the sky, went over the earth all around, went over the seven Karshvares.

90. 'Who first lifted up Haomas, in a mortar inlaid with stars and made of a heavenly substance. Ahura Mazda longed for him, the Amesha-Spentas longed for him, for the well-shapen body of him whom the swift-horsed sun awakes for prayer from afar [2].

91. ' Hail to Mithra, the lord of wide pastures, who has a thousand ears and ten thousand eyes! Thou art worthy of sacrifice and prayer : mayest thou have sacrifice and prayer in the houses of men! Hail to the man who shall offer thee a sacrifice, with the holy wood in his hand, the baresma in his hand, the holy meat in his hand, the holy mortar in his hand [3], with his hands well-washed, with the mortar well-washed, with the bundles of baresma tied up, the Haoma uplifted, and the Ahuna Vairya sung through.

92. 'The holy Ahura Mazda confessed that religion and so did Vohu-Manô, so did Asha-Vahista, so did Khshathra-Vairya, so did Spenta-Ârmaiti, so

---

[1] Haoma ; cf. Yasna IX, 26 [81].
[2] For the morning service in the Gâh Usahîn.
[3] Cf. Vend. III, 1.

did Haurvatâ*t* and Ameretâ*t* ; and all the Amesha-Spe*n*tas longed for and confessed his religion. The kind Mazda conferred upon him the mastership of the world ; and [so did they [1]] who saw thee amongst all creatures the right lord and master of the world, the best cleanser of these creatures.

93. 'So mayest thou in both worlds, mayest thou keep us in both worlds, O Mithra, lord of wide pastures! both in this material world and in the world of the spirit, from the fiend of Death, from the fiend Aêshma [2], from the fiendish hordes, that lift up the spear of havoc, and from the onsets of Aêshma, wherein the evil-doing Aêshma rushes along with Vîdôtu [3], made by the Daêvas.

94. 'So mayest thou, O Mithra, lord of wide pastures! give swiftness to our teams, strength to our own bodies, and that we may watch with full success those who hate us, smite down our foes, and destroy at one stroke our adversaries, our enemies and those who hate us [4].

'For his brightness and glory, I will offer him a sacrifice worth being heard . . . .

XXIV.

95. 'We sacrifice unto Mithra, the lord of wide pastures, ... sleepless, and ever awake ;

'Who goes over the earth, all her breadth over, after the setting of the sun [5], touches both ends of

---

[1] The Amesha-Spe*n*tas.
[2] See Vend. Introd. IV, 22.   [3] See ibid.
[4] See Yt. V, 53; X, 11, 114; V, 53.
[5] It should seem as if Mithra was supposed to retrace his steps during the night. The Hindus supposed that the sun had a bright face and a dark one, and that during the night it returned from the west to the east with its dark face turned towards the earth.

this wide, round earth, whose ends lie afar, and surveys everything that is between the earth and the heavens,

96. 'Swinging in his hands a club with a hundred knots, a hundred edges, that rushes forwards and fells men down; a club cast out of red brass, of strong, golden brass; the strongest of all weapons, the most victorious of all weapons[1];

97. 'From whom Angra Mainyu, who is all death, flees away in fear; from whom Aêshma, the evil-doing Peshôtanu[2], flees away in fear; from whom the long-handed Bûshyãsta[3] flees away in fear; from whom all the Daêvas unseen and the Varenya fiends flee away in fear[4].

98. 'Oh! may we never fall across the rush of Mithra, the lord of wide pastures, when in anger[5]! May Mithra, the lord of wide pastures, never smite us in his anger; he who stands up upon this earth as the strongest of all gods, the most valiant of all gods, the most energetic of all gods, the swiftest of all gods, the most fiend-smiting of all gods, he, Mithra, the lord of wide pastures[6].

'For his brightness and glory, I will offer him a sacrifice worth being heard . . . .

XXV.

99. 'We sacrifice unto Mithra, the lord of wide pastures, ... sleepless, and ever awake;

'From whom all the Daêvas unseen and the Varenya fiends flee away in fear[7].

---

[1] Cf. § 132.
[3] See ibid. IV, 24.
[5] Cf. Yt. X, 69.
[7] Cf. § 97.

[2] See Vend. Introd. V, 19.
[4] Cf. § 69.
[6] §§ 97–98 = §§ 134–135.

'The lord of nations, Mithra, the lord of wide pastures, drives forward at the right-hand side of this wide, round earth, whose ends lie afar.

100. 'At his right hand drives the good, holy Sraosha; at his left hand drives the tall and strong Rashnu; on all sides around him drive the waters, the plants, and the Fravashis of the faithful.

101. 'In his might, he ever brings to them falcon-feathered arrows, and, when driving, he himself comes there, where are nations, enemy to Mithra, he, first and foremost, strikes blows with his club on the horse and his rider; he throws fear and fright upon the horse and his rider.

'For his brightness and glory, I will offer him a sacrifice worth being heard . . . .

XXVI.

102. 'We sacrifice unto Mithra, the lord of wide pastures, ... sleepless, and ever awake;

'The warrior of the white horse, of the sharp spear, the long spear, the quick arrows; foreseeing and clever;

103. 'Whom Ahura Mazda has established to maintain and look over all this moving [1] world, and who maintains and looks over all this moving world; who, never sleeping, wakefully guards the creation of Mazda; who, never sleeping, wakefully maintains the creation of Mazda.

'For his brightness and glory, I will offer him a sacrifice worth being heard . . . .

---

[1] Fravôis; Parsi tradition translates large: frâz (tr. Phl.), buland (Asp., Yasna LVII, 15 [LVI, 7, 3]).

XXVII.

104. 'We sacrifice unto Mithra, the lord of wide pastures, ... sleepless, and ever awake;

'Whose long arms, strong with Mithra-strength, encompass what he seizes in the easternmost river [1] and what he beats with the westernmost river [2], what is by the Sanaka [3] of the Rangha and what is by the boundary of the earth [4].

105. 'And thou, O Mithra! encompassing all this around, do thou reach it, all over, with thy arms.

'The man without glory [5], led astray from the right way, grieves in his heart; the man without glory thinks thus in himself: " That careless Mithra does not see all the evil that is done, nor all the lies that are told."

106. 'But I think thus in my heart:

' " Should the evil thoughts of the earthly man be a hundred times worse, they would not rise so high as the good thoughts of the heavenly Mithra;

' " Should the evil words of the earthly man be a hundred times worse, they would not rise so high as the good words of the heavenly Mithra;

---

[1] The Sind.

[2] The Rangha or Tigris. The words âgeurvayêiti and nighnê, 'he seizes, he beats,' are the words used of the priest laying the Haoma in the mortar and pounding it with the pestle (Yasna, X, 2 [4–5]). The Sind and the Rangha are thus compared with the two parts of the Hâvana, the land between is the Haoma, and Mithra's arms are the arms of the priest.

[3] Sanakê, an ἅπαξ λεγόμενον; opposed to the aodhas of the Rangha, Yt. XII, 19.

[4] The Arabian sea (?). Cf. Yt. XII, 21.

[5] Who has not a ray of the celestial light: here, the man of little faith.

' " Should the evil deeds of the earthly man be a hundred times worse, they would not rise so high as the good deeds of the heavenly Mithra ;

107. ' "Should the heavenly wisdom[1] in the earthly man be a hundred times greater, it would not rise so high as the heavenly wisdom in the heavenly Mithra ;

' "And thus, should the ears of the earthly man hear a hundred times better, he would not hear so well as the heavenly Mithra, whose ear hears well, who has a thousand senses, and sees every man that tells a lie."

' Mithra stands up in his strength, he drives in the awfulness of royalty, and sends from his eyes beautiful looks that shine from afar, (saying) :

108. ' "Who will offer me a sacrifice? Who will lie unto me? Who thinks me a god worthy of a good sacrifice? Who thinks me worthy only of a bad sacrifice? To whom shall I, in my might, impart brightness and glory? To whom bodily health? To whom shall I, in my might, impart riches and full weal? Whom shall I bless by raising him a virtuous[2] offspring?

109. ' " To whom shall I give in return, without his thinking of it, the awful sovereignty, beautifully arrayed, with many armies, and most perfect ; the sovereignty of an all-powerful tyrant, who fells down heads, valiant, smiting, and unsmitten ; who orders chastisement to be done and his order is done at once, which he has ordered in his anger ? "

' O Mithra! when thou art offended and not satisfied, he[3] soothes thy mind, and makes Mithra satisfied.

---

[1] See above, p. 4, n. 5.   [2] Âsna : Sansk. su*s*îla (p. 34, n. 4).
[3] He who offers thee a good sacrifice ; cf. § 108.

110. ' " To whom shall I, in my might, impart sickness and death? To whom shall I impart poverty and sterility [1]? Of whom shall I at one stroke cut off the offspring?

111. ' " From whom shall I take away, without his thinking of it, the awful sovereignty, beautifully arrayed, with many armies, and most perfect; the sovereignty of an all-powerful tyrant, who fells down heads, valiant, smiting, and unsmitten; who orders chastisement to be done and his order is done at once, which he has ordered in his anger?"

' O Mithra! while thou art satisfied and not angry, he moves thy heart to anger [2], and makes Mithra unsatisfied.

' For his brightness and glory, I will offer him a sacrifice worth being heard . . . .

XXVIII.

112. ' We sacrifice unto Mithra, the lord of wide pastures, ... sleepless, and ever awake;

A warrior with a silver helm [3], a golden cuirass [3], who kills with the poniard, strong, valiant, lord of the borough. Bright are the ways of Mithra, by which he goes towards the country, when, wishing well, he turns its plains and vales to pasture grounds,

113. ' And then cattle and males come to graze, as many as he wants.

' May Mithra and Ahura [4], the high gods, come to us for help, when the poniard lifts up its voice

---

[1] Doubtful.

[2] He who offers thee a bad sacrifice.   [3] Doubtful.

[4] See Vend. Introd. IV, 8.

aloud [1], when the nostrils of the horses quiver, when the poniards . . . . [2], when the strings of the bows whistle and shoot sharp arrows ; then the brood of those whose libations are hated fall smitten to the ground, with their hair torn off.

114. 'So mayest thou, O Mithra, lord of wide pastures! give swiftness to our teams, strength to our own bodies, and that we may watch with full success those who hate us, smite down our foes, and destroy at one stroke our adversaries, our enemies, and those who hate us [3].

' For his brightness and glory, I will offer him a sacrifice worth being heard . . . .

XXIX.

115. ' We sacrifice unto Mithra, the lord of wide pastures, ... sleepless, and ever awake.

' O Mithra, lord of wide pastures! thou master of the house, of the borough, of the town, of the country, thou Zarathu*s*trôtema [4]!

116. ' Mithra is twentyfold [5] between two friends or two relations ;

' Mithra is thirtyfold between two men of the same group [6] ;

' Mithra is fortyfold between two partners [7] ;

---

[1] When it clashes with another.   [2] Kahvân.

[3] See Yt. V, 53 ; X, 11, 94.

[4] The chief of the sacerdotal order, the so-called Maubedân-maused.

[5] Or 'the contract is twentyfold . . . . ,' that is, twenty times more strictly binding than between any two strangers. This passage is one of the most important of the Avesta, as a short account of the social constitution and morals of Zoroastrian Iran.

[6] Of the same gild (svapaṅkti, ap. Neriosengh).

[7] Hadha-gaêtha, co-proprietors of a gaêtha (a rural estate).

'Mithra is fiftyfold between wife and husband [1];

'Mithra is sixtyfold between two pupils (of the same master);

'Mithra is seventyfold between the pupil and his master;

'Mithra is eightyfold between the son-in-law and his father-in-law;

'Mithra is ninetyfold between two brothers;

117. 'Mithra is a hundredfold between the father and the son;

'Mithra is a thousandfold between two nations [2];

'Mithra is ten thousandfold when connected with the Law of Mazda [3], and then he will be every day [4] of victorious strength [5].

118. 'May I come unto thee with a prayer that goes lowly or goes highly! As this sun rises up above the Hara Berezaiti and then fulfils its career, so may I, O Spitama! with a prayer that goes lowly or goes highly, rise up above the will of the fiend Angra Mainyu [6]!

'For his brightness and glory, I will offer him a sacrifice worth being heard . . . .

XXX.

119. 'We sacrifice unto Mithra, the lord of wide pastures, ... sleepless, and ever awake.

'Offer up a sacrifice unto Mithra, O Spitama! and order thy pupils to do the same.

---

[1] Doubtful.

[2] A fair recognition of the jus gentium.

[3] The contract between the faithful and the Law, the covenant (?).

[4] Reading [h]amahê ayãn.

[5] The last clause is doubtful; the text is corrupt.

[6] Prayer follows Mithra in his career, rising and setting with him.

' Let the worshipper of Mazda sacrifice unto thee [1]
with small cattle, with black cattle, with flying birds,
gliding forward on wings.

120. 'To Mithra all the faithful worshippers of
Mazda must give strength and energy with offered
and proffered Haomas, which the Zaotar proffers
unto him and gives in sacrifice [2]. Let the faithful
man drink of the libations cleanly prepared, which
if he does, if he offers them unto Mithra, the lord of
wide pastures, Mithra will be pleased with him and
without anger.'

121. Zarathustra asked him : ' O Ahura Mazda!
how shall the faithful man drink the libations cleanly
prepared, which if he does and he offers them unto
Mithra, the lord of wide pastures, Mithra will be
pleased with him and without anger?'

122. Ahura Mazda answered: ' Let them wash
their bodies three days and three nights; let them
undergo thirty strokes [3] for the sacrifice and prayer
unto Mithra, the lord of wide pastures. Let them
wash their bodies two days and two nights; let them
undergo twenty strokes for the sacrifice and prayer
unto Mithra, the lord of wide pastures. Let no

---

[1] Mithra.

[2] The translation of this sentence is conjectural.

[3] Thirty strokes with the Sraoshô-karana (upâzana; see Vend.
Introd. V, 19); it is an expiation (âkayayanta) which purges
them from their sins and makes them fit for offering a sacrifice to
Mithra. One may find in this passage the origin of the painful
trials through which the adepts of the Mithriac mysteries had to
go before being admitted to initiation (οὐκ ἂν οὖν εἰς αὐτὸν δυνή-
σαιτό τις τελεσθῆναι, εἰ μὴ διά τινων βαθμῶν παρελθὼν τῶν κολάσεων
δείξει ἑαυτὸν ὅσιον καὶ ἀπαθῆ, Suidas s. v., ap. Windischmann, über
Mithra, 68 seq.).

man drink of these libations who does not know the
staota y,êsnya[1]: Vîspê ratavô[2].

'For his brightness and glory, I will offer him a sacrifice worth
being heard . . . .

XXXI.

123. 'We sacrifice unto Mithra, the lord of wide pastures, ...
sleepless, and ever awake;

'To whom Ahura Mazda offered up a sacrifice in
the shining Garô-nmâna[3].

124. 'With his arms lifted up towards Immortality[4], Mithra, the lord of wide pastures, drives
forward from the shining Garô-nmâna, in a beautiful
chariot that drives on, ever-swift, adorned with all
sorts of ornaments, and made of gold.

125. 'Four stallions draw that chariot, all of the
same white colour, living on heavenly food[5] and
undying. The hoofs of their fore-feet are shod with
gold, the hoofs of their hind-feet are shod with
silver; all are yoked to the same pole, and wear
the yoke[6] and the cross-beams of the yoke[6],
fastened with hooks[6] of Khshathra vairya[7] to a
beautiful . . . .[8]

126. 'At his right hand drives Rashnu-Razi*s*ta[9],
the most beneficent and most well-shapen.

---

[1] The sutûd yê*s*t; the last chapters of the Yasna, from LVIII
[LVII] to end, according to Anquetil (Zend-Avesta I, 2, 232).
[2] The first words of the Vispêrad.
[3] Paradise.
[4] Towards the abode of the Immortals.
[5] Fed with ambrosia (ἀμβρόσιον εἶδαρ) like Poseidon's steeds
(Il. XIII, 35; cf. Ovid, Metam. IV, 214).
[6] Doubtful (simãm*k*a simôithrãm*k*a).
[7] Metal. See Vend. Introd. IV, 33.
[8] Upairispâta.   [9] See Yt. XII.

'At his left hand drives the most upright *K*ista [1], the holy one,'bearing libations in her hands, clothed with white clothes, and white herself; and the cursing thought [2] of the Law of Mazda.

127. 'Çlose by him drives the strong cursing thought [2] of the wise man, opposing foes in the shape of a boar, a sharp-toothed he-boar, a sharp-jawed boar, that kills at one stroke, pursuing, wrathful, with a dripping face [3], strong and swift to run, and rushing all around [4].

'Behind him drives Âtar [5], all in a blaze, and the awful kingly Glory.

128. 'On a side of the chariot of Mithra, the lord of wide pastures, stand a thousand bows well-made, with a string of cowgut; they go through the heavenly space [6], they fall through the heavenly space upon the skulls of the Daêvas.

129. 'On a side of the chariot of Mithra, the lord of wide pastures, stand a thousand vulture-feathered arrows, with a golden mouth [7], with a horn shaft, with a brass tail, and well-made. They go through the heavenly space, they fall through the heavenly space upon the skulls of the Daêvas.

130. 'On a side of the chariot of Mithra, the lord of wide pastures, stand a thousand spears well-made and sharp-piercing. They go through the heavenly space, they fall through the heavenly space upon the skulls of the Daêvas.

'On a side of the chariot of Mithra, the lord of

---

[1] See Yt. XVI.   [2] See above, p. 12, note 13.   [3] Cf. Yt. X, 70.

[4] Or better, rushing before (pâiri-vâza; cf. the translations of pairi-da*h*vyu, Yt. X, 144 and pairi-vâra, Yt. I, 19). Cf. Yt. XIV, 15.

[5] The Genius of Fire.   [6] See p. 95, note 1.   [7] A golden point.

wide pastures, stand a thousand steel-hammers, two-
edged, well-made. They go through the heavenly
space, they fall through the heavenly space upon
the skulls of the Daêvas.

131. 'On a side of the chariot of Mithra, the lord
of wide pastures, stand a thousand swords, two-
edged and well-made. They go through the heavenly space, they fall through the heavenly space
upon the skulls of the Daêvas.

'On a side of the chariot of Mithra, the lord of
wide pastures, stand a thousand maces of iron, well-
made. They go through the heavenly space, they
fall through the heavenly space upon the skulls of
the Daêvas.

132. 'On a side of the chariot of Mithra, the lord
of wide pastures, stands a beautiful well-falling club,
with a hundred knots, a hundred edges, that rushes
forward and fells men down; a club cast out of
red brass, of strong, golden brass; the strongest of
all weapons, the most victorious of all weapons[1]. It
goes through the heavenly space[2], it falls through
the heavenly space upon the skulls of the Daêvas.

133. 'After he has smitten the Daêvas, after he
has smitten down the men who lied unto Mithra,
Mithra, the lord of wide pastures, drives forward
through Arezahê and Savahê, through Fradadhafshu
and Vîdadhafshu, through Vourubareʂti and Vouru-
ʒareʂti, through this our Karshvare, the bright
*Hv*aniratha[3].

134. 'Angra Mainyu, who is all death, flees away
in fear; Aêshma, the evil-doing Peshotanu, flees

---

[1] Cf. Yt. X, 96.   [2] The text has, they go . . . .
[3] See above, p. 123, note 5.

away in fear ; the long-handed Bûshyãsta flees away
in fear ; all the Daêvas unseen and the Varenya
fiends flee away in fear.

135. 'Oḥ! may we never fall across the rush of
Mithra, the lord of wide pastures, when in anger!
May Mithra, the lord of wide pastures, never smite
us in his anger; he who stands up upon this earth
as the strongest of all gods, the most valiant of all
gods, the most energetic of all gods, the swiftest of
all gods, the most fiend-smiting of all gods, he,
Mithra, the lord of wide pastures[1].

'For his brightness and glory, I will offer him a sacrifice worth
being heard . . . .

XXXII.

136. ' We sacrifice unto Mithra, the lord of wide pastures, ...
sleepless, and ever awake ;

' For whom white stallions, yoked to his chariot,
draw it, on one golden wheel, with a full shining
axle.

137. 'If Mithra takes his libations to his own
dwelling[2], " Happy that man, I think,"—said Ahura
Mazda,—" O holy Zarathustra! for whom a holy
priest, as pious as any in the world[3], who is the
Word incarnate, offers up a sacrifice unto Mithra with
bundles of baresma and with the [proper] words.

' " Straight to that man, I think, will Mithra come,
to visit his dwelling,

138. ' " When Mithra's boons will come to him, as
he follows God's teaching, and thinks according to
God's teaching.

'"Woe to that man, I think,"—said Ahura Mazda,—

---

[1] §§ 134–135 = §§ 97–98.   [2] Cf. Yt. X, 32.
[3] Doubtful. Possibly, ' of a pious conscience.'

"O holy Zarathu*s*tra! for whom an unholy priest, not pious [1], who is not the Word incarnate, stands behind the baresma, however full may be the bundles of baresma he ties, however long may be the sacrifice he performs."

139. 'He does not delight Ahura Mazda, nor the other Amesha-Spe*n*tas, nor Mithra, the lord of wide pastures, he who thus scorns Mazda, and the other Amesha-Spe*n*tas, and Mithra, the lord of wide pastures, and the Law, and Rashnu, and Ar*s*tâ*t*, who makes the world grow, who makes the world increase.

'For his brightness and glory, I will offer him a sacrifice worth being heard . . . .

XXXIII.

140. 'We sacrifice unto Mithra, the lord of wide pastures, ... sleepless, and ever awake.

'I will offer up a sacrifice unto the good Mithra, O Spitama! unto the strong, heavenly god, who is foremost, highly merciful, and peerless; whose house is above [2], a stout and strong warrior;

141. 'Victorious and armed with a well-fashioned weapon, watchful in darkness and undeceivable. He is the stoutest of the stoutest, he is the strongest of the strongest, he is the most intelligent of the gods, he is victorious and endowed with Glory: he, of the ten thousand eyes, of the ten thousand spies, the powerful, all-knowing, undeceivable god.

'For his brightness and glory, I will offer him a sacrifice worth being heard . . . .

---

[1] An unqualified priest; cf. Vend. IX, 47–57; XVIII, 1 seq.
[2] Or, 'whose house is great.'

XXXIV.

142. 'We sacrifice unto Mithra, the lord of wide pastures, ...
sleepless, and ever awake ;

'Who, with his manifold knowledge, powerfully
increases the creation of Spe*n*ta Mainyu, and is a
well-created and most great Yazata, self-shining like
the moon, when he makes his own body shine ;

143. 'Whose face is flashing with light like the
face of the star Ti*s*trya [1] ; whose chariot is embraced
by that goddess who is foremost amongst those who
have no deceit in them [2], O Spitama! who is fairer
than any creature in the world, and full of light to
shine. I will worship that chariot, wrought by the
Maker, Ahura Mazda, inlaid with stars and made of
a heavenly substance; (the chariot) of Mithra, who
has ten thousand spies, the powerful, all-knowing,
undeceivable god.

'For his brightness and glory, I will offer him a sacrifice worth
being heard . . . .

XXXV.

144. 'We sacrifice unto Mithra, the lord of wide
pastures, who is truth-speaking, a chief in assemblies,
with a thousand ears, well-shapen, with a thousand
eyes, high, with full knowledge, strong, sleepless, and
ever awake.

'We sacrifice unto the Mithra around countries [3] ;
'We sacrifice unto the Mithra within countries;

---

[1] See Yt. VIII. [2] Ashi Vanguhi (?); cf. § 68.
[3] Who watches around countries : aiwida*h*v*yûm is translated
مهر بیرامون شهر ها (Pers. tr. of Mihir Nyâyi*s*).

'We sacrifice unto the Mithra in this country[1];
'We sacrifice unto the Mithra above countries;
'We sacrifice unto the Mithra under countries;
'We sacrifice unto the Mithra before countries[2];
'We sacrifice unto the Mithra behind countries.

145. 'We sacrifice unto Mithra and Ahura, the two great, imperishable, holy gods[3]; and unto the stars, and the moon, and the sun, with the trees that yield up baresma[4]. We sacrifice unto Mithra, the lord of all countries.

'For his brightness and glory, I will offer unto him a sacrifice worth being heard, namely, unto Mithra, the lord of wide pastures.

'Yathâ ahû vairyô: The will of the Lord is the law of holiness . . . .

'I bless the sacrifice and prayer, and the strength and vigour of Mithra, the lord of wide pastures, who has a thousand ears, ten thousand eyes, a Yazata invoked by his own name; and that of Râma Hvâstra[5].

'Ashem Vohû: Holiness is the best of all good . . . .
'[Give] unto that man[6] brightness and glory, ... give him the bright, all-happy, blissful abode of the holy Ones!'

---

[1] Âdaḥvyûm : است شهر این در که مهرکه ; cf. Yasna XXVI, 9 [28].
[2] Pairidaḥvyûm : است شهر هر پیش که.
[3] Cf. Vend. Introd. IV, 8.   [4] Cf. Vend. p. 22, note 2.
[5] Cf. Sîrôzah I, 16.   [6] Who sacrifices to Mithra.

XI. SRÔSH YAST HÂDHÔKHT.

There are two Yasts dedicated to Sraosha, the angel of divine worship [1]: one is a part of the Yasna (LVII [LVI]), and this, the other, is called the Srôsh Yast Hâdhôkht. Whether it belonged to the so-called Hâdhôkht Nosk [2], one of the twenty-one Nosks of which the original Avesta was formed [3], or whether it was recited in the Hâdhôkht sacrifice [4], a particular liturgy, is a matter on which we have no sufficient information.

The two Yasts have a few developments in common (see §§ 8–9, 10–13): the Hâdhôkht is more liturgical, the Yasna Yast is more descriptive, and has to a greater degree the poetical imagery of a Yast. The Srôsh Yast Hâdhôkht is recited every day, during any gâh except the Rapitvîn. A Pahlavi translation of this Yast is extant (East India Office, XII, 102 ; Paris, Supplément Persan, XXXIII, 259 ; edited in Études Iraniennes, II), and Anquetil mentions a Sanskrit translation.

---

0. May Ahura Mazda be rejoiced !....

Ashem Vohû : Holiness is the best of all good ....

I confess myself a worshipper of Mazda, a follower of Zarathustra, one who hates the Daêvas and obeys the laws of Ahura ;

For sacrifice, prayer, propitiation, and glorification unto [Hâvani], the holy and master of holiness ....

Unto the holy, strong Sraosha, who is the incarnate Word, a mighty-speared and lordly god,

Be propitiation, with sacrifice, prayer, propitiation, and glorification.

Yathâ ahû vairyô: The will of the Lord is the law of holiness ....

---

[1] Cf. Vend. Introd. IV, 31.   [2] Ibid. III, 3.
[3] See an account of the Hâdhôkht Nosk in the Dînkart (West, Pahlavi Texts, I, 225, note) ; cf. Introd. to Yt. XXI.
[4] Cf. § 18, note.

I.

1. We sacrifice unto the holy, tall-formed, fiend-smiting Sraosha, who makes the world increase, the holy and master of holiness.

Good prayer, excellent prayer to the worlds [1], O Zarathu*s*tra!

2. This it is that takes away the friendship of the fiend and fiends, of the he-fiend and of the she-fiend; it turns away in giddiness their eyes, minds, ears [2], hands, feet, mouths, and tongues [3]; as good prayer, without deceit and without harm, is Manly Courage [4], and turns away the Dru*g* [5].

3. The holy Sraosha, the best protector of the poor, is fiend-smiting; he is the best smiter of the Dru*g*.

The faithful one who pronounces most words of blessing is the most victorious in victory; the Mãthra Spe*n*ta takes best the unseen Dru*g* away. The Ahuna Vairya [6] is the best fiend-smiter among all spells; the word of truth is the fighter [7] that is the best of all fiend-smiters.

The Law of the worshippers of Mazda is the truest giver of all the good things, of all those that are the offspring of the good principle; and so is the Law of Zarathu*s*tra.

4. And he who should pronounce that word [8], O Zarathu*s*tra! either a man or a woman, with a mind all intent on holiness, with words all intent on

---

[1] 'Has been taught to the world, namely, the Law' (Pahl. Comm.).

[2] Doubtful.   [3] Derezvã: Pahl. hûzvân; cf. Yt. I, 28.

[4] Is the same with it, is as powerful.

[5] Doubtful (vârethrem dâre*s*tâ . . . . zak drû*g* vartî dâstârtûm).

[6] See p. 23.

[7] Or, 'is the best of all fiend-smiters in battle.'

[8] This chapter (Pahl. Comm.).

holiness, with deeds all intent on holiness, when he is in fear either of high waters or of the darkness of a rainy night;

Or at the fords of a river, or at the branching-off of roads ;

Or in the meeting together of the faithful, or the rushing together of the worshippers of the Daêvas [1];

5. Whether on the road [2] or in the law [3] he has to fear, not in that day nor in that night shall the tormenting fiend, who wants to torment him, prevail to throw upon him the look of his evil eye, and the malice of the thief [4] who carries off cattle shall not reach him.

6. Pronounce then that word, O Zarathustra! that word to be spoken [5], when thou fall upon the idolaters [6] and thieves and Daêvas rushing together. Then the malice of the wicked worshippers of the Daêvas, of the Yâtus and their followers, of the Pairikas and their followers, will be affrighted and rush away. Down are the Daêvas! Down are the Daêva-worshippers, and they take back their mouths from biting [7].

---

[1] Different words are used, as usual, to express the same conflict, according as it refers to the faithful or to the idolaters.

[2] Aipi-ayanãm: madam râs.

[3] Arethyanãm: dâdistân (from aretha, meaning dînâ, dâdistân).

[4] Gadha: nrisamsa (Neriosengh); the Pahlavi has ﻴ, a Saka, a Scythe.

[5] The praise of Sraosha.

[6] Keresaska: krasîâk; cf. Neriosengh ad Yasna IX, 24 [75]; that name was in the later periods applied to Christians, as if keresa were the name of Christ; cf. Bahman Yast II, 19 ; III, 2.

[7] Doubtful.

7. And therefore we take around us the holy-natured Sraosha, the holy, the fiend-smiter, as one does with shepherds' dogs; therefore we sacrifice unto the holy-natured Sraosha, the holy, the fiend-smiter, with good thoughts, good words, and good deeds.

8 [1]. For his brightness and glory, for his strength and victorious power, for his offering sacrifices unto the gods [2], I will offer him a sacrifice worth being heard. I will offer up libations unto the holy Sraosha, unto the great Ashi Vanguhi [3], and unto Nairyô-sangha [4], the tall-formed.

So may the holy Sraosha, the fiend-smiter, come to us for help!

9. We worship the holy Sraosha; we worship the great master, Ahura Mazda, who is supreme in holiness, who is the foremost to do deeds of holiness.

We worship all the words [5] of Zarathustra, and all the good deeds, those done and those to be done.

Yênhê hâtãm: All those beings of whom Ahura Mazda . . . .

II.

10 [6]. We sacrifice unto the holy, tall-formed, fiend-smiting Sraosha, who makes the world increase, the holy and master of holiness;

Who strikes the evil-doing [7] man, who strikes the evil-doing woman; who smites the fiendish

---

[1] §§ 8–9 = Yasna LVII, 3–4 [LVI, 1, 6–12].
[2] See Vend. Introd. IV, 31.   [3] See Yt. XVII.
[4] See Vend. XXII, 7 [22] and Sîrôzah I, 9.
[5] The words of the law.
[6] §§ 10–13 = Yasna LVII, 15–18 [LVI, 7].
[7] Cf. Yt. I, 19.

Dru*g*, and is̆ most strong and world-destroying; who maintains and looks over all this moving[1] world;

11. Who, never sleeping, wakefully guards the creation of Mazda; who, never sleeping, wakefully maintains the creation of Mazda; who protects all the material world with his club uplifted, from the hour when the sun is down;

12. Who never more did enjoy sleep from the time when the two Spirits made the world, namely, the good Spirit and the evil One; who every day, every night, fights with the Mâzainya Daêvas.

13. He bows not for fear and fright before the Daêvas: before him all the Daêvas bow for fear and fright reluctantly, and rush away to darkness[2].

For his brightness and glory, for his strength and victorious power . . . .[3]

III.

14. Yathâ ahû vairyô: The will of the Lord is the law of holiness . . . .

We sacrifice unto the holy, tall-formed, fiend-smiting Sraosha, who makes the world increase, the holy and master of holiness;

Who with peace and friendship[4] watches the Dru*g* and the most beneficent Spirit: so that the Amesha-Spe*n*tas may go along the seven Karshvares of the earth[5]; who is the teacher of the

---

[1] Cf. above, p. 145, note 1.   [2] To hell.
[3] As above, §§ 8–9.   [4] To the creation of Ormazd.
[5] Doubtful. The Yasna has: 'Through whose strength, victorious power, wisdom, and knowledge the Amesha-Spe*n*tas go (avãn; Phl. sâtûnand) along the seven Karshvares of the earth' (LVII, 23 [LVI, 10, 2]).

Law[1] : he himself was taught it by Ahura Mazda, the holy One.

For his brightness and glory, for his strength and victorious power . . . .

IV.

15. Yathâ ahû vairyô: The will of the Lord is the law of holiness . . . .

We sacrifice unto the holy, tall-formed, fiend-smiting Sraosha, who makes the world increase, the holy and master of holiness ;

Whom the holy Ahura Mazda has created to withstand Aêshma, the fiend of the wounding spear ; we sacrifice unto Peace, whose breath is friendly, and unto the two withstanders of sin and guilt[2],

16. The friends of the holy Sraosha ;

The friends of Rashnu Razi*s*ta [3] ;

The friends of the good Law of the worshippers of Mazda ;

The friends of Ar*s*tâ*t*[4], who makes the world grow, who makes the world increase, who makes the world prosper ;

The friends of Ashi Vanguhi [5] ;

The friends of the good *K*isti [6] ;

The friends of the most right *K*ista [7] ;

---

[1] He teaches the law to the three saviours to come, Oshêdar Bâmî, Oshêdar Mâh, and Soshyôs (Yasna LVII, 24 [LVI, 10, 2]; Phl. tr.).

[2] Pare*s*tas*k*a mravay*âo*s*k*a, to be corrected, according to various readings, into staretas*k*a mavay*âo*s*k*a or something like it ; the two genii here alluded to are Anâstareta and Amuyamna, Sinlessness and Innocence, who are invoked in company with Akh*s*ti hamvai*n*ti in Vispêrad VIII, 4.

[3] See Yt. XII.
[4] See Yt. XVII.
[5] See Vend. XIX, 39.
[6] See ibid.
[7] See Yt. XVI, 1.

17. The friends of all gods;
The friends of the Mãthra Spenta;
The friends of the fiend-destroying Law;
The friends of the long-traditional teaching;
The friends of the Amesha-Spentas;
The friends of ourselves, the Saoshyants[1], the two-footed part of the holy creation;
The friends of all the beings of the holy world.

For his brightness and glory, for his strength and victorious power . . . .

V.

18. Yathâ ahû vairyô: The will of the Lord is the law of holiness . . . .
We sacrifice unto the holy, tall-formed, fiend-smiting Sraosha, who makes the world increase, the holy and master of holiness;

The first [Sraosha], the next, the middle, and the highest; with the first sacrifice, with the next, with the middle, and with the highest[2]. We sacrifice unto all [the moments][3] of the holy and strong Sraosha, who is the incarnate Word;

19. The strong Sraosha, of the manly courage, the warrior of the strong arms, who breaks the skulls of the Daêvas; who smites with heavy blows[4] and is strong to smite; the holy Sraosha, who smites

---

[1] The faithful, as helping through their good deeds in the work of final restoration, to be performed by Saoshyant (cf. Yt. XIII, 17).

[2] The first sacrifice is the Yasna sacrifice; the next (literally, superior) is the Vispêrad; the middle sacrifice is the Hâdhôkht [and] êvak hômâst; the highest sacrifice is the Dvâzdah hômâst (Pahl. Comm.). Sraosha is called the first, next, middle, and highest, accordingly as he presides over one or the other of those sacrifices. For a definition of the êvak hômâst and Dvâzdah hômâst, see West, Pahlavi Texts, I, 212, note 5.

[3] Vîspãn, translated harvisp zamân.

[4] Literally, the smiter who smites with smitings.

with heavy blows; we sacrifice unto the crushing Ascendant of both the holy Sraosha and Arƨti [1].

20. We sacrifice for all the houses protected by Sraosha, where the holy Sraosha is dear and friendly treated and satisfied, as well as the faithful man [2], rich in good thoughts, rich in good words, rich in good deeds.

21. We sacrifice unto the body of the holy Sraosha;

We sacrifice unto the body of Rashnu Raziƨta;

We sacrifice unto the body of Mithra, the lord of wide pastures;

We sacrifice unto the body of the holy wind;

We sacrifice unto the body of the good Law of the worshippers of Mazda;

We sacrifice unto the body of Arƨtâ/, who makes the world grow, who makes the world increase, who makes the world prosper;

We sacrifice unto the body of Ashi Vanguhi;

We sacrifice unto the body of the good Kisti;

We sacrifice unto the body of the most right Kista;

We sacrifice unto the bodies of all the gods;

22. We sacrifice unto the body of the Mãthra Speñta;

We sacrifice unto the body of the fiend-destroying Law;

We sacrifice unto the body of the long-traditional teaching;

We sacrifice unto the bodies of the Amesha-Speñtas;

---

[1] The same as Arƨtâ/. Cf. Yasna LVII, 34–35 [LVI, 13, 3–7].
[2] He receives alms (the ashô-dâd).

We sacrifice unto the bodies of ourselves, the Saoshya*nt*s, the two-footed part of the holy creation;

We sacrifice unto the bodies of all the beings of the holy world [1].

For his brightness and glory, for his strength and victorious power ....

23. Yathâ ahû vairyô: The will of the Lord is the law of holiness ....

I bless the sacrifice and prayer, the strength and vigour of the holy, strong Sraosha, who is the incarnate Word, a mighty-speared and lordly god.

[Give] unto that man [2] brightness and glory, ... give him the bright, all-happy, blissful abode of the holy Ones!

---

[1] Cf. §§ 16–17.   [2] Who sacrifices to Sraosha.

XII. RASHN YAST.

Rashnu Razista, 'the truest True,' is the Genius of Truth: he is one of the three judges of the departed, with Mithra and Sraosha: he holds the balance in which the deeds of men are weighed after their death: 'he makes no unjust balance . . . . , neither for the pious nor yet the wicked, neither for lords nor yet rulers ; as much as a hair's breadth he will not vary, and he shows no favour [1].' He is an offshoot either of Mithra, the God of Truth and the avenger of lies, or of Ahura Mazda himself, the all-knowing lord (§ 2 seq.).

This Yast seems to be an appeal made to Rashnu to come and attend the performance of the var nîrang or ordeal (see p. 170, note 3), of which Rashnu, as the Genius of Truth, was the natural witness and arbiter (cf. Vend. IV, 54–55 [154–156]). As a god of Truth must know everything and be present everywhere, he is called from whatever part of the world he may actually be in. This brings about an enumeration of all the parts of the world, from this earth (§§ 9–22) to the highest heaven (§ 37), passing through the Albôrz (§§ 23–26), the star region (§§ 26–32), the moon region (§ 33), and the sun region (§ 34 ; cf. p. 73, note 2).

This Yast is recited on the days of Rashn, Murdâd, Âshtâd, and Zemyâd (the 18th, 7th, 26th, and 28th of the month).

---

0. May Ahura Mazda be rejoiced! . . . .
Ashem Vohû: Holiness is the best of all good . . . .
I confess myself a worshipper of Mazda, a follower of Zara-thustra, one who hates the Daêvas and obeys the laws of Ahura ;
For sacrifice, prayer, propitiation, and glorification unto [Hâvani], the holy and master of holiness.

Unto Rashnu Razista ; unto Arstât, who makes the world grow, who makes the world increase ; unto the true-spoken speech, that makes the world grow [2];

---

[1] Minokhirad II, 120–121 (tr. West).
[2] Sîrôzah I, 18.

Be propitiation, with sacrifice, prayer, propitiation, and glorification.

Yathâ ahû vairyô: The will of the Lord is the law of holiness . . . .

I.

1. The holy (Zarathustra) asked him[1]: 'O holy Ahura Mazda! I ask thee; answer me with words of truth, thou who knowest the truth. Thou art undeceivable, thou hast an undeceivable understanding; thou art undeceivable, as thou knowest everything.

'What of the Holy Word is created true? what is created progress-making? what is fit to discern? what is healthful? what is wise? what is happy and more powerful to destroy than all other creatures[2]?'

2. Ahura Mazda answered: 'I will declare that unto thee, O pure, holy Spitama!

'The most glorious Holy Word (itself), this is what in the Holy Word is created true, what is created progress making, what is fit to discern, what is healthful, wise, and happy, what is more powerful to destroy than all other creatures.'

3. Ahura Mazda said: 'Bind up a three-twigged baresma against the way of the sun. [Address] unto me, Ahura Mazda, these words: "We invoke, we bless [Ahura][3]; I invoke the friendship [of Ahura] towards this var[4] prepared, towards the fire and the baresma, towards the full boiling [milk[5]], towards the var[4] of oil and the sap[6] of the plants."

---

[1] Ahura Mazda. [2] Cf. Yt. I, 1 seq.

[3] The text is apparently corrupt and has literally, 'We invoke, we bless m e, Ahura Mazda.'

[4] See following page, note 3.

[5] Possibly, waters; cf. Yt. V, 132 and Vend. IV, 46 [128], 54 [154] seq.

[6] Literally, the fat.

4. 'Then I, Ahura Mazda, shall come for help unto thee, towards this var prepared, towards the fire and the baresma, towards the full boiling [milk], towards the var of oil and the sap of the plants ;

'Along with the fiend-smiting Wind, along with the cursing thought of the wise [1], along with the kingly Glory, along with Saoka [2], made by Mazda.

5. 'We invoke, we bless Rashnu, the strong ; I invoke his friendship towards this var [3] prepared, towards the fire and the baresma, towards the full boiling [milk], towards the var of oil and the sap of the plants.

6. 'Then Rashnu the tall, the strong, will come for help unto thee, towards this var prepared, towards the fire and the baresma, towards the full boiling [milk], towards the var of oil and the sap of the plants :

'Along with the fiend-smiting Wind, along with the cursing thought of the wise, along with the kingly Glory, along with Saoka, made by Mazda.

7. 'O thou, holy Rashnu! O most true Rashnu! most beneficent Rashnu! most knowing Rashnu! most discerning Rashnu! most fore-knowing Rashnu! most far-seeing Rashnu! Rashnu, the

---

[1] See p. 12, note 13.   [2] See Vend. XXII, 3.

[3] Varô; this seems to be the Var nîrang or ordeal which is alluded to in several passages of the Avesta ; cf. Afrîgân I, 9 ; Yasna XXXI, 3 b (see Pahl. Comm.; cf. Comm. ad XXXIV, 4 a); cf. Vend. IV, 46, 55. According to the Dînkart, there were thirty-three kinds of var ordeals (Haug, Ardâ Vîrâf, p. 145); the most common was to pour melted copper upon the breast of the man whose truth was to be tested : if he went off uninjured, he was considered to have spoken the truth. Cf. Vend. Introd. III, 9.

best doer of justice [1]! Rashnu, the best smiter of thieves;

8. 'The uninjured, the best killer, smiter, destroyer of thieves and bandits! in whatever part of the world thou art watching the doings [2] of men and making the account . . . . [3].

II.

9. 'Whether thou, O holy Rashnu! art in the Karshvare Arezahi [4], we invoke, we bless Rashnu, the strong. I invoke his friendship towards this var prepared [5] . . . . in whatever part of the world thou art.

III.

10. 'Whether thou, O holy Rashnu! art in the Karshvare Savahi [4], we invoke, we bless Rashnu. I invoke his friendship towards this var prepared . . . . in whatever part of the world thou art.

IV.

11. 'Whether thou, O holy Rashnu! art in the Karshvare Fradadhafshu [4], we invoke, we bless Rashnu, the strong. I invoke his friendship towards this var prepared . . . . in whatever part of the world thou art.

V.

12. 'Whether thou, O holy Rashnu! art in the

---

[1] Arethama*t*-bairishta: aretha is dînâ, dâdistân (law, justice).

[2] Ke*s*a=kartârî (Pahl. Comm. ad Vend. XXI, 3 [14]).

[3] I cannot make anything of the rest of the sentence hadhanâ tanasu*s*; cf. § 38.

[4] See Yt. X, 15, note 5.   [5] The rest as in §§ 5–8.

Karshvare Vîdadhafshu[1], we invoke, we bless
Rashnu, the strong. I invoke his friendship towards
this var prepared . . . . in whatever part of the
world thou art.

VI.

13. 'Whether thou, O holy Rashn ! **art** in the
Karshvare Vouru-bare*s*ti[1], we **invoke**, we bless
Rashnu, the strong. I invoke his friendship towards
this var prepared . . . . in whatever part of the
world thou art.

VII.

14. 'Whether thou, O holy Rashnu! art in the
Karshvare Vouru-*g*are*s*ti[1], we invoke, we bless
Rashnu, the strong. I invoke his friendship towards
this var prepared . . . . in whatever part of the
world thou art.

VIII.

15. 'Whether thou, O holy Rashnu! art in this
Karshvare, the bright *H*vaniratha[1], we invoke, we
bless Rashnu, the strong. I invoke his friendship
towards this var prepared . . . . in whatever part
of the world thou art.

IX.

16. 'Whether thou, O holy Rashnu! art in the
sea Vouru-Kasha[2], we invoke, we bless Rashnu, the
strong. I invoke his friendship towards this var
prepared . . . . in whatever part of the world
thou art.

---

[1] See Yt. X, 15, note 5.   [2] See p. 54, note 6.

X.

17. 'Whether thou, O holy Rashnu! art on the tree of the eagle [1], that stands in the middle of the sea Vouru-Kasha, that is called the tree of good remedies, the tree of powerful remedies, the tree of all remedies, and on which rest the seeds of all plants; we invoke, we bless Rashnu, the strong.   I invoke his friendship towards this var prepared....

XI.

18. 'Whether thou, O holy Rashnu! art on the Aodhas [2] of the Rangha, we invoke, we bless Rashnu, the strong.   I invoke his friendship towards this var prepared . . . .

XII.

19. 'Whether thou, O holy Rashnu! art on the Sanaka [3] of the Rangha, we invoke, we bless Rashnu, the strong.   I invoke his friendship towards this var prepared . . . .

---

[1] The Saêna, in later mythology the Sînamrû or Sîmûrgh; his 'resting-place is on the tree which is Jad-bêsh (opposed to harm) of all seeds; and always when he rises aloft, a thousand twigs will shoot forth from that tree; and when he alights, he will break off the thousand twigs, and he sheds their seed therefrom. And the bird Chañmrôsh for ever sits in that vicinity; and his work is this, that he collects that seed which sheds from the tree of all seeds, which is Jad-bêsh, and conveys it there where Tishtar seizes the water, so that Tishtar may seize the water with that seed of all kinds, and may rain it on the world with the rain' (Minokhirad LXII, 37; tr. West).

[2] By the floods (? Vend. I, 26); it has probably a geographical meaning; cf. the following paragraph; perhaps the marshy country at the mouth of the Tigris.

[3] Cf. Yt. X, 104; aodhas and sanaka may refer to the southern and northern basin of the Tigris.

XIII.

20. 'Whether thou, O holy Rashnu! art at one of the angles of this earth, we invoke, we bless Rashnu. I invoke his friendship towards this var prepared . . . .

XIV.

21. 'Whether thou, O holy Rashnu! art at the boundary of this earth, we invoke, we bless Rashnu. I invoke his friendship towards this var prepared . . . .

XV.

22. 'Whether thou, O holy Rashnu! art in any place of this earth, we invoke, we bless Rashnu. I invoke his friendship towards this var prepared . . . .

XVI.

23. 'Whether thou, O holy Rashnu! art on the Hara Berezaiti, the bright mountain around which the many (stars) revolve, where come neither night nor darkness, no cold wind and no hot wind, no deathful sickness, no uncleanness made by the Daêvas, and the clouds cannot reach up unto the Haraiti Bareza [1]; we invoke, we bless **Rashnu**. I invoke his friendship towards this var prepared . . . .

XVII.

24. 'Whether thou, O holy Rashnu! art upon the highest Hukairya, of the deep precipices [2], made of gold, wherefrom this river of mine, Ardvi Sûra Anâhita, leaps from a thousand times the height of a man, we invoke, we bless Rashnu, the strong. I invoke his friendship towards this var prepared . . . .

---

[1] Cf. Yt. X, 50.

[2] Reading vîspô-vaêmem; cf. Yt. V, 96, note 7.

XVIII.

25. 'Whether thou, O holy Rashnu! art upon the Taêra of the height Haraiti, around which the stars, the moon, and the sun revolve[1], we invoke, we bless Rashnu, the strong. I invoke his friendship towards this var prepared . . . .

XIX.

26. 'Whether thou, O holy Rashnu! art in the star Vana*nt*[2], made by Mazda, we invoke, we bless Rashnu, the strong. I invoke his friendship towards this var prepared . . . .

XX.

27. 'Whether thou, O holy Rashnu! art in the bright and glorious star Ti*s*trya[3], we invoke, we bless Rashnu, the strong. I invoke his friendship towards the var prepared . . . .

XXI.

28. 'Whether thou, O holy Rashnu! art in the group of the Haptôiri*n*ga stars[3], we invoke, we bless Rashnu, the strong. I invoke his friendship towards this var prepared . . . .

XXII.

29. 'Whether thou, O holy Rashnu! art in those stars that have the seed of the waters in them[4], we

---

[1] See Bund. V, 3 seq.; cf. Yt. X, 13, 50.

[2] Cf. Yt. XX and Yt. VIII, 12. [3] Cf. Yt. VIII, 12.

[4] 'The star of water essence is for the increase of water; and the star of earth essence, for the increase of earth; and the star of tree essence, for the increase of trees; and the star of cattle essence,

invoke, we bless Rashnu, the strong.   I invoke his
friendship towards this var prepared . . . .

XXIII.

30. 'Whether thou, O holy Rashnu! art in those
stars that have the seed of the earth in them [1], we
invoke, we bless Rashnu, the strong.   I invoke his
friendship towards this var prepared . . . .

XXIV.

31. 'Whether thou, O holy Rashnu! art in those
stars that have the seed of the plants in them [1], we
invoke, we bless Rashnu, the strong.   I invoke his
friendship towards this var prepared . . . .

XXV.

32. 'Whether thou, O holy Rashnu! art in the
stars that belong to the Good Spirit [2], we invoke,
we bless Rashnu, the strong.   I invoke his friendship towards this var prepared . . . .

XXVI.

33. 'Whether thou, O holy Rashnu! art in the
moon which has the seed of the Bull in it [3], we invoke, we bless Rashnu, the strong.   I invoke his
friendship towards this var prepared . . . .

---

for the increase of cattle; and the essence of water, and earth, and
trees, and cattle is created for the increase of man' (Minokhirad
XLIX, 7, tr. West).

[1] See preceding note.

[2] Excluding the planets which belong to Ahriman (Minokhirad
VIII, 19; Bund. III, 25; V, 1).

[3] See above, p. 8, note 8.

XXVII.

34. 'Whether thou, O holy Rashnu! art in the swift-horsed sun, we invoke, we bless Rashnu, the strong. I invoke his friendship towards this var prepared . . . .

XXVIII.

35. 'Whether thou, O holy Rashnu! art in the sovereign endless Light, we invoke, we bless Rashnu, the strong. I invoke his friendship towards this var prepared . . . .

XXIX.

36. 'Whether thou, O holy Rashnu! art in the bright, all-happy, blissful abode of the holy Ones, we invoke, we bless Rashnu, the strong. I invoke his friendship towards this var prepared . . . .

XXX.

37. 'Whether thou, O holy Rashnu! art in the shining Garô-demâna [1], we invoke, we bless Rashnu, the strong. I invoke his friendship towards this var prepared . . . .

XXXI.

38. 'Whether thou, O holy Rashnu! art . . . . [2] we invoke, we bless Rashnu, the strong. I invoke his friendship towards this var prepared . . . .

39. 'For his brightness and glory, I will offer unto him a sacrifice worth being heard . . . .

---

[1] The highest heaven, the abode of Ormazd.
[2] ? Upa hadhana hadhanâ tanasus; cf. § 8, p. 171, note 3.

'Yê*n*hê hâtãm: All those beings of whom Ahura Mazda . . . .
40. 'Yathâ ahû vairyô: The will of the Lord is the law of
holiness . . . .

'I bless the sacrifice and prayer, and the strength
and vigour of Rashnu Razi*s*ta; of Ar*s*tâ*t*, who
makes the world grow, who makes the world increase; and of the true-spoken speech that makes
the world grow.

'Ashem Vohû: Holiness is the best of all good . . . .
'[Give] unto that man[1] brightness and glory, give him health of
body, ... give him the bright, all-happy, blissful abode of the
holy Ones.'

---

[1] Who shall have worshipped Rashnu.

XIII. FARVARDÎN YA*ST*.

The Fravashi is the inner power in every being that maintains
it and makes it grow and subsist. Originally the Fravashis were
the same as the Pit*ri*s of the Hindus or the Manes of the Latins,
that is to say, the everlasting and deified souls of the dead (see
§§ 49–52); but in course of time they gained a wider domain, and
not only men, but gods and even physical objects, like the sky and
the earth, &c. (§§ 85–86), had each a Fravashi (see Ormazd et
Ahriman, §§ 111–113).

This Ya*st* is to be divided into two parts. The former part
(§§ 1–84) is a glorification of the powers and attributes of the
Fravashis in general; the latter part (§§ 85–158) is an enumeration
of the Fravashis of the most celebrated heroes of Mazdeism, from
the first man, Gaya Maretan, down to the last, Saoshya*nt*.

This latter part is like a Homer's catalogue of Mazdeism.
The greatest part of the historical legends of Iran lies here con-
densed into a register of proper names. This enumeration is
divided into seven chapters:

The first (XXIV, §§ 85–95) contains the names of several gods,
of the first man, Gaya Maretan, the first law-giver, Zarathu*st*ra, and
his first disciple, Maidhyô-m*a*ungha;

The second part (XXV, §§ 96–110) contains the names of the
disciples of Zarathu*st*ra, most of them belonging to the epical
cyclus of Vîstâspa (Gu*st*âsp);

The third part (XXVI, §§ 111–117) is of uncertain character,
and no name contained in it is found in the epical legends;

The fourth part (XXVII, §§ 118–128) seems to be devoted to
the heroes of the other Karshvares and to mythical beings, born
or unborn (cf. §§ 121, 122, 127, 128);

The fifth part (XXVIII, § 129) is devoted to Saoshya*nt* alone;

The sixth part (XXIX, §§ 130–138) is devoted to the heroes
before the time of Zarathu*st*ra;

The seventh part (XXX, §§ 139–142) is devoted to the holy
women of Mazdeism from Hvôvi, Zarathu*st*ra's wife, down to
Srûta*t*-fedhri, Vanghu-fedhri, and Ereda*t*-fedhri, the future mothers
of his three unborn sons.

The second, third, and fourth enumerations all end with the

N 2

name of Astva*t*-ereta (that is to say, Saoshya*nt*), which shows that they do not refer to successive generations, but to three independent branches, which are each developed apart down to the time of the Saviour.

---

0. May Ahura Mazda be rejoiced! . . . .
Ashem Vohû: Holiness is the best of all good . . . .
I confess myself a worshipper of Mazda, a follower of Zarathu*s*tra, one who hates the Daêvas and obeys the laws of Ahura;
For sacrifice, prayer, propitiation, and glorification unto [Hâvani], the holy and master of holiness.

Unto the awful, overpowering Fravashis of the faithful; unto the Fravashis of the men of the primitive law [1]; unto the Fravashis of the next-of-kin,

Be propitiation, with sacrifice, prayer, propitiation, and glorification.
Yathâ ahû vairyô: The will of the Lord is the law of holiness . . . .

I.

1. Ahura Mazda spake unto Spitama Zarathu*s*tra, saying: 'Do thou proclaim, O pure Zarathu*s*tra! the vigour and strength, the glory, the help and the joy that are in the Fravashis of the faithful, the awful and overpowering Fravashis; do thou tell how they come to help me, how they bring assistance unto me, the awful Fravashis of the faithful [2].

2. 'Through their brightness and glory, O Zarathu*s*tra! I maintain that sky, there above, shining and seen afar, and encompassing this earth all around.

3. 'It looks like a palace, that stands built of a

---

[1] The so-called paoiryô-*t*kaêsha: the primitive law is what 'is considered as the true Mazdayasnian religion in all ages, both before and after the time of Zaratûst' (West, Pahlavi Texts, I, 242, note 1); cf. § 150.
[2] Cf. § 19.

heavenly substance[1], firmly established, with ends that lie afar, shining in its body of ruby over the three-thirds (of the earth)[2]; it is like a garment inlaid with stars, made of a heavenly substance, that Mazda puts on, along with Mithra and Rashnu and Spenta-Ârmaiti, and on no side can the eye perceive the end of it.

4. 'Through their brightness and glory, O Zarathustra! I maintain Ardvi Sûra Anâhita, the wide-expanding and health-giving, who hates the Daêvas and obeys the laws of Ahura, who is worthy of sacrifice in the material world, worthy of prayer in the material world; the life-increasing and holy, the flocks-increasing and holy, the fold-increasing and holy, the wealth-increasing and holy, the country-increasing and holy[3];

5[4]. 'Who makes the seed of all males pure, who makes the womb of all females pure for bringing forth, who makes all females bring forth in safety, who puts milk in the breasts of all females in the right measure and the right quality;

6. 'The large river, known afar, that is as large as the whole of all the waters that run along the earth; that runs powerfully from the height Hukairya down to the sea Vouru-Kasha.

7. 'All the shores of the sea Vouru-Kasha are boiling over, all the middle of it is boiling over,

---

[1] Reading mainyu-tâstô; cf. Yt. X, 90, 143, and in this very paragraph vanghanem mainyu-tâstem.

[2] A division of the earth different from and older than the division into seven Karshvares; cf. Yasna XI, 7 [21]; this division was derived by analogy from the tripartite division of the universe (earth, atmosphere, and heaven).

[3] Yt. V, 1.   [4] §§ 5–8 = Yt. V, 2–5.

when she runs down there, when she streams down
there, she, Ardvi Sûra Anâhita, who has a thousand
cells and a thousand channels; the extent of each of
those cells, of each of those channels, is as much
as a man can ride in forty days, riding on a good
horse.

8. 'From this river of mine alone flow all the
waters that spread all over the seven Karshvares;
this river of mine alone goes on bringing waters,
both in summer and in winter. This river of mine
purifies the seed in males, the womb in females, the
milk in females' breasts [1].

9. 'Through their brightness and glory, O Zarathustra! I maintain the wide earth made by Ahura,
the large and broad earth, that bears so much that
is fine, that bears all the bodily world, the live and
the dead, and the high mountains, rich in pastures
and waters;

10. 'Upon which run the many streams and
rivers; upon which the many kinds of plants grow
up from the ground, to nourish animals and men,
to nourish the Aryan nations, to nourish the five
kinds of animals [2], and to help the faithful.

11. 'Through their brightness and glory, O Zarathustra! I maintain in the womb the child that has
been conceived, so that it does not die from the

---

[1] §§ 4–8 = Yt. V, 1–5.

[2] There are five classes of animals: those living in waters
(upâpa), those living under the ground (upasma=upa-zema),
the flying ones (fraptargat), the running ones (ravaskarant), the
grazing ones (kangranghâk); Vispêrad I, 1 seq.; Yt. XIII, 74.
The representatives of those several classes are the kar mâhî
fish, the ermine, the karsipt, the hare, and the ass-goat (Pahl.
Comm. ad Visp. l. l.).

assaults of Vîdôtu [1], and I develop in it [2] the bones, the hair, the . . . . [3], the entrails, the feet, and the sexual organs.

12. 'Had not the awful Fravashis of the faithful given help unto me, those animals and men of mine, of which there are such excellent kinds, would not subsist; strength would belong to the Dru*g*, the dominion would belong to the Dru*g*, the material world would belong to the Dru*g*.

13. 'Between the earth and the sky the immaterial creatures would be harassed by the Dru*g*; between the earth and the sky the immaterial creatures would be smitten by the Dru*g*; and never afterwards would Angra-Mainyu give way to the blows of Spe*n*ta-Mainyu.

14. 'Through their brightness and glory the waters run and flow forward from the never-failing springs; through their brightness and glory the plants grow up from the earth, by the never-failing springs; through their brightness and glory the winds blow, driving down the clouds towards the never-failing springs.

15. 'Through their brightness and glory the females conceive offspring; through their brightness and glory they bring forth in safety; it is through their brightness and glory when they become blessed with children.

16. 'Through their brightness and glory a man is born who is a chief in assemblies and meetings [4], who listens well [5] to the (holy) words, whom Wisdom

---

[1] See Vend. IV, 40 [137].   [2] Doubtful.
[3] ? Derewda.   [4] A ποιμὴν λαῶν.
[5] Who learns well, who has the gaoshô-srûta khratu.

holds dear[1], and who returns a victor from discussions with Gaotema, the heretic[2].

'Through their brightness and glory the sun goes his way; through their brightness and glory the moon goes her way; through their brightness and glory the stars go their way.

17. 'In fearful battles they are the wisest for help, the Fravashis of the faithful.

'The most powerful amongst the Fravashis of the faithful, O Spitama! are those of the men of the primitive law[3] or those of the Saoshyants[4] not yet born, who are to restore the world. Of the others, the Fravashis of the living faithful are more powerful, O Zarathustra! than those of the dead, O Spitama!

18. 'And the man who in life shall treat the Fravashis of the faithful well, will become a ruler of the country with full power, and a chief most strong; so shall any man of you become, who shall treat Mithra well, the lord of wide pastures, and Arstât, who makes the world grow, who makes the world increase.

19. 'Thus do I proclaim unto thee, O pure Spitama! the vigour and strength, the glory, the help, and the joy that are in the Fravashis of the faithful,

---

[1] Or, 'who wishes for wisdom' (lore; khratukâta=khratu-kinah).

[2] Yô nâidhyanghô gaotemahê parô ayau parstôit avâiti. This seems to be an allusion to controversies with the Buddhists or Gotama's disciples, whose religion had obtained a footing in the western parts of Iran as early as the second century before Christ. Nâidhyanghô means a heretic, an Ashemaogha (see Pahl. Comm. ad Yasna XXXIV, 8).

[3] See above, p. 180, note 1.   [4] See above, p. 165, note 1.

the awful and overpowering Fravashis; and how
they come to help me, how they bring assistance
unto me, the awful Fravashis of the faithful [1].'

II.

20. Ahura Mazda spake unto Spitama Zarathustra, saying: 'If in this material world, O Spitama Zarathustra! thou happenest to come upon
frightful roads, full of dangers and fears, O Zarathustra! and thou fearest for thyself, then do thou
recite these words, then proclaim these fiend-smiting
words, O Zarathustra!

21. '"I praise, I invoke, I meditate upon, and we
sacrifice unto the good, strong, beneficent Fravashis
of the faithful. We worship the Fravashis of the
masters of the houses, those of the lords of the
boroughs, those of the lords of the towns, those of
the lords of the countries, those of the Zarathustrô-
temas [2]; the Fravashis of those that are, the Fravashis of those that have been, the Fravashis of
those that will be; all the Fravashis of all nations [3],
and most friendly the Fravashis of the friendly
nations;

22. '"Who maintain the sky, who maintain the
waters, who maintain the earth, who maintain the
cattle, who maintain in the womb the child that has
been conceived, so that it does not die from the
assaults of Vîdôtu, and develop in it the bones, the
hair, the . . . ., the entrails, the feet, and the sexual
organs [4];

23. '"Who are much-bringing, who move with

---

[1] Cf. § 1.
[2] See Yt. X, 115, note.
[3] See § 143, text and note.
[4] See § 11.

awfulness, well-moving, swiftly moving, quickly
moving, who move when invoked ; who are to be
invoked in the conquest of good, who are to be invoked in fights against foes, who are to be invoked
in battles ;

24. ' "Who give victory to their invoker, who give
boons to their lover, who give health to the sick
man, who give good Glory to the faithful man that
brings libations and invokes them with a sacrifice
and words of propitiation [1] ;

25. ' "Who turn to that side where are faithful
men, most devoted to holiness, and where is the
greatest piety [2], where the faithful man is rejoiced [3],
and where the faithful man is not ill-treated [4]." '

III.

26. We worship the good, strong, beneficent Fravashis of the faithful, who are the mightiest of drivers,
the lightest of those driving forwards, the slowest
of the retiring [5], the safest [5] of all bridges, the least-
erring [5] of all weapons and arms [6], and who never
turn their backs [7].

27. At once, wherever they come, we worship
them, the good ones, the excellent ones, the good,
the strong, the beneficent Fravashis of the faithful.
They are to be invoked when the bundles of
baresma are tied ; they are to be invoked in fights
against foes, in battles [8], and there where gallant
men strive to conquer foes.

---

[1] Cf. § 40.

[2] Fréritau: cf. fréreti=farnâmisn, âdesa (Yasna VIII, 2 [4]).

[3] With alms (ashô-dâd).   [4] Cf. § 36.

[5] Doubtful.   [6] Defensive arms.

[7] To flee.   [8] Cf. § 23.

28. Mazda invoked them for help, when he fixed the sky and the waters and the earth and the plants; when Spe*n*ta-Mainyu fixed the sky, when he fixed the waters, when the earth, when the cattle, when the plants, when the child conceived in the womb, so that it should not die from the assaults of Vîdôtu, and developed in it the bones, the hair, the . . . . , the entrails, the feet, and the sexual organs [1].

29. Spe*n*ta-Mainyu maintained the sky, and they sustained it from below, they, the strong Fravashis, who sit in silence, gazing with sharp looks; whose eyes and ears are powerful, who bring long joy, high and high-girded; well-moving and moving afar, loud-snorting [2], possessing riches and a high renown.

IV.

30. We worship the good, strong, beneficent Fravashis of the faithful; whose friendship is good, and who know how to benefit; whose friendship lasts long; who like to stay in the abode where they are not harmed by its dwellers; who are good, beautiful afar [3], health-giving, of high renown, conquering in battle, and who never do harm first.

V.

31. We worship the good, strong, beneficent Fravashis of the faithful; whose will is dreadful unto those who vex them; powerfully working and most beneficent; who in battle break the dread arms of their foes and haters.

---

[1] Cf. §§ 11, 22.

[2] They are compared to horses; cf. Yt. VIII, 2.

[3] Their beauty is seen afar. One manuscript has 'known afar;' another, 'whose eyesight reaches far.'

VI.

32. We worship the good, strong, beneficent Fravashis of the faithful; liberal, valiant, and full of strength, not to be seized by thought, welfare-giving, kind, and health-giving, following with Ashi's remedies, as far as the earth extends, as the rivers stretch, as the sun rises [1].

VII.

33. We worship the good, strong, beneficent Fravashis of the faithful, who gallantly and bravely fight, causing havoc, wounding [2], breaking to pieces all the malice of the malicious, Daêvas and men, and smiting powerfully in battle, at their wish and will.

34. You kindly deliver the Victory made by Ahura, and the crushing Ascendant, most beneficently, to those countries where you, the good ones, unharmed and rejoiced, unoppressed and unoffended, have been held worthy of sacrifice and prayer, and proceed the way of your wish.

VIII.

35. We worship the good, strong, beneficent Fravashis of the faithful, of high renown, smiting in battle, most strong, shield-bearing and harmless to those who are true, whom both the pursuing and the fleeing invoke for help: the pursuer invokes

---

[1] All the beneficent powers hidden in the earth, in the waters, and in the sun, and which Ashi Vanguhi (Yt. XVII) imparts to man.

[2] Doubtful: urvaênaitîs.

them for a swift race, and for a swift race does the fleer invoke them ;

36. Who turn to that side where are faithful men, most devoted to holiness, and where is the greatest piety, where the faithful man is rejoiced, and where the faithful man is not ill-treated [1].

IX.

37. We worship the good, strong, beneficent Fravashis of the faithful, who form many battalions, girded with weapons [2], lifting up spears, and full of sheen; who in fearful battles come rushing along where the gallant heroes [3] go and assail the Dânus [4].

38. There you destroy the victorious strength of the Turanian Dânus; there you destroy the malice of the Turanian Dânus; through you the chiefs [5] are of high intellect [6] and most successful; they, the gallant heroes [3], the gallant Saoshyants [7], the gallant conquerors of the offspring of the Dânus chiefs of myriads, who wound with stones [8].

X.

39. We worship the good, strong, beneficent Fravashis of the faithful, who rout the two wings of an army standing in battle array, who make the centre swerve, and swiftly pursue onwards, to help the faithful and to distress the doers of evil deeds.

XI.

40. We worship the good, strong, beneficent

---

[1] Cf. § 25. [2] Yâstô-zayau. [3] Doubtful.
[4] Yt. V, 72. [5] Doubtful.
[6] Hvîra; see Études Iraniennes, II, 183.
[7] Cf. p. 165, note 1. [8] Doubtful (asabana).

Fravashis of the faithful; awful, overpowering, and victorious, smiting in battle, sorely wounding, blowing away (the foes), moving along to and fro, of good renown, fair of body, godly of soul, and holy; who give victory to their invoker, who give boons to their lover, who give health to the sick man[1];

41. Who give good glory to him who worships them with a sacrifice, as that man did worship them, the holy Zarathustra, the chief of the material world, the head of the two-footed race, in whatever struggle he had to enter, in whatever distress he did fear;

42. Who, when well invoked, enjoy bliss in the heavens; who, when well invoked, come forward from the heavens, who are the heads[2] of that sky above, possessing the well-shapen Strength, the Victory made by Ahura, the crushing Ascendant, and Welfare[3], the wealth-bringing, boon-bringing, holy, well fed, worthy of sacrifice and prayer in the perfection of holiness.

43. They shed Satavaêsa[4] between the earth and the sky, him to whom the waters belong[5], who listens to appeals and makes the waters flow and the plants grow up, to nourish animals and men, to nourish the Aryan nations, to nourish the five kinds of animals[6], and to help the faithful[7].

44. Satavaêsa comes down and flows between the earth and the sky, he to whom the waters belong, who listens to appeals and makes the waters and the plants grow up, fair, radiant, and full of

---

[1] Cf. § 24.
[2] 'The chief creatures;' cf. Gâh II, 8.
[3] Saoka; cf. Sîrôzah I, 3, note.
[4] Cf. Yt. VIII, 9, and 34, note.
[5] Tat-âpem.
[6] See above, p. 182, note 2.
[7] Cf. § 10.

light, to nourish animals and men, to nourish the Aryan nations, to nourish the five kinds of animals, and to help the faithful.

XII.

45. We worship the good, strong, beneficent Fravashis of the faithful; with helms of brass, with weapons of brass, with armour [1] of brass; who struggle in the fights for victory in garments of light, arraying the battles and bringing them forwards, to kill thousands of Daêvas.

When the wind blows from behind them [2] and brings their breath unto men,

46. Then men know where blows the breath of victory : and they pay pious homage unto the good, strong, beneficent Fravashis of the faithful, with their hearts prepared and their arms uplifted.

47. Whichever side they have been first worshipped in the fulness of faith of a devoted heart [3], to that side turn the awful Fravashis of the faithful, along with Mithra and Rashnu and the awful cursing thought [4] of the wise and the victorious wind.

48. And those nations are smitten at one stroke by their fifties and their hundreds, by their hundreds and their thousands, by their thousands and their tens of thousands, by their tens of thousands and their myriads of myriads, against which turn the awful Fravashis of the faithful, along with Mithra and Rashnu, and the awful cursing thought of the wise and the victorious wind.

---

[1] Doubtful.
[2] Literally, blows them within.
[3] Cf. Yt. X, 9.
[4] See above, p. 12, note 12.

XIII.

49. We worship the good, strong, beneficent
Fravashis of the faithful, who come and go through
the borough at the time of the Hamaspathmaêdha[1];
they go along there for ten nights, asking thus[2]:

50. 'Who will praise us? Who will offer us a
sacrifice? Who will meditate upon us? Who will
bless us[3]? Who will receive us with meat and
clothes in his hand[4] and with a prayer worthy of
bliss[5]? Of which of us will the name be taken for
invocation[6]? Of which of you will the soul be worshipped by you with a sacrifice[7]? To whom will
this gift of ours be given, that he may have never-
failing food for ever and ever?'

51. And the man who offers them up a sacrifice,

---

[1] The sixth and last Gâhambâr (see Âfrîgân Gâhambâr), or the last
ten days of the year (10th–20th March), including the last five days
of the last month, Sapendârmad, and the five complementary days.
These last ten days should be spent in deeds of charity, religious
banquets (gasan), and ceremonies in memory of the dead. It was
also at the approach of the spring that the Romans and the
Athenians used to offer annual sacrifices to the dead; the Romans
in February 'qui tunc extremus anni mensis erat' (Cicero, De
Legibus, II, 21), the Athenians on the third day of the Anthesterion
feast (in the same month). The souls of the dead were supposed to
partake of the new life then beginning to circulate through nature,
that had also been dead during the long months of winter.

[2] Perhaps: asking for help, thus.

[3] Frînât: who will pronounce the Âfrîn?

[4] To be given in alms to poor Mazdayasnians (ashô-dâd).

[5] Asha-nasa: that makes him reach the condition of one of
the blessed (ahlâyîh ârzânîk, Vend. XVIII, 6 [17]): the Sanskrit
translation has, 'that is to say, that makes him worthy of a great
reward.'

[6] As in the invocations from § 87 to the end.

[7] An allusion to the formula: 'I sacrifice to the Fravashi of my
own soul,' Yasna XXIII, 4 [6].

with meat and clothes in his hand, with a prayer
worthy of bliss, the awful Fravashis of the faithful,
satisfied, unharmed, and unoffended, bless thus :

52. 'May there be in this house flocks of animals
and men! May there be a swift horse and a solid
chariot! May there be a man who knows how to
praise God [1] and rule in an assembly, who will offer
us sacrifices with meat and clothes in his hand, and
with a prayer worthy of bliss [2].'

XIV.

53. We worship the good, strong, beneficent
Fravashis of the faithful, who show beautiful paths
to the waters, made by Mazda, which had stood
before for a long time in the same place without
flowing [3] :

54. And now they flow along the path made by
Mazda, along the way made by the gods, the watery
way appointed to them, at the wish of Ahura Mazda,
at the wish of the Amesha-Spentas.

XV.

55. We worship the good, strong, beneficent
Fravashis of the faithful, who show a beautiful
growth to the fertile [4] plants, which had stood before
for a long time in the same place without growing :

56. And now they grow up along the path made

---

[1] Stâhyô : stutikaro (Sansk. tr.; cf. Âtash Nyâyis, 10).

[2] §§ 49–52 are a part of the so-called Âfrîgân Dahmân (a prayer
recited in honour of the dead); a Sanskrit translation of that
Âfrîgân has been published by Burnouf in his Études zendes.

[3] In winter.

[4] Doubtful. The word is *hva*wrîra, which Aspendiârji makes
synonymous with *hv*âpara, kind, merciful (Vispêrad XXI
[XXIV], 1).

by Mazda, along the way made by the gods, in the
time appointed to them, at the wish of Ahura
Mazda, at the wish of the Amesha-Spentas.

XVI.

57. We worship the good, strong, beneficent
Fravashis of the faithful, who showed their paths to
the stars, the moon, the sun, and the endless lights,
that had stood before for a long time in the same
place, without moving forwards, through the oppression of the Daêvas and the assaults of the Daêvas [1].

58. And now they move around in their far-
revolving circle for ever, till they come to the time
of the good restoration of the world.

XVII.

59. We worship the good, strong, beneficent
Fravashis of the faithful, who watch over the bright
sea Vouru-Kasha [2], to the number of ninety thousand, and nine thousand, and nine hundred, and
ninety-nine.

XVIII.

60. We worship the good, strong, beneficent
Fravashis of the faithful, who watch over the stars
Haptôiringa [3], to the number of ninety thousand,
and nine thousand, and nine hundred, and ninety-
nine.

XIX.

61. We worship the good, strong, beneficent
Fravashis of the faithful, who watch over the body

---

[1] Bundahis VI, 3.

[2] To keep the white Hôm there from the evil beings that try
to destroy it (Minokhirad LXII, 28).

[3] See above, p. 97, note 4.

of Keresâsp̃a, the son of Sâma[1], the club-bearer with plaited hair, to the number of ninety thousand, and nine thousand, and nine hundred, and ninety-nine.

XX.

62. We worship the good, strong, beneficent Fravashis of the faithful, who watch over the seed of the holy Zarathustra[2], to the number of ninety thousand, and nine thousand, and nine hundred, and ninety-nine.

XXI.

63. We worship the good, strong, beneficent Fravashis of the faithful, who fight at the right hand of the reigning lord, if he rejoices the faithful[3] and if the awful Fravashis of the faithful are not hurt by him, if they are rejoiced by him, unharmed and unoffended.

XXII.

64. We worship the good, strong, beneficent Fravashis of the faithful, who are greater, who are

---

[1] Keresâspa lies asleep in the plain of Pêsyânsâi; 'the glory (far) of heaven stands over him for the purpose that, when Az-i-Dahâk becomes unfettered, he may arise and slay him; and a myriad guardian spirits of the righteous are as a protection to him' (Bundahis XXIX, 8; tr. West).

[2] 'Zaratûst went near unto Hvôv (Hvôgvi, his wife) three times, and each time the seed went to the ground; the angel Nêryôsang received the brilliance and strength of that seed, delivered-it with care to the angel Anâhîd, and in time will blend it with a mother' (Bundahis XXXII, 8). A maid, Eredat-fedhri, bathing in Lake Kâsava, will conceive by that seed and bring forth the Saviour Saoshyant; his two fore-runners, Ukhshyat-ereta and Ukhshyat-nemah, will be born in the same way of Srûtat-fedhri and Vanghu-fedhri (Yt. XIII, 141–142).

[3] With alms.

O 2

stronger, who are swifter, who are more powerful, who are more victorious, who are more healing, who are more effective than can be expressed by words; who run by tens of thousands into the midst of the Myazdas.

65. And when the waters come up from the sea Vouru-Kasha, O Spitama Zarathustra! along with the Glory made by Mazda [1], then forwards come the awful Fravashis of the faithful, many and many hundreds, many and many thousands, many and many tens of thousands,

66. Seeking water for their own kindred, for their own borough, for their own town, for their own country, and saying thus: 'May our own country have a good store and full joy!'

67. They fight in the battles that are fought in their own place and land, each according to the place and house where he dwelt (of yore) [2]: they look like a gallant warrior who, girded up and watchful, fights for the hoard he has treasured up.

68. And those of them who win bring waters to their own kindred, to their own borough, to their own town, to their own country, saying thus: 'May my country grow and increase!'

69. And when the all-powerful sovereign of a country has been surprised by his foes and haters, he invokes them, the awful Fravashis of the faithful.

70. And they come to his help, if they have not been hurt by him, if they have been rejoiced by him, if they have not been harmed nor offended, the awful Fravashis of the faithful: they come flying unto him, it seems as if they were well-winged birds.

---

[1] Cf. Yt. XIX, 56 seq.; VIII, 34.   [2] Doubtful.

71. They come in as a weapon and as a shield, to keep him behind and to keep him in front, from the Drug unseen, from the female Varenya fiend, from the evil-doer bent on mischief, and from that fiend who is all death, Angra Mainyu. It will be as if there were a thousand men watching over one man [1];

72. So that neither the sword well-thrust, neither the club well-falling, nor the arrow well-shot, nor the spear well-darted, nor the stones flung from the arm shall destroy him.

73. They come on this side, they come on that side, never resting, the good, powerful, beneficent Fravashis of the faithful, asking for help thus: 'Who will praise us? Who will offer us a sacrifice? Who will meditate upon us? Who will bless us? Who will receive us with meat and clothes in his hand and with a prayer worthy of bliss? Of which of us will the name be taken for invocation? Of which of you will the soul be worshipped by you with a sacrifice? To whom will that gift of ours be given, that he may have never-failing food for ever and ever [2]?'

74. We worship the perception [3]; we worship the intellect; we worship the conscience; we worship those of the Saoshyants [4];

We worship the souls; those of the tame animals; those of the wild animals; those of the animals that live in the waters; those of the animals that live under the ground; those of the flying ones; those of the running ones; those of the grazing ones [5].

---

[1] Cf. Yt. I, 19.   [2] Cf. § 50.
[3] Âsna = âzana (?).   [4] Cf. p. 165, note 1.
[5] Cf. Yt. XIII, 10.

We worship their Fravashis[1].

75. We worship the Fravashis.

We worship them, the liberal;

We worship them, the valiant; we worship them, the most valiant;

We worship them, the beneficent; we worship them, the most beneficent;

We worship them, the powerful;

We worship them, the most strong;

We worship them, the light; we worship them, the most light;

We worship them, the effective; we worship them, the most effective.

76. They are the most effective amongst the creatures of the two Spirits, they the good, strong, beneficent Fravashis of the faithful, who stood holding fast when the two Spirits created the world, the Good Spirit and the Evil One[2].

77. When Angra Mainyu broke into the creation of the good holiness, then came in across Vohu Manô and Âtar[3].

78. They destroyed the malice of the fiend Angra Mainyu, so that the waters did not stop flowing nor did the plants stop growing; but at once the most beneficent waters of the creator and

---

[1] There seems to be in this paragraph a distinction of five faculties of the soul, âsna, mana, daêna, urvan, fravashi. The usual classification, as given in this Yast, § 149, and in later Parsism (Spiegel, Die traditionelle Literatur der Parsen, p. 172), is: ahu, spirit of life (?); daêna, conscience; baodhô, perception; urvan, the soul; fravashi.

[2] The Fravashis, 'on war horses and spear in hand, were around the sky . . . . and no passage was found by the evil spirit, who rushed back' (Bund. VI, 3–4; tr. West).

[3] Cf. Ormazd et Ahriman, § 107.

ruler, Ahura Mazda, flowed forward and his plants went on growing.

79. We worship all the waters;

We worship all the plants;

We worship all the good, strong, beneficent Fravashis of the faithful.

We worship the waters by their names [1];

We worship the plants by their names [2];

We worship the good, strong, beneficent Fravashis of the faithful by their names.

80. Of all those ancient Fravashis, we worship the Fravashi of Ahura Mazda; who is the greatest, the best, the fairest, the most solid, the wisest, the finest of body and supreme in holiness [3];

81. Whose soul is the Mãthra Spenta, who is white, shining, seen afar; and we worship the beautiful forms, the active forms wherewith he clothes the Amesha-Spentas; we worship the swift-horsed sun.

XXIII.

82. We worship the good, strong, beneficent Fravashis of the Amesha-Spentas, the bright ones, whose looks perform what they wish, the tall, quickly coming to do, strong, and lordly, who are undecaying and holy;

83. Who are all seven of one thought, who are all seven of one speech, who are all seven of one deed; whose thought is the same, whose speech is the same, whose deed is the same, whose father and

---

[1] That is to say, after their different kinds (described in Yasna XXXVIII, 3, 5 [7-9, 13-14]; LXVIII, 8 [LXVII, 15]; and Bund. XXI).

[2] After their kinds (Bund. XXVII).   [3] Cf. Yasna I, 1.

commander is the same, namely, the Maker, Ahura Mazda;

84. Who see one another's soul thinking of good thoughts, thinking of good words, thinking of good deeds, thinking of Garô-nmâna, and whose ways [1] are shining as they go down towards the libations [2].

XXIV.

85. We worship the good, strong, beneficent Fravashis: that of the most rejoicing [3] fire, the beneficent and assembly-making [4]; and that of the holy, strong Sraosha [5], who is the incarnate Word, a mighty-speared and lordly god; and that of Nairyô-sangha [6].

86. And that of Rashnu Razista [7];

That of Mithra [8], the lord of wide pastures;

That of the Mãthra-Spenta [9];

That of the sky;

That of the waters;

That of the earth;

That of the plants;

That of the Bull [10];

That of the living man [11];

That of the holy creation [12].

87. We worship the Fravashi of Gaya Maretan [13],

---

[1] The Vedic devayâna.   [2] Cf. Yt. XIX, 15, 17.
[3] Urvâzista. As a proper name Urvâzista is the name of the fire in plants (Yasna XVII, 11 [65], and Bund. XVII, 1).
[4] At the hearth and the altar.   [5] See Yt. XI.
[6] See Vend. XXII, 7.   [7] See Yt. XII.
[8] See Yt. X.   [9] The Holy Word.   [10] See Sîrôzah I, 12.
[11] Of mankind; possibly, of Gaya (Maretan).
[12] Doubtful.
[13] The first man. On the myths of Gaya Maretan, see Ormazd et Ahriman, §§ 129-135.

who first listened unto the thought and teaching of
Ahura Mazda; of whom Ahura formed the race of
the Aryan nations, the seed of the Aryan nations.

We worship the piety and the Fravashi of the
holy Zarathustra;

88. Who first thought what is good, who first
spoke what is good, who first did what is good; who
was the first Priest, the first Warrior, the first
Plougher of the ground [1]; who first knew and first
taught; who first possessed [2] and first took possession of the Bull [3], of Holiness [4], of the Word, the
obedience to the Word, and dominion, and all the
good things made by Mazda, that are the offspring
of the good Principle;

89. Who was the first Priest, the first Warrior,
the first Plougher of the ground; who first took the
turning of the wheel [5] from the hands of the Daêva
and of the cold-hearted man; who first in the material
world pronounced the praise of Asha [6], thus bringing
the Daêvas to naught, and confessed himself a
worshipper of Mazda, a follower of Zarathustra, one
who hates the Daêvas, and obeys the laws of
Ahura.

90. Who first in the material world said the
word that destroys the Daêvas, the law of Ahura;
who first in the material world proclaimed the word
that destroys the Daêvas, the law of Ahura; who

---

[1] As having established those three classes. His three earthly
sons, Isat-vâstra, Urvatat-nara, and Hvare-kithra (§ 98), were the
chiefs of the three classes. Cf. Vend. Introd. III, 15, note 3.

[2] Doubtful.   [3] Cf. Yasna XXIX, 8.

[4] The divine Order, Asha.

[5] The wheel of sovereignty (?); cf. Yt. X, 67; this expression
smacks of Buddhism.

[6] Who first pronounced the Ashem Vohû; cf. Yt. XXI.

first in the material world declared all the creation
of the Daêvas unworthy of sacrifice and prayer;
who was strong, giving all the good things of life,
the first bearer of the Law amongst the nations;

91. In whom was heard the whole Mãthra, the
word of holiness; who was the lord and master of
the world [1], the praiser of the most great, most good
and most fair Asha [2]; who had a revelation of the
Law, that most excellent of all beings;

92. For whom the Amesha-Spe*n*tas longed, in
one accord with the sun, in the fulness of faith of a
devoted heart; they longed for him, as the lord and
master of the world, as the praiser of the most great,
most good, and most fair Asha, as having a revelation of the Law, that most excellent of all beings;

93. In whose birth and growth the waters and
the plants rejoiced; in whose birth and growth the
waters and the plants grew; in whose birth and
growth all the creatures of the good creations cried
out, Hail [3]!

94. 'Hail to us! for he is born, the Âthravan,
Spitama Zarathu*s*tra. Zarathu*s*tra will offer us
sacrifices with libations and bundles of baresma;
and there will the good Law of the worshippers of
Mazda come and spread through all the seven
Karshvares of the earth.

95. 'There will Mithra, the lord of wide pastures,
increase all the excellences of our countries, and
allay their troubles; there will the powerful Apãm-
Napâ*t* [4] increase all the excellences of our countries,
and allay their troubles.'

---

[1] Material lord and spiritual master.
[2] The reciter of the Ashem Vohû.
[3] Cf. Vend. XIX, 46 [143].   [4] See Sîrôzah I, 9, note.

We worship the piety and Fravashi of Maidhyô-maungha, the son of Arâsti [1], who first listened unto the word and teaching of Zarathustra.

XXV.

96. We worship the Fravashi of the holy Asmô-*hv*anva*nt* [2];

We worship the Fravashi of the holy Asan-*hv*anva*nt*.

We worship the Fravashi of the holy Gavayan.

We worship the Fravashi of the holy Parsha*t*-ga*us* [3], the son of Frâta;

We worship the Fravashi of the holy Vohvasti, the son of Snaoya;

We worship the Fravashi of the holy Isva*t*, the son of Varâza.

97. We worship the Fravashi of the holy Saêna, the son of Ahûm-stu*t* [4], who first appeared upon this earth with a hundred pupils [5].

We worship the Fravashi of the holy Fradhi-daya.

We worship the Fravashi of the holy Usmânara, the son of Paêshata.

---

[1] Maidhyô-m*a*ungha was the cousin and first disciple of Zara-thustra; Zarathustra's father, Pourushaspa, and Ârâsti were brothers (Bund. XXXII, 3); cf. Yasna LI [L], 19.

[2] Cf. p. 33, note 2; Yt. XXII, 37.

[3] Another Parsa*t*-ga*us* is mentioned § 126.

[4] Possibly, 'the holy falcon, praiser of the lord;' thus the Law was brought to the Var of Yima by the bird Karsipta (Vend. II, 42), who recites the Avesta in the language of birds (Bund. XIX, 16): the Saêna-bird (Sîmurgh) became in later literature a mythical incarnation of Supreme wisdom (see the Mantik uttair and Dabistân I, 55).

[5] Who was the first regular teacher, the first aêthrapaiti.

We worship the Fravashi of the holy Vohu-
rao*k*ah, the son of Frânya;
We worship the Fravashi of the holy Ashô-
rao*k*ah, the son of Frânya;
We worship the Fravashi of the holy Varesmô-
rao*k*ah, the son of Frânya.

98. We worship the Fravashi of the holy Isa*t*-
vâstra, the son of Zarathu*s*tra;
We worship the Fravashi of the holy Urvata*t*-
nara, the son of Zarathu*s*tra;
We worship the Fravashi of the holy *Hv*are-
*k*ithra, the son of Zarathu*s*tra[1].
We worship the Fravashi of the holy Daêvô-
*t*bi*s*, the son of Takhma.
We worship the Fravashi of the holy Thrimith-
wa*nt*, the son of Spitâma[2].
We worship the Fravashi of the holy D*a*ungha,
the son of Zairita.

99. We worship the Fravashi of the holy king
Vîstâspa[3]; the gallant one, who was the incarnate

---

[1] 'By Zaratûst were begotten three sons and three daughters;
one son was Isa*dv*âstar, one Aûrvata*d*-nar, and one Khûrshê*d*-
*k*îhar; as Isa*dv*âstar was chief of the priests he became the
Môbad of Môbads, and passed away in the hundredth year of
the religion; Aûrvata*d*-nar was an agriculturist, and the chief of the
enclosure formed by Yim, which is below the earth (see Vend. II,
43 [141]); Khûrshê*d*-*k*îhar was a warrior, commander of the army
of Pêshyôtanû, son of Vi*s*tâsp (see Yt. XXIV, 4), and dwells in
Kangde*z*; and of the three daughters the name of one was Frên,
of one Srît, and of one Pôru*k*îst (see Yt. XIII, 139). Aûrvata*d*-nar
and Khûrshê*d*-*k*îhar were from a serving (*k*akar) wife, the rest
were from a privileged (pâ*d*akhshah) wife' (Bund. XXXII, 5–6;
tr. West).

[2] According to Anquetil, 'the threefold seed of Spitama Zarathu*s*tra;' cf. above, § 62.

[3] The king of Bactra, the champion of Zoroastrism; cf. Yt. V,
98, 108.

Word, the mighty-speared, and lordly one; who, driving the Drug[1] before him, sought wide room for the holy religion; who, driving the Drug[1] before him, made wide room for the holy religion, who made himself the arm and support of this law of Ahura, of this law of Zarathustra.

100. Who took her[2], standing bound[3], from the hands of the Hunus[4], and established her to sit in the middle [of the world], high ruling, never falling back, holy, nourished with plenty of cattle and pastures, blessed with plenty of cattle and pastures[4].

101. We worship the Fravashi of the holy Zairivairi[5];

We worship the Fravashi of the holy Yukhtavairi;

We worship the Fravashi of the holy Srîraokhshan;

We worship the Fravashi of the holy Keresaokhshan;

We worship the Fravashi of the holy Vanâra;

We worship the Fravashi of the holy Varâza;

We worship the Fravashi of the holy Bûgisravah[6];

---

[1] Druga paurvanka, possibly, 'with the spear pushed forwards' (reading druka).

[2] Daêna, the religion.　　　　[3] Cf. Yt. II, 15.

[4] A generic name of the people called elsewhere Varedhakas (Yt. IX, 31; XVII, 51) or Hvyaonas (ibid. and XIX, 87). The Hunus have been compared with the Hunni; but it is not certain that this is a proper name; it may be a disparaging denomination, meaning the brood (hunu=Sansk. sûnu; cf. Yt. X, 113).

[5] Zarîr, the brother of Vîstâspa and son of Aurvat-aspa (see Yt. V, 112). The ten following seem to be the names of the other sons of Aurvat-aspa (Bund. XXXI, 29).

[6] Possibly the same with Pât-Khosrav, a brother to Vîstâspa in the Yâdkâr-î Zarîrân, as Mr. West informs me.

We worship the Fravashi of the holy Berezy-arsti;

We worship the Fravashi of the holy Tîzyarsti;

We worship the Fravashi of the holy Perethu-arsti;

We worship the Fravashi of the holy Vîzyarsti.

102. We worship the Fravashi of the holy Naptya;

We worship the Fravashi of the holy Vazâspa;

We worship the Fravashi of the holy Habâspa.

We worship the Fravashi of the holy Vistauru ¹, the son of Naotara.

We worship the Fravashi of the holy Fras-hãm-vareta ²;

We worship the Fravashi of the holy Frashô-kareta.

We worship the Fravashi of the holy Âtare-vanu;

We worship the Fravashi of the holy Âtare-pâta;

We worship the Fravashi of the holy Âtare-dâta;

We worship the Fravashi of the holy Âtare-kithra;

---

¹ Gustahm, the son of Nodar; see Yt. V, 76. Strangely enough, Tusa is not mentioned here, unless he is the same with one of the preceding names: possibly the words 'the son of Naotara' (Nao-tairyâna) refer to all the four.

² Possibly Frashîdvard فرشیدورد (misspelt from a Pahlavi form Frasânvard ﻡﺋﻳﺋﻮﻭﻟﻪ (?); the Yâdkâr-î Zarîrân, as Mr. West informs me, has ﻡﺋﻳﻮﻭﻟﻪ and ﻡﺋﻳﺦﻮﻭﻟﻪ). Frashîdvard was a son of Gus-tâsp: he was killed by one of Argâsp's heroes and avenged by his brother Isfendyâr (Speñtô-dâta). The following names would belong to his brothers: most of them contain the word Âtar, in honour of the newly-adopted worship of fire.

We worship the Fravashi of the holy Âtare-
*h*varenah;

We worship the Fravashi of the holy Âtare-
savah;

We worship the Fravashi of the holy Âtare-
za*n*tu;

We worship the Fravashi of the holy Âtare-
danghu.

103. We worship the Fravashi of the holy
Hu*s*kyaothna;

We worship the Fravashi of the holy Pi*s*k-
yaothna;

We worship the Fravashi of the holy and gallant
Spe*n*tô-dâta [1].

We worship the Fravashi of the holy Bastavairi [2];

We worship the Fravashi of the holy Kavârazem [3].

We worship the Fravashi of the holy Frasha-
o*s*tra [4], the son of Hvôva;

We worship the Fravashi of the holy *G*âmâspa [5],
the son of Hvôva;

---

[1] Isfendyâr, the heroic son of Gûstâsp, killed by Rustem.

[2] In the Yâ*d*kâr-î Zarîrân, according to Mr. West, Bastvar, the
son of Zairivairi, whose death he avenges on his murderer Vîdrafs.
This makes Bastavairi identical with the Nastûr نستور of Firdausi
(read Bastûr بستور).

[3] Kavârazem is the Gurezm of later tradition (گرزم), 'the
jealous brother of Isfendyâr, whom he slandered to his father and
caused to be thrown into prison' (Burhân qâti'h). Firdausi (IV, 432)
has only that he was a relation to Gûstâsp: شنیدم که گشتـاسپ‌را
خویش بود. See Études Iraniennes, II, 230.

[4] Who gave his daughter, Hvôvi, in marriage to Zarathu*s*tra
(Yasna L [XLIX], 4, 17).

[5] See Yt. V, 68.

We worship the Fravashi of the holy Avâraostri [1].

104. We worship the Fravashi of the holy
Huskyaothna, the son of Frashaostra ;
We worship the Fravashi of the holy *Hv*âdaêna,
the son of Frashaostra.

We worship the Fravashi of the holy Hanghaurv*a*ungh, the son of *G*âmâspa [2] ;
We worship the Fravashi of the holy Vareshna,
the son of Hanghaurv*a*ungh.

We worship the Fravashi of the holy Vohu-
nemah, the son of Avâraostri,
To withstand evil dreams, to withstand evil
visions, to withstand evil . . . . [3], to withstand the
evil Pairikas.

105. We worship the Fravashi of the holy
Mãthravâka, the son of Sîmaê*z*i, the Aêthrapati,
the Hamidhpati [4], who was able to smite down
most of the evil, unfaithful Ashemaoghas, that
shout the hymns [5], and acknowledge no lord and no
master [6], the dreadful ones whose Fravashis are
to be broken [7]; to withstand the evil done by the
faithful [8].

---

[1] Another brother to Frashaostra (?).

[2] The son of *G*âmâsp in the Shâh Nâmah is called Girâmî and
Garâmîk-kar*d* in the Yâ*d*kâr-î Zarîrân.

[3] ? Aoiwra.

[4] Aêthrapati, in Parsi hêrbad, a priest, whose special function
is to teach; his pupils were called aêthrya. Aêthrapati meant
literally 'the master of the hearth' (cf. hêrkodah, fire-temple).
Hamidhpati is literally 'the master of the sacrificial log.'

[5] Doubtful.

[6] No temporal lord (ahu) and no spiritual master (ratu).

[7] Doubtful (avas*k*asta-fravashinãm).

[8] The evil done by Zoroastrians. This Mãthravâka ('Proclaimer

106. We worship the Fravashi of the holy Asha-stu, the son of Maidhyô-m*a*ungha [1].

We worship the Fravashi of the holy Avare-thrabah, the son of Râstare-vagha*nt*.

We worship the Fravashi of the holy Bûg*ra*, the son of Dâzgarâspa.

We worship the Fravashi of the holy Zbaurva*nt*;

We worship the Fravashi of the holy and gallant Karesna [2], the son of Zbaurva*nt*; who was the incarnate Word, mighty-speared and lordly;

107. In whose house did walk the good, beautiful, shining Ashi Vanguhi, in the shape of a maid fair of body, most strong, tall-formed, high-up girded, pure, nobly born of a glorious seed [3]; who, rushing to the battle, knew how to make room for himself with his own arms; who, rushing to the battle, knew how to fight the foe with his own arms [4].

108. We worship the Fravashi of the holy Vîrâspa, the son of Karesna;

We worship the Fravashi of the holy Âzâta, the son of Karesna:

We worship the Fravashi of the holy Frâyaodha, the son of Karesna.

We worship the Fravashi of the holy and good Arshya; Arshya, the chief in assemblies, the most energetic of the worshippers of Mazda.

---

of the Holy Word') was apparently a great doctor and confounder of heresies.

[1] See above, § 95.

[2] Possibly the eponym of that great Kâren family, which played so great a part in the history of the Sassanian times, and traced its origin to the time of Gûs*t*âsp (Noeldeke, Geschichte der Perser zur Zeit der Sasaniden, p. 437).

[3] Cf. Yt. V, 64.   [4] Cf. Yt. XIII, 99.

We worship the Fravashi of the holy Dâraya*t*-ratha;
We worship the Fravashi of the holy Frâya*t*-ratha;
We worship the Fravashi of the holy Skâraya*t*-ratha.

109. We worship the Fravashi of the holy Ar*sv*a*nt*;
We worship the Fravashi of the holy Vyar*sv*a*nt*;
We worship the Fravashi of the holy Paityar*s*-va*nt*.

We worship the Fravashi of the holy Amru [1];
We worship the Fravashi of the holy *K*amru [1].

We worship the Fravashi of the holy Drâtha;
We worship the Fravashi of the holy Paiti-drâtha;
We worship the Fravashi of the holy Paiti-vangha.

We worship the Fravashi of the holy Frashâ-vakhsha.

We worship the Fravashi of the holy Nemô-vanghu, the son of Vaêdhayangha.

110. We worship the Fravashi of the holy Vîsadha.

We worship the Fravashi of the holy Ashâ-vanghu, the son of Biva*n*dangha [2];
We worship the Fravashi of the holy *G*arô-danghu, the son of Pairi*s*tîra [2];

---

[1] Amru and *K*amru are apparently the two mythical birds mentioned above under the names of Sîn-amru (the Amru-falcon) and *K*âmrô*s* (p. 173, note 1).

[2] Mr. West compares Ashâvanghu, the son of Biva*n*dangha, and *G*arôdanghu, the son of Pairi*s*tîra, with the two high-priests of the Karshvares of Arezahi and Savahi, whose names are, in the

We worship the Fravashi of the holy Nere-myazdana, the son of .Âthwyôza.

We worship the Fravashi of the holy Berezisnu, the son of Ara;

We worship the Fravashi of the holy Kasupatu, the son of Ara.

We worship the Fravashi of the holy Frya.

We worship the Fravashi of the holy ASTVAT-ERETA [1].

XXVI.

111. We worship the Fravashi of the holy Gaopi-vanghu.

We worship the Fravashi of the holy and gallant Hãm-baretar vanghvãm [2].

We worship the Fravashi of the holy Staotar-Vahistahê-Ashyêhê [3].

We worship the Fravashi of the holy Pouru-dhâkhsti, the son of Khstâvaênya;

We worship the Fravashi of the holy Khshoi-wrâspa, the son of Khstâvaênya.

112. We worship the Fravashi of the holy Ayô-asti, the son of Pouru-dhâkhsti [4];

We worship the Fravashi of the holy Vohv-asti, the son of Pouru-dhâkhsti;

Bundahis, Ashâshagahad-ê Hvandkân and Hoazarôdathhri-ê Parê-styarô (Bund. XXIX, 1, notes 4 and 5).

[1] Saoshyant; cf. §§ 117, 128.

[2] Possibly, 'the holy Hãm-baretar vanghvãm, the son of Takhma.' His name means, 'the gatherer of good things.'

[3] This name means, 'the praiser of excellent holiness' (the reciter of the Ashem Vohû).

[4] See preceding paragraph.

We worship the Fravashi of the holy Gayadhâsti, the son of Pouru-dhâkhsti;

We worship the Fravashi of the holy Asha-vaz-
dah, the son of Pouru-dhâkhsti[1];

We worship the Fravashi of the holy Urûdhu,
the son of Pouru-dhâkhsti.

We worship the Fravashi of the holy Khshathrô-
kinah, the son of Khshvôiwrâspa[2].

113. We worship the Fravashi of the holy
Ashâhura, the son of Gîsti.

We worship the Fravashi of the holy Frâyazanta;

We worship the Fravashi of the holy Frenah,
the son of Frâyazanta;

We worship the Fravashi of the holy Garô-
vanghu, the son of Frâyazanta.

We worship the Fravashis of the holy Ashavazdah and Thrita, the sons of Sâyuzdri[3].

We worship the Fravashi of the holy Vohu-
raokah, the son of Varakasa.

We worship the Fravashi of the holy Aregan-
ghant, the Turanian[4].

We worship the Fravashi of the holy Usinemah.

114. We worship the Fravashi of the holy
Yukhtâspa.

We worship the Fravashi of the holy Asha-
skyaothna, the son of Gayadhâsti[5].

---

[1] One of the seven immortals, rulers in *Hv*aniratha; cf. Yt. V,
72, text and notes, and Yt. XIII, 120, 124.

[2] See preceding paragraph.

[3] See Yt. V, 72. The text has 'the Fravashi;' cf. Yt. V, 116,
note, and Yt. XIII, 115.

[4] Cf. Yt. XIII, 143. Possibly, the son of Tûra.

[5] Cf. § 112.

We worship the Fravashi of the holy Vohu-nemah, the son of Katu;

We worship the Fravashi of the holy Vohu-vazdah, the son of Katu.

We worship the Fravashi of the holy Asha-saredha, the son of Asha-sairyã*k*;

We worship the Fravashi of the holy Asha-saredha, the son of Zairyã*k*.

We worship the Fravashi of the holy *K*âkhshni.

We worship the Fravashi of the holy Syâvâspi.

We worship the Fravashi of the holy Pouru*s*ti, the son of Kavi.

115. We worship the Fravashi of the holy Varesmapa, the son of *G*anara.

We worship the Fravashi of the holy Nanârâsti, the son of Paêshatah;

We worship the Fravashi of the holy Zarazdâti, the son of Paêshatah.

We worship the Fravashi of the holy Gaêvani, the son of Vohu-nemah [1].

We worship the Fravashis of the holy Arezva and Srûta-spâdha.

We worship the Fravashis [2] of the holy Zrayah and Spe*n*tô-khratu.

We worship the Fravashi of the holy Var*s*ni, the son of Vâgereza.

We worship the Fravashi of the holy Frâ*k*ya, the son of Taurvâti.

We worship the Fravashi of the holy Vahmaê-dâta, the son of Mãthravâka [3].

---

[1] There are two men of this name; one is the son of Katu (§ 114), the other is the son of Avârao*s*tri (§ 104).

[2] The text has 'the Fravashi;' cf. preceding page, note 3.

[3] See § 105.

We worship the Fravashi of the holy U*s*tra, the
son of Sadhanah.

116. We worship the Fravashi of the holy
Danghu-srûta ;
We worship the Fravashi of the holy Danghu-
frâdhah.

We worship the Fravashi of the holy Aspô-
padhô-makh*s*ti ;
We worship the Fravashi of the holy Payanghrô-
makh*s*ti.

We worship the Fravashi of the holy U*s*tâza*n*ta.

We worship the Fravashi of the holy Asha-
savah ;
We worship the Fravashi of the holy Ashô-
urvatha.

We worship the Fravashi of the holy Haomô-
*hv*arenah.

117. We worship the Fravashi of the holy
Frava.

We worship the Fravashi of the holy Usnâka.

We worship the Fravashi of the holy *Hv*anva*nt*.

We worship the Fravashi of the holy Daênô-
vazah.

We worship the Fravashi of the holy Are*g*aona.

We worship the Fravashi of the holy Aiwi-
*hv*arenah.

We worship the Fravashi of the holy Huyazata.

We worship the Fravashi of the holy Hare-
dhaspa.

We worship the Fravashi of the holy Pâzinah.

We worship the Fravashi of the holy *Hv*âkhsha-
thra.

We worship the Fravashi of the holy Ashô-
paoirya.

We worship the Fravashi of the holy ASTVAT-
ERETA [1].

XXVII.

118. We worship the Fravashi of the holy
Hug*a*u.
We worship the Fravashi of the holy Anghuyu.
We worship the Fravashi of the holy Gâuri;
We worship the Fravashi of the holy Yû*s*ta, the
son of Gâuri.
We worship the Fravashi of the holy Mãzdrâ-
vanghu;
We worship the Fravashi of the holy Srîrâ-
vanghu.
We worship the Fravashi of the holy Âyûta.
We worship the Fravashi of the holy Sûrô-
yazata.
119. We worship the Fravashi of the holy
Eredhwa.
We worship the Fravashi of the holy Kavi.
We worship the Fravashi of the holy Ukhshan,
the son of the great Vîdi-sravah, known afar [2].
We worship the Fravashi of the holy Vanghu-
dhâta, the son of *Hv*adhâta;
We worship the Fravashi of the holy Uzya, the
son of Vanghu-dhâta;
We worship the Fravashi of the holy Frya.
120. We worship the Fravashi of the holy one
whose name is Ashem-yêNhê-rao*k*au;
We worship the Fravashi of the holy one whose
name is Ashem-yêNhê-vereza;

---

[1] Saoshya*nt*; cf. §§ 110, 128.
[2] Perhaps, Ukhshan, the conqueror of glory, known afar, son of
Berezva*nt*.

We worship the Fravashi of the holy one whose name is Ashem-yahmâi-uṣtâ [1].

We worship the Fravashi of the holy Yôiṣta [2], of the Fryâna house.

We worship the Fravashi of the holy Usmânara, the son of Paêshatah Paitisrîra [3], to withstand the evil done by one's kindred [4].

121. We worship the Fravashi of the holy Spiti [5], the son of Uspãsnu;
We worship the Fravashi of the holy Erezrâspa, the son of Uspãsnu [6].

We worship the Fravashi of the holy Usadhan, the son of Mazdayasna.

We worship the Fravashi of the holy Frâdat-vanghu, the son of Stivaṇt.

We worship the Fravashi of the holy Raoḵas-ḵaêshman [7];
We worship the Fravashi of the holy Hvare-ḵaêshman [7].

We worship the Fravashi of the holy Frasrû-târa;
We worship the Fravashi of the holy Vîsrûtâra.

We worship the Fravashi of the holy Baremna.

---

[1] One of the immortals, rulers in Hvaniratha: he is said to belong to the Fryâna family (Dâdistân XC, 3); he resides in the district of the river Nâîvtâk (Bund. XXIX, 5).

[2] See Yt. V, 81.

[3] Paitisrîra is perhaps an epithet (most beautiful?), added to distinguish Paêshatah from the hero mentioned in § 115.

[4] An allusion to some legend of domestic feud of which Paêshatah was the hero.

[5] The high-priest of the Fradadhafshu Karshvare (Spîtoîd-i Aûspôsînân; Bund. XXIX, 1; tr. West, note 6).

[6] The high-priest of the Vîdadhafshu Karshvare (Aîrîz-râsp Aûspôsînân; see ibid., note 7).

[7] Cf. § 128.

We worship the Fravashi of the holy Vîsrûta.

122. We worship the Fravashi of the holy *H*vaspa[1];
We worship the Fravashi of the holy *K*athwar-aspa[2].

We worship the Fravashi of the holy Dawrâ-maêshi.

We worship the Fravashi of the holy Fraora-ostra, the son of Kaosha.

We worship the Fravashi of the holy Frînâspa, the son of Kaêva.

We worship the Fravashi of the holy Frâda*t*-nara, the son of Gravâratu.

We worship the Fravashi of the holy Vohu-u*s*tra, the son of Ãkhnangha.

We worship the Fravashi of the holy Vîvare-shva*nt*, the son of Ainyu.

123. We worship the Fravashi of the holy Frârâzi, the son of Tûra[3].

We worship the Fravashi of the holy Stipi, the son of Rava*nt*.

We worship the Fravashi of the holy Parsha*nt*a, the son of Ga*n*darewa.

We worship the Fravashi of the holy Avahya, the son of Spe*nt*a.

We worship the Fravashi of the holy Aêta, the son of Mâyu;

---

[1] Probably the same with Huvâsp, the high-priest in the Vouru-bare*s*ti Karshvare (Bund. XXIX, 1; tr. West, note 8).

[2] Possibly the same with the high-priest in the Vouru-*g*are*s*ti karshvare, *K*akhravâk (ibid., note 9). *K*akhravâk is the generic name of the bird Karshipta (Pahl. Comm. ad II, 42 [139]); it must stand here by mistake for *K*ahârâsp.

[3] Or, 'the Turanian;' cf. § 113.

We worship the Fravashi of the holy Yaêtus-gau, the son of Vyâtana.

We worship the Fravashi of the holy Garsta, the son of Kavi.

124. We worship the Fravashi of the holy Pouru-bangha, the son of Zaosha.

We worship the Fravashi of the holy Vohu-dâta, the son of Kâta.

We worship the Fravashi of the holy Baungha, the son of Saungha.

We worship the Fravashis [1] of the holy Hvareza and Ankasa.

We worship the Fravashi of the holy Aravaostra, the son of Erezvat-danghu.

We worship the Fravashi of the holy Frâkithra, the son of Berezvant.

We worship the Fravashi of the holy Vohu-peresa, the son of Ainyu.

125. We worship the Fravashi of the holy Parô-dasma, the son of Dâstâghni, a Mîza man of the Mîza land.

We worship the Fravashis of the holy Fratîra and Baêshatastîra.

We worship the Fravashi of the holy and pure Avare-gau, the son of Aoighimatastîra.

We worship the Fravashi of the holy Gaomant, the son of Zavan, a Raozdya man of the Raozdya land.

We worship the Fravashi of the holy Thrit, the son of Aêvo-saredha-fyaêsta, a Tanya man of the Tanya land.

---

[1] The text has 'the Fravashi;' cf. §§ 113, 127.

126. We worship the Fravashi of the holy Tîrô-nakathwa, of the Uspaê*s*ta-Saêna house [1].

We worship the Fravashi of the holy Utayuti Vi*t*-kavi, the son of Zighri, of the Saêna house [1]; We worship the Fravashi of the holy Frôhakafra, the son of Merezîshmya, of the Saêna house [1].

We worship the Fravashi of the holy Varesmô-rao*k*ah, the son of Perethu-afzem.

1.27. We worship the Fravashis [2] of the holy Asha-nemah and Vîda*t*-g*a*u, of this country.

We worship the Fravashis [2] of the holy Parsha*t*-g*a*u and Dâzgara-g*a*u, of the Apakhshîra country.

We worship the Fravashi of the holy Hufra-vâkh*s*, of the Kahrkana house [1].

We worship the Fravashi of the holy Akayadha, of the Pîdha house [1].

We worship the Fravashi of the holy *G*âmâspa, the younger [3].

We worship the Fravashi of the holy Maidhyô-m*a*ungha, the younger [4].

We worship the Fravashi of the holy Urvata*t*-nara, the younger [5].

128. We worship the Fravashi of the holy Rao*k*as-*k*aê*s*man;

We worship the Fravashi of the holy *Hv*are-*k*aê*s*man;

We worship the Fravashi of the holy Frâda*t*-*hv*arenah;

---

[1] See Études Iraniennes, II, 142.
[2] The text has ‘the Fravashi;’ cf. § 113.
[3] Different from *G*âmâspa, the son of Hvôva (§ 103).
[4] Different from Maidhyô-m*a*ungha, the son of Ârâsti (§ 95).
[5] Different from Urvata*t*-nara, the son of Zarathu*s*tra (§ 98).

We worship the Fravashi of the holy Vareda*t*-*hv*arenah ;

We worship the Fravashi of the holy Vouru-nemah ;

We worship the Fravashi of the holy Vouru-savah [1] ;

We worship the Fravashi of the holy Ukhshya*t*-ereta [2] ;

We worship the Fravashi of the holy Ukhshya*t*-nemah [3] ;

We worship the Fravashi of the holy ASTVA*T*-ERETA [4] ;

XXVIII.

129. Whose name will be the victorious SAO-SHYA*NT* and whose name will be Astva*t*-ereta. He will be SAOSHYA*NT* (the Beneficent One), because he will benefit the whole bodily world; he will be ASTVA*T*-ERETA (he who makes the bodily creatures

---

[1] The six foremost helpers of Saoshya*nt*, each in one of the six Karshvares: ' It is said that in the fifty-seven years, which are the period of the raising of the dead, Rôshanô-*k*ashm in Arzâh, Khûr-*k*ashm in Savâh, Frâda*d*-gadman (Frâda*t*-*hv*arenô, Increaser of Glory) in Fradad*â*fsh, Vâredad-gadman (Vareda*t*-*hv*arenô, Multiplier of Glory) in Vîdad*â*fsh, Kâmak-vakhshi*s*n (Vouru-nemô, Prayer-loving) in Vôrûbar*s*t, and Kâmak-sû*d* (Vouru-savô, Weal-loving) in Vôrû-*g*ar*s*t, while Sôshâns in the illustrious and pure Khvanîras is connected with them, are immortal. The completely good sense, perfect hearing, and full glory of those seven producers of the renovation are so miraculous that they converse from region unto region, every one together with the six others ' (Dâdistân XXXVI, 5–6 ; tr. West).

[2] The first brother and forerunner to Saoshya*nt*, the Oshedar mâh of later tradition (see above, p. 196, note 2 ; cf. § 141, note).

[3] The second brother and forerunner to Saoshya*nt*, the Oshedar bâmî of later tradition (ibid.; cf. § 142, note).

[4] Saoshya*nt*; cf. following paragraph and §§ 110, 117.

rise up), because as a bodily creature and as a living creature he will stand against the destruction of the bodily creatures, to withstand the Dru*g* of the two-footed brood, to withstand the evil done by the faithful [1].

XXIX.

130. We worship the Fravashi of the holy Yima [2], the son of Vîvangha*nt*; the valiant Yima, who had flocks at his wish [3]; to stand against the oppression caused by the Daêvas, against the drought that destroys pastures, and against death that creeps unseen [4].

131. We worship the Fravashi of the holy Thraêtaona, of the Âthwya house [5]; to stand against itch, hot fever, humours, cold fever, and incontinency [6], to stand against the evil done by the Serpent [7].

We worship the Fravashi of the holy Aoshnara, the son of Pouru-*g*îra [8].

We worship the Fravashi of the holy Uzava, the son of Tûmâspa [9].

---

[1] He will suppress both the destructive power of the men of the Dru*g* (idolaters and the like) and the errors of Mazdayas-nians (?).

[2] See above, p. 25, note 4.

[3] Vouru-vãthwa; cf. Études Iraniennes, II, 182.

[4] As he made waters and trees undrying, cattle and men undying.

[5] See above, p. 61, note 1.

[6] As the inventor of medicine; see Vend. XX, Introd.

[7] Disease, being a poison, comes from the Serpent; see ibid.

[8] Or 'Aoshnara, full of wisdom;' cf. Yt. XXIII, 2, and West, Pahlavi Texts, II, 171, note 3.

[9] Called in the Shâh Nâmah Zab, son of Tahmâsp, who appears to have been a son of Nodar (Bund. XXXI, 23).

We worship the Fravashi of the holy Aghraê-ratha, the demi-man[1].

We worship the ·Fravashi of the holy Manus-*k*ithra, the son of Airyu[2].

132. We worship the Fravashi of the holy king Kavâta[3];

We worship the Fravashi of the holy king Aipivanghu[4];

We worship the Fravashi of the holy king Usadhan[5];

We worship the Fravashi of the holy king Arshan[5];

We worship the Fravashi of the holy king Pisanah[5];

We worship the Fravashi of the holy king Byârshan[5];

We worship the Fravashi of the holy king Syâvarshan[6];

We worship the Fravashi of the holy king Husravah[6];

133. For the well-shapened Strength[7], for the Victory made by Ahura, for the crushing Ascendant; for the righteousness of the law, for the innocence of

---

[1] See above, p. 114, note 7 (Yt. IX, 18).

[2] Airyu, the youngest of the three sons of Thraêtaona (see p. 61, note 1), was killed by his brothers and avenged by his son Manus-*k*ithra, who succeeded Thraêtaona.

[3] Kavâta, Kai Qobâd in the Shâh Nâmah, an adoptive son to Uzava, according to Bund. XXXI, 24.

[4] Kaî-Apîveh in the Bundahis; he was the son of Kai Qobâd.

[5] Usadhan, Arshan, Pisanah, and Byârshan were the four sons of Aipivanghu; they are called in Firdausi Kai Kaus, Kai Arish, Kai Pashîn, and Kai Armîn. Kai Kaus alone came to the throne.

[6] Syâvakhsh and Khosrav; see above, p. 64, note 1.

[7] To become possessed of Strength, Victory, &c., as Husravah did.

the law, for the unconquerable power of the law; for the extermination of the enemies at one stroke;

134. And for the vigour of health, for the Glory made by Mazda, for the health of the body, and for a good, virtuous offspring, wise, chief in assemblies, bright, and clear-eyed, that frees [their father] from the pangs [of hell], of good intellect; and for that part in the blessed world that falls to wisdom and to those who do not follow impiety;

135. For a dominion full of splendour, for a long, long life, and for all boons and remedies; to withstand the Yâtus and Pairikas, the oppressors, the blind, and the deaf; to withstand the evil done by oppressors [1].

136. We worship the Fravashi of the holy Keresâspa [2], the Sâma [3], the club-bearer with plaited hair; to withstand the dreadful arm and the hordes with the wide battle array, with the many spears, with the straight spears, with the spears uplifted, bearing the spears of havoc; to withstand the dreadful brigand who works destruction [4], the man-slayer who has no mercy; to withstand the evil done by the brigand.

137. We worship the Fravashi of the holy Âkhrûra [5], the son of Husravah;

To withstand the wicked one that deceives his friend and the niggard that causes the destruction of the world [6].

---

[1] Like Frangrasyan; cf. p. 64, note 1.

[2] See Yt. V, 37; XV, 27; XIX, 38.

[3] Belonging to the Sâma family (Yasna IX, 10).

[4] Like the nine highwaymen killed by Keresâspa, Yt. XIX, 41.

[5] Not mentioned in the Shâh Nâmah; Khosrav was succeeded by a distant relation, Lôhrasp.

[6] An allusion to the lost legend of Âkhrûra; see, however, West, Pahlavi Texts, II, 375.

We worship the Fravashi of the holy and gallant
Haoshyangha;

To withstand the Mâzainya Daêvas and the Varenya fiends; to withstand the evil done by the
Daêvas [1].

138. We worship the Fravashi of the holy Fra-
dhâkh*s*ti, the son of the jar [2],

To withstand Aêshma, the fiend of the wounding
spear, and the Daêvas that grow through Aêshma;
to withstand the evil done by Aêshma.

XXX.

139. We worship the Fravashi of the holy
Hvôvi [3].

We worship the Fravashi of the holy Fr*e*ni;
We worship the Fravashi of the holy Thriti;
We worship the Fravashi of the holy Pouru-
*k*ista [4].

We worship the Fravashi of the holy Hutaosa [5];
We worship the Fravashi of the holy Huma [6].
We worship the Fravashi of the holy Zairi*k*i.

---

[1] See Yt. V, 21–23.

[2] Khumbya, one of the immortals in *H*vaniratha; he resides in
the Pê*s*yânsaî plain: ' he is *H*vembya for this reason, because they
brought him up in a *h*vemb (jar) for fear of Khashm' (Bund.
XXIX, 5). He answers pretty well to the Agastya and Vasish*th*a of
the Vedic legend (see Ormazd et Ahriman, § 177).

[3] One of the three wives of Zarathu*s*tra, the daughter of Frasha-
o*s*tra; she is the supposed mother of Saoshya*nt* and his brothers
(see p. 195, note 2).

[4] The three daughters of Zarathu*s*tra and sisters to Isa*dv*âstar
(see p. 204, note 1).

[5] Vî*s*tâspa's wife; see Yt. IX, 26, and XVII, 46.

[6] Vî*s*tâspa's daughter, Humâi, in the Shâh Nâmah.

We worship the Fravashi of the holy Vîspa-taurvashi.

We worship the Fravashi of the holy Ustavaiti.

We worship the Fravashi of the holy Tusnâ-maiti.

140. We worship the Fravashi of the holy Freni, the wife of Usenemah [1];

We worship the Fravashi of the holy Freni, the wife of the son of Frâyazanta [2];

We worship the Fravashi of the holy Freni, the wife of the son of Khshôiwrâspa [3];

We worship the Fravashi of the holy Freni, the wife of Gayadhâsti [4].

We worship the Fravashi of the holy Asabani, the wife of Pourudhâkhsti [5].

We worship the Fravashi of the holy Ukhsh-yeinti, the wife of Staotar-Vahistahê-Ashyêhê [6].

141. We worship the Fravashi of the holy maid Vadhût.

We worship the Fravashi of the holy maid Gaghrûdh.

We worship the Fravashi of the holy maid Franghâdh.

We worship the Fravashi of the holy maid Urû-dhayant.

We worship the Fravashi of the holy maid Paê-sanghanu.

We worship the Fravashi of the holy Hvaredhi.

We worship the Fravashi of the holy Hukithra.

We worship the Fravashi of the holy Kanuka.

---

[1] See § 113. [2] Of Frenah or Garô-vanghu, § 113.
[3] Of Khshathrô-kinah, § 112. [4] See § 112.
[5] See § 111. [6] Ibid.

[23] Q

We worship the Fravashi of the holy maid Srûta*t*-fedhri[1].

142. We worship the Fravashi of the holy maid Vanghu-fedhri[2];

We worship the Fravashi of the holy maid Ereda*t*-fedhri[3], who is called Vîspa-taurvairi. She is Vîspa-taurvairi (the all-destroying) because she will bring him forth, who will destroy the malice of Daêvas and men, to withstand the evil done by the *G*ahi[4].

143. We worship the Fravashis of the holy men in the Aryan countries;

We worship the Fravashis of the holy women in the Aryan countries.

We worship the Fravashis of the holy men in the Turanian countries[5];

We worship the Fravashis of the holy women in the Turanian countries.

We worship the Fravashis of the holy men in the Sairimyan countries[6];

---

[1] Ukhshya*t*-ereta's mother (see above, § 126); the Saddar Bundahi*s* (Études Iraniennes, II, 209) calls her Bad, from the last part of her name (fedhri for padhri, and states that, bathing in Lake Kãsava, she will become pregnant from the seed of Zarathu*s*tra, that is preserved there (see above, p. 195, note 2), and she will bring forth a son, Oshedar bâmî.

[2] Ukhshya*t*-nemah's mother, called Vah Bad in the Saddar; she will conceive in the same way as Srûta*t*-fedhri.

[3] Saoshya*nt*'s mother.

[4] Cf. Vend. XIX, 5, and Introd. IV, 39–40.

[5] Gôgô*s*asp (a commentator to the Avesta) says, 'There are holy men in all religions, as appears from the words tûiryanãm da*h*vyunãm [We worship the Fravashis of the holy men in the Turanian countries],' (Pahl. Comm. ad Vend. III, end; and Vend. V, 38 [122]); cf. above, §§ 113, 123.

[6] The countries inherited by Sairima (Selm), the third son of

We worship the Fravashis of the holy women in the Sairimyan countries.

144. We worship the Fravashis of the holy men in the Sâini countries [1];

We worship the Fravashis of the holy women in the Sâini countries.

We worship the Fravashis of the holy men in the Dâhi countries [2];

We worship the Fravashis of the holy women in the Dâhi countries.

We worship the Fravashis of the holy men in all countries;

We worship the Fravashis of the holy women in all countries.

145. We worship all the good, awful, beneficent Fravashis of the faithful, from Gaya Maretan down to the victorious Saoshyant [3]. May the Fravashis of the faithful come quickly to us! May they come to our help!

146. They protect us when in distress with manifest assistance, with the assistance of Ahura Mazda and of the holy, powerful Sraosha, and with the Mãthra-Spenta, the all-knowing, who hates the Daêvas with a mighty hate, a friend of Ahura Mazda, whom Zarathustra worshipped so greatly in the material world.

147. May the good waters and the plants and

Thraêtaona, as Turan and Iran were inherited by Tûra and Airyu. Selm's heritage was Rûm, that is to say, Europa and Western Asia.

[1] China (Bund. XV, 29).

[2] Perhaps the Dahae (Pliny VI, 17; Aeneis VIII, 728) or Δάαι (Strabo), called Ta-hia by Chinese geographers, on the south of the Oxus.

[3] From the first man to the last.

the Fravashis of the faithful abide down here! May
you be rejoiced and well received in this house!
Here are the Âthravans of the countries [1], thinking
of good holiness. Our hands are lifted up for
asking help, and for offering a sacrifice unto you,
O most beneficent Fravashis!

148. We worship the Fravashis of all the holy
men and holy women whose souls are worthy of sacrifice [2], whose Fravashis are worthy of invocation.

We worship the Fravashis of all the holy men
and holy women, our sacrificing to whom makes us
good in the eyes of Ahura Mazda: of all of those we
have heard that Zarathustra is the first and best, as a
follower of Ahura and as a performer of the law.

149. We worship the spirit, conscience, perception, soul, and Fravashi [3] of men of the primitive
law [4], of the first who listened to the teaching (of
Ahura), holy men and holy women, who struggled
for holiness [5]; we worship the spirit, conscience, perception, soul, and Fravashi of our next-of-kin, holy
men and holy women, who struggled for holiness [5].

150. We worship the men of the primitive law
who will be in these houses, boroughs, towns, and
countries;

We worship the men of the primitive law who
have been in these houses, boroughs, towns, and
countries;

We worship the men of the primitive law who are
in these houses, boroughs, towns, and countries.

151. We worship the men of the primitive law

---

[1] Itinerant priests are received here.
[2] Doubtful.   [3] Cf. p. 198, note 1.
[4] The Paoiryô-tkaêsas; see p. 180, note 1.
[5] For the triumph of the Zoroastrian law.

in all houses, boroughs, towns, and countries, who obtained these houses, who obtained these boroughs, who obtained these towns, who obtained these countries, who obtained holiness, who obtained the Mãthra, who obtained the [blessedness of the] soul, who obtained all the perfections of goodness.

152. We worship Zarathustra, the lord and master of all the material world, the man of the primitive law; the wisest of all beings, the best-ruling of all beings, the brightest of all beings, the most glorious of all beings, the most worthy of sacrifice amongst all beings, the most worthy of prayer amongst all beings, the most worthy of propitiation amongst all beings, the most worthy of glorification amongst all beings, whom we call well-desired and worthy of sacrifice and prayer as much as any being can be, in the perfection of his holiness.

153. We worship this earth;

We worship those heavens;

We worship those good things that stand between (the earth and the heavens) and that are worthy of sacrifice and prayer and are to be worshipped by the faithful man.

154. We worship the souls of the wild beasts and of the tame [1].

We worship the souls of the holy men and women, born at any time, whose consciences struggle, or will struggle, or have struggled, for the good.

---

[1] Daitika, Persian دد; Neriosengh has 'that go by herds,' paṅktikârin. Aidyu; the Pahlavi translation has ayyâr, 'that are of help' (domesticated?); Neriosengh has misread it as suvâr and translated açvacârin. The expression daitika aidyu answers to the Persian دد ودام, meaning all sorts of animals (see Études Iraniennes, II, 150).

155. We worship the spirit, conscience, perception, soul, and Fravashi of the holy men and holy women who struggle, will struggle, or have struggled, and teach the Law, and who have struggled for holiness.

Yênhê hâtãm: All those beings to whom Ahura Mazda . . . .
Yathâ ahû vairyô: The will of the Lord is the law of holiness . . . .

156. The Fravashis of the faithful, awful and overpowering, awful and victorious; the Fravashis of the men of the primitive law; the Fravashis of the next-of-kin; may these Fravashis come satisfied into this house; may they walk satisfied through this house!

157. May they, being satisfied, bless this house with the presence of the kind Ashi Vanguhi! May they leave this house satisfied! May they carry back from here hymns and worship to the Maker, Ahura Mazda, and the Amesha-Spentas! May they not leave this house of us, the worshippers of Mazda, complaining!

158. Yathâ ahû vairyô: The will of the Lord is the law of holiness . . . .

I bless the sacrifice and prayer, and the strength and vigour of the awful, overpowering Fravashis of the faithful; of the Fravashis of the men of the primitive law; of the Fravashis of the next-of-kin.

Ashem Vohû: Holiness is the best of all good . . . .
[Give] unto that man[1] brightness and glory, ... give him the bright, all-happy, blissful abode of the holy Ones.

---

[1] Who shall worship the Fravashis.

XIV. BAHRÂM YAST.

Regarding Bahrâm (Verethraghna), the Genius of Victory, see Vend. Introd. V, 8.

This Yast can be divided into four parts:—

I (§§ 1–28). An enumeration of the ten incarnations in which Verethraghna appeared to Zarathustra (as a wind, § 2; as a bull, § 7; as a horse, § 9; as a camel, § 11; as a boar, § 15; as a youth, § 17; as a raven, § 19; as a ram, § 23; as a buck, § 25; and as a man, § 27).

II (§§ 30–33). The powers given by Verethraghna to his worshipper, Zarathustra.

III (§§ 34–46). The magical powers, ascribed to the raven's feather, of striking terror into an army and dispersing it (the raven being the seventh incarnation of Verethraghna).

IV (§§ 47–64). The glorification of Verethraghna.

---

o. May Ahura Mazda be rejoiced! . . . .

Ashem Vohû: Holiness is the best of all good . . . .

I confess myself a worshipper of Mazda, a follower of Zarathustra, one who hates the Daêvas and obeys the laws of Ahura;

For sacrifice, prayer, propitiation, and glorification unto [Hâvani], the holy and master of holiness . . . .

Unto Verethraghna, made by Mazda, and unto the crushing Ascendant [1];

Be propitiation, with sacrifice, prayer, propitiation, and glorification.

Yathâ ahû vairyô: The will of the Lord is the law of holiness . . . .

I.

1. We sacrifice unto Verethraghna, made by Ahura.

Zarathustra asked Ahura Mazda: 'Ahura Mazda, most beneficent Spirit, Maker of the material world, thou Holy One!

---

[1] Sîrôzah I, 20.

'Who is the best-armed of the heavenly gods?'
Ahura Mazda answered: 'It is Verethraghna,
made by Ahura, O Spitama Zarathustra!'

2. Verethraghna, made by Ahura, came to him
first, running in the shape of a strong, beautiful
wind, made by Mazda; he bore the good Glory,
made by Mazda, the Glory made by Mazda, that is
both health and strength.

3. Then he, who is the strongest[1], said unto him [2]:
'I am the strongest in strength; I am the most victorious in victory; I am the most glorious in Glory;
I am the most favouring in favour; I am the best
giver of welfare; I am the best-healing in health-
giving.

4. 'And I shall destroy the malice of all the
malicious, the malice of Daêvas and men, of the
Yâtus and Pairikas, of the oppressors, the blind,
and the deaf.

5. 'For his brightness and glory, I will offer unto
him a sacrifice worth being heard; namely, unto
Verethraghna, made by Ahura. We worship Verethraghna, made by Ahura, with an offering of libations, according to the primitive ordinances of
Ahura; with the Haoma and meat, the baresma,
the wisdom of the tongue, the holy spells, the
speech, the deeds, the libations, and the rightly-
spoken words.

'Yênhê hâtãm: All those beings of whom Ahura Mazda ....

II.

6. 'We sacrifice unto Verethraghna, made by
Ahura.'

---

[1] Verethraghna.   [2] Zarathustra.

Zarathustra 'asked Ahura Mazda : ' Ahura Mazda, most beneficent Spirit, Maker of the material world, thou Holy One!

' Who is, the best-armed of the heavenly Gods ? '

Ahura Mazda answered : ' It is Verethraghna, made by Ahura, O Spitama Zarathustra!'

7. Verethraghna, made by Ahura, came to him the second time, running in the shape of a beautiful bull, with yellow ears and golden horns ; upon whose horns floated the well-shapen Strength, and Victory, beautiful of form, made by Ahura : thus did he come, bearing the good Glory, made by Mazda, the Glory made by Mazda, that is both health and strength.

Then he, who is the strongest, said unto him : ' I am the strongest in strength . . . .[1],

'And I shall destroy the malice of all malicious . . . .[2]'

For his brightness and glory, I will offer unto him a sacrifice worth being heard . . . .[3]

III.

8. We sacrifice unto Verethraghna, made by Ahura.

Zarathustra asked Ahura Mazda : ' Ahura Mazda, most beneficent Spirit, Maker of the material world, thou Holy One!

' Who is the best-armed of the heavenly gods ? '

Ahura Mazda answered : ' It is Verethraghna, made by Ahura, O Spitama Zarathustra!'

9. Verethraghna, made by Ahura, came to him the third time, running in the shape of a white, beautiful horse, with yellow ears and a golden caparison ; upon whose forehead floated the well-shapen Strength,

---

[1] As above, § 3. [2] As above, § 4. [3] As above, § 5.

and Victory, beautiful of form, made by Ahura : thus did he come, bearing the good Glory, made by Mazda, that is both health and strength.

Then he, who is the strongest, said unto him : ' I am the strongest in strength . . . .

'And I shall destroy the malice of all malicious . . . .'

For his brightness and glory, I will offer unto him a sacrifice worth being heard . . . .

IV.

10. We sacrifice unto Verethraghna, made by Ahura.

Zarathuʃtra asked Ahura Mazda : ' Ahura Mazda, most beneficent Spirit, Maker of the material world, thou Holy One!

' Who is the best-armed of the heavenly gods ? '

Ahura Mazda answered : ' It is Verethraghna, made by Ahura, O Spitama Zarathuʃtra !'

11. Verethraghna, made by Ahura, came to him the fourth time, running in the shape of a burden-bearing [1] camel, sharp-toothed [2], swift . . . . [3], stamping forwards, long-haired, and living in the abodes of men [4];

12. Who of all males in rut shows greatest strength and greatest fire, when he goes to his females. Of all females those are best kept whom a burden-bearing camel keeps, who has thick forelegs and large humps, ... [5], quick-eyed, long-headed, bright, tall, and strong ;

13. Whose piercing look goes afar . . . . [6], even in the dark of the night; who throws white foam

---

[1] Doubtful (vadharôiʃ).
[2] Doubtful (dadãsôiʃ).
[3] ? Urvatô; cf. § 19.
[4] Tame, domesticated.
[5] ? Smarʃnô.
[6] ? Haitahê.

along his mouth; well-kneed, well-footed, standing
with the countenance of an all-powerful master:

Thus did Verethraghna come, bearing the good
Glory made by Mazda, the Glory made by
Mazda . ... .

V.

14. We sacrifice unto Verethraghna, made by
Ahura.

Zarathustra asked Ahura Mazda : ' Ahura Mazda,
most beneficent Spirit, Maker of the material world,
thou Holy One!

' Who is the best-armed of the heavenly gods ? '

Ahura Mazda answered : ' It is Verethraghna,
made by Ahura, O Spitama Zarathustra !'

15. Verethraghna, made by Ahura, came to him
the fifth time, running in the shape of a boar, opposing the foes, a sharp-toothed he-boar, a sharp-jawed
boar, that kills at one stroke, pursuing, wrathful,
with a dripping face [1], strong, and swift to run, and
rushing all around [2].

Thus did Verethraghna come, bearing the good
Glory made by Mazda, the Glory made by
Mazda . . . .

VI.

16. We sacrifice unto Verethraghna, made by
Ahura.

Zarathustra asked Ahura Mazda : ' Ahura Mazda,
most beneficent Spirit, Maker of the material world,
thou Holy One!

' Who is the best-armed of the heavenly gods ? '

Ahura Mazda answered : ' It is Verethraghna,
made by Ahura, O Spitama Zarathustra !'

---

[1] Cf. Yt. X, 70. [2] Or better, rushing before. Cf. Yt. X, 127.

17. Verethraghna, made by Ahura, came to him the sixth time, running in the shape of a beautiful youth of fifteen, shining, clear-eyed, thin-heeled.

Thus did Verethraghna come, bearing the good Glory made by Mazda, the Glory made by Mazda . . . .

VII.

18. We sacrifice unto Verethraghna, made by Ahura.

Zarathustra asked Ahura Mazda : 'Ahura Mazda, most beneficent Spirit, Maker of the material world, thou Holy One!

'Who is the best-armed of the heavenly gods?'

Ahura Mazda answered: 'It is Verethraghna, made by Ahura, O Spitama Zarathustra!'

19. Verethraghna, made by Ahura, came to him the seventh time, running in the shape of a raven that . . . .[1] below and . . . .[1] above, and that is the swiftest of all birds, the lightest of the flying creatures.

20. He alone of living things,—he or none,—overtakes the flight of an arrow, however well it has been shot. He flies up joyfully at the first break of dawn, wishing the night to be no more, wishing the dawn, that has not yet come, to come [2].

21. He grazes the hidden ways [3] of the mountains, he grazes the tops of the mountains, he grazes the depths of the vales, he grazes the summits [4] of the trees, listening to the voices of the birds.

---

[1] ? Urvatô, pishatô.

[2] The raven was sacred to Apollo. The priests of the sun in Persia are said to have been named ravens (Porphyrius). Cf. Georgica I, 45.

[3] Reading vîgâtavô.   [4] Doubtful.

Thus did Verethraghna come, bearing the good Glory made by Mazda[1], the Glory made by Mazda . . . .

VIII.

22. We sacrifice unto Verethraghna, made by Ahura.

Zarathustra asked Ahura Mazda : 'Ahura Mazda, most beneficent Spirit, Maker of the material world, thou Holy One!

'Who is the best-armed of the heavenly gods?'

Ahura Mazda answered : 'It is Verethraghna, made by Ahura, O Spitama Zarathustra!'

23. Verethraghna, made by Ahura, came to him the eighth time, running in the shape of a wild, beautiful ram, with horns bent round[2].

Thus did Verethraghna come, bearing the good Glory made by Mazda[3], the Glory made by Mazda . . . .

IX.

24. We sacrifice unto Verethraghna, made by Ahura.

Zarathustra asked Ahura Mazda : 'Ahura Mazda, most beneficent Spirit, Maker of the material world, thou Holy One!

'Who is the best-armed of the heavenly gods?'

Ahura Mazda answered : 'It is Verethraghna, made by Ahura, O Spitama Zarathustra!'

---

[1] The royal Glory is described flying in the shape of a raven, Yt. XIX, 35.

[2] Doubtful.

[3] While Ardashîr, the founder of the Sasanian dynasty, was flying from Ardavân, a beautiful wild ram ran after him and overtook him, and Ardavân understood from this that the kingly Glory had left him and had passed over to his rival (Shâh Nâmah, Ardashîr; Kâr Nâmakî Artachshîr, tr. Noeldeke, p. 45).

25. Verethraghna, made by Ahura, came to him the ninth time, running in the shape of a beautiful, fighting buck, with sharp horns.

Thus did Verethraghna come, bearing the good Glory made by Mazda, the Glory made by Mazda . . . .

X.

26. We sacrifice unto Verethraghna, made by Ahura.

Zarathustra asked Ahura Mazda : 'Ahura Mazda, most beneficent Spirit, Maker of the material world, thou Holy One!

'Who is the best-armed of the heavenly gods ?'

Ahura Mazda answered : 'It is Verethraghna, made by Ahura, O Spitama Zarathustra !'

27. Verethraghna, made by Ahura, came to him the tenth time, running in the shape of a man, bright and beautiful, made by Mazda : he held a sword with a golden blade, inlaid with all sorts of ornaments.

Thus did Verethraghna come, bearing the good Glory made by Mazda, the Glory made by Mazda . . . .

XI.

28. We sacrifice unto Verethraghna, made by Ahura, who makes virility, who makes death, who makes resurrection, who possesses peace, who has a free way.

Unto him did the holy Zarathustra offer up a sacrifice, [asking] for victorious thinking, victorious speaking, victorious doing, victorious addressing, and victorious answering.

29. Verethraghna, made by Ahura, gave him the

fountains of manliness[1], the strength of the arms,
the health of the whole body, the sturdiness of the
whole body, and the eye-sight of the Kara fish[2],
that lives beneath the waters and can measure[3] a
rippling of the water, not thicker than a hair, in the
Rangha whose ends lie afar, whose depth is a thousand times the height of a man[4].

For his brightness and glory, I will offer unto him a sacrifice
worth being heard . . . .

XII.

30. We sacrifice unto Verethraghna, made by
Ahura, who makes virility, who makes death, who
makes resurrection, who possesses peace, who has
a free way.

Unto him did the holy Zarathustra offer up a
sacrifice, [asking] for victorious thinking, victorious
speaking, victorious doing, victorious addressing,
and victorious answering.

31. Verethraghna, made by Ahura, gave him the
fountains of manliness, the strength of the arms, the
health of the whole body, the sturdiness of the whole
body, and the eye-sight of the male horse, that, in
the dark of the night, in its first half[5] and through
the rain, can perceive a horse's hair lying on the
ground and knows whether it is from the head or
from the tail[6].

---

[1] Erezi, Pahl. gond (Old Zand-Pahlavi Dictionary, p. 11).

[2] See Vendîdâd XIX, 42.   [3] Possibly, perceive.

[4] Cf. Yt. XVI, 7, and Bundahis XVIII, 6: 'those fish . . . .
know the scratch of a needle's point (or better hole) by which the
water shall increase, or by which it is diminishing' (tr. West).

[5] Avakhshaityau, the night before hu-vakhsha (before the
time when the light begins to grow; midnight).

[6] Cf. Yt. XVI, 10, and Bundahis XIX, 32: 'Regarding the Arab

For his brightness and glory, I will offer unto him a sacrifice worth being heard . . . .

XIII.

32. We sacrifice unto Verethraghna, made by Ahura, who makes virility, who makes death, who makes resurrection, who possesses peace, who has a free way.

Unto him did the holy Zarathuℛtra sacrifice, [asking] for victorious thinking, victorious speaking, victorious doing, victorious addressing, and victorious answering.

33. Verethraghna, made by Ahura, gave him the fountains of virility, the strength of the arms, the health of the whole body, the sturdiness of the whole body, and the eye-sight of the vulture with a golden collar[1], that, from as far as nine districts, can perceive a piece of flesh not thicker than the fist, giving just as much light as a needle gives, as the point of a needle gives[2].

For his brightness and glory, I will offer unto him a sacrifice worth being heard . . . .

XIV.

34. We sacrifice unto Verethraghna, made by Ahura.

Zarathuℛtra asked Ahura Mazda: 'Ahura Mazda, most beneficent Spirit, Maker of the material world, thou Holy One!

---

horse, they say that if, in a dark night, a single hair occurs on the ground, he sees it' (tr. West).

[1] Possibly the Gypaetus, the vautour doré.

[2] 'Even from his highest flight, he (the vulture) sees when flesh the size of a fist is on the ground' (Bund. XIX, 31; tr. West). Cf. Horapollo (I, 11).

'If I have a curse thrown upon me, a spell told upon me by the many men who hate me, what is the remedy for it?'

35. Ahura Mazda answered: 'Take thou a feather of that bird with . . . . [1] feathers, the Vâre*n*gana, O Spitama Zarathu*s*tra! With that feather thou shalt rub thy own body [2], with that feather thou shalt curse back thy enemies.

·36. 'If a man holds a bone of that strong bird, or a feather of that strong bird, no one can smite or turn to flight that fortunate man. The feather of that bird of birds brings him help; it brings unto him the homage of men, it maintains in him his glory.

37. 'Then the sovereign, the lord of countries, will no longer kill his [3] hundreds, though he is a killer of men; the . . . . [4] will not kill at one stroke; he alone smites and goes forwards.

38. 'All tremble before him who holds the feather, they tremble therefore before me; all my enemies tremble before me and fear my strength and victorious force and the fierceness established in my body.

39. 'He [5] carries the chariot of the lords; he carries the chariots of the lordly ones, the chariots of the sovereigns. He carried the chariot of Kavi

---

[1] Peshô-parena. The Vâre*n*gana is the same bird as the Vâra-ghna, the raven.

[2] The feather of the Vâre*n*gana plays here the same part as the Sîmurgh's feather in the Shâh Nâmah. When Rûdâbah's flank was opened to bring forth Rustem, her wound was healed by rubbing it with a Sîmurgh's feather; Rustem, wounded to death by Isfendyâr, was cured in the same manner.

[3] Of him who holds that feather.

[4] ? Vaêsaêpa.   [5] That bird.

Usa [1]; upon his wings runs the male horse [2], runs the burden-bearing camel, runs the water of the river.

40. 'Him rode the gallant Thraêtaona, who smote A*z*i Dahâka, the three-mouthed, the three-headed, the six-eyed, who had a thousand senses; that most powerful, fiendish Dru*g*, that demon, baleful to the world, the strongest Dru*g* that Angra Mainyu created against the material world, to destroy the world of the good principle [3].

'For his brightness and glory, I will offer unto him a sacrifice worth being heard . . . .

XV.

41. 'We sacrifice to Verethraghna, made by Ahura.

'Verethraghna confounds the glory of this house with its wealth in cattle. He is like that great bird, the Saêna [4]; he is like the big clouds, full of water, that beat the mountains.

'For his brightness and glory, I will offer unto him a sacrifice worth being heard . . . .

XVI.

42. 'We sacrifice to Verethraghna, made by Ahura.'

Zarathu*s*tra asked Ahura Mazda: 'Ahura Mazda, most beneficent Spirit, Maker of the material world, thou Holy One!

'Where is it that we must invoke the name of Verethraghna, made by Ahura? Where is it that

---

[1] Kai Kaus; when he tried to ascend to heaven on a throne carried by eagles (Journal Asiatique, 1881, I, 513).

[2] A metaphor to express the swiftness of the wind, of the camel, and of the rivers.

[3] Cf. Yt. V, 34.   [4] The Sîmurgh; cf. p. 241, note 2.

we must praise him? That we must humbly praise him?'

43. Ahura Mazda answered: 'When armies meet together in full array, O Spitama Zarathustra! (asking) which of the two is the party that conquers[1] and is not crushed, that smites and is not smitten;

44. 'Do thou throw[1] four feathers[2] in the way. Whichever of the two will first worship the well-shapen Strength, and Verethraghna, beautiful of form, made by Mazda, on his side will victory stand.

45. 'I will bless Strength and Victory, the two keepers, the two good keepers, the two maintainers; the two who . . . .[3], the two who . . . .[3], the two who . . . .[3]; the two who forgive, the two who strike off, the two who forget[4].

46. 'O Zarathustra! let not that spell be shown to any one, except by the father to his son, or by the brother to his brother from the same womb, or by the Âthravan to his pupil[5]. These are words that are awful and powerful, awful and assembly-ruling, awful and victorious, awful and healing; these are words that save the head that was lost and chant away the uplifted weapon.'

XVII.

47. We sacrifice to Verethraghna, made by Ahura: who goes along the armies arrayed, and goes here

---

[1] Doubtful.

[2] Or an arrow feathered with four Vârengana's feathers.

[3] Â-dhwaozen, vî-dhwaozen, fra-dhwaozen.

[4] Âmarezen, cf. آمرزیدن; vîmarezen, cf. Yt. I, 2; fra marezen, cf. فرموش.

[5] Cf. Yt. IV, 10.

and there asking, along with Mithra and Rashnu:
'Who is it who lies unto Mithra? Who is it who
thrusts [his oath] against Rashnu [1]? To whom shall
I, in my might, impart illness and death [2]?'

48 [3]. Ahura Mazda said: 'If men sacrifice unto
Verethraghna, made by Ahura, if the due sacrifice
and prayer is offered unto him just as it ought to
be performed in the perfection of holiness, never
will a hostile horde enter the Aryan countries, nor
any plague, nor leprosy, nor venomous plants,
nor the chariot of a foe, nor the uplifted spear of
a foe.'

49 [4]. Zarathustra asked: 'What is then, O Ahura
Mazda! the sacrifice and invocation in honour of
Verethraghna, made by Ahura, as it ought to be
performed in the perfection of holiness?'

50. Ahura Mazda answered: 'Let the Aryan
nations bring libations unto him; let the Aryan
nations tie bundles of baresma for him; let the
Aryan nations cook for him a head of cattle, either
white, or black, or of any other colour, but all of
one and the same colour.

51. 'Let not a murderer take of those offerings,
nor a whore, nor a . . . . , who does not sing
the Gâthâs, who spreads death in the world and
withstands the law of Mazda, the law of Zarathustra.

52. 'If a murderer take of those offerings, or a
whore, or a . . . . , who does not sing the Gâthâs,
then Verethraghna, made by Ahura, takes back his
healing virtues.

---

[1] Against truth.
[2] Cf. Yt. X, 108 seq.
[3] § 48; cf. Yt. VIII, 56.
[4] §§ 49–53 = Yt. VIII, 57–61.

53. 'Plagues will ever pour upon the Aryan nations; hostile hordes will ever fall upon the Aryan nations; the Aryans will be smitten by their fifties and their hundreds, by their hundreds and their thousands, by their thousands and their tens of thousands, by their tens of thousands and their myriads of myriads.'

54. There Verethraghna, made by Ahura, proclaimed thus: 'The Soul of the Bull[1], the wise creature, does not receive from man due sacrifice and prayer; for now the Daêvas and the worshippers of the Daêvas make blood flow and spill it like water;

55. 'For now the . . . .[2] Daêvas and the worshippers of the Daêvas bring to the fire the plant that is called Haperesi, the wood that is called Neme*t*ka[3];

56. '(Therefore) when the . . . .[2] Daêvas and the worshippers of the Daêvas bow their backs, bend their waists, and arrange all their limbs[4], they think they will smite and smite not, they think they will kill and kill not; and then the... Daêvas and the worshippers of the Daêvas have their minds confounded and their eyes made giddy[5].'

For his brightness and glory, I will offer unto him a sacrifice worth being heard . . . .

---

[1] Gôsûrûn or Drvâspa; see Yt. IX. The destruction of any living being is an injury to Drvâspa.

[2] ? Vyâmbura.

[3] The Haperesi and the Neme*t*ka are probably some species of green wood; it is forbidden to put green wood in the fire as it kills it, and injures the Genius of Water at the same time.

[4] In order to strike.

[5] The general meaning of the last four clauses is that the impious are defeated.

XVIII.

57. We sacrifice to Verethraghna, made by Ahura.

I offer up Haoma, who saves one's head [1]; I offer up the victorious Haoma; I offer him up, the good protector; I offer up Haoma, who is a protector to my body, as a man who shall drink [2] of him shall win and prevail [3] over his enemies in battle;

58. That I may smite this army, that I may smite down this army, that I may cut in pieces this army that is coming behind me.

For his brightness and glory, I will offer unto him a sacrifice worth being heard . . . .

XIX.

59. We sacrifice to Verethraghna, made by Ahura.

The prince and his son and his sons who are chiefs of myriads [4] offer him up a bright . . . . [5] [saying]: 'He is strong, and Victorious is his name; he is victorious, and Strong is his name;'

60. That I may be as constantly victorious as any one of all the Aryans [6]; that I may smite this army, that I may smite down this army, that I may cut in pieces this army that is coming behind me.

For his brightness and glory, I will offer unto him a sacrifice worth being heard . . . .

---

[1] ? Sâiri-baoghem; cf. § 46.

[2] Nivazaiti; literally, swallow (? frôt ô bun burtan, Vend. V, 8 [26]).

[3] Literally, overtake.   [4] Cf. Yt. V, 85.

[5] ? Asânem sighûirê.   [6] Cf. Yt. V, 69.

XX.

61. We sacrifice to Verethraghna, made by Ahura.

Yathâ ahû vairyô: The will of the Lord is the law of holiness . . . .

In the ox is our strength, in the ox is our need [1]; in the ox is our speech, in the ox is our victory; in the ox is our food, in the ox is our clothing; in the ox is tillage, that makes food grow for us.

For his brightness and glory, I will offer unto him a sacrifice worth being heard . . . .

XXI.

62. We sacrifice to Verethraghna, made by Ahura; Who breaks the columns asunder, who cuts the columns to pieces, who wounds the columns, who makes the columns shake; who comes and breaks the columns asunder, who comes and cuts the columns to pieces, who comes and wounds the columns, who comes and makes the columns shake, both of Daêvas and men, of the Yâtus and Pairikas, of the oppressors, the blind, and the deaf.

For his brightness and glory, I will offer unto him a sacrifice worth being heard . . . .

XXII.

63. We sacrifice to Verethraghna, made by Ahura. When Verethraghna, made by Ahura, binds the hands, confounds the eye-sight, takes the hearing

---

[1] From Yasna X, 20 (62), where, instead of the words, ' in the ox is our strength (amem), in the ox is our need,' the text has, ' in the ox is his need, in the ox is our need,' meaning, ' when we give him his need (water and grass), he gives us our need (milk and calves),' (Pahl. tr.).

from the ears of the Mithradruges [1] marching in columns, allied by cities, they can no longer move their feet, they can no longer withstand.

For his brightness and glory, I will offer unto him a sacrifice worth being heard . . . .

64. Yathâ ahû vairyô: The will of the Lord is the law of holiness . . . .

I bless the sacrifice and prayer, and the strength and vigour of Verethraghna, made by Mazda; and of the crushing Ascendant.

Ashem Vohû: Holiness is the best of all good . . . .

[Give] unto that man [2] brightness and glory, ... give him the bright, all-happy, blissful abode of the holy Ones.

---

[1] See p. 120, note 2.
[2] Who shall offer a sacrifice to Verethraghna.

XV. RÂM YAST.

This Yast bears the name of Râma *Hv*âstra, the Genius who presides over the 21st day of the month (Sîrôzah, § 21), and is devoted to his Hamkâr, Vayu.

Regarding Râma *Hv*âstra, the Genius that gives good abodes and good pastures, and his connection with Vayu, see Vend. Introd. IV, and Études Iraniennes, II, 187.

This Yast can be divided into two parts. The first part (§§ 1–140) contains an enumeration of worshippers who sacrificed to Vayu : Ahura Mazda (§ 2), Haoshyangha (§ 7), Takhma Urupa (§ 11), Yima (§ 15), Azi Dahâka (§ 19), Thraêtaona (§ 23), Keresâspa (§ 27), Aurvasâra (§ 31), Hutaosa (§ 35), and Iranian maids (§ 39). The second part (§§ 42–58) contains a special enumeration and glorification of the many names of Vayu (§§ 42–50).

---

0. May Ahura Mazda be rejoiced! . . . .

Ashem Vohû: Holiness is the best of all good . . . .

I confess myself a worshipper of Mazda, a follower of Zarathustra, one who hates the Daêvas, and obeys the laws of Ahura ; For sacrifice, prayer, propitiation, and glorification unto [Hâvani], the holy and master of holiness . . . .

Unto Râma *Hv*âstra, unto Vayu who works highly and is more powerful to afflict than all other creatures [1],

Be propitiation from me, for sacrifice, prayer, propitiation, and glorification.

Yathâ ahû vairyô: The will of the Lord is the law of holiness . . . .

I.

1. I will sacrifice to the Waters and to Him who divides them [2]. I will sacrifice to Peace, whose breath is friendly, and to Weal, both of them.

---

[1] Cf. Sîrôzah I, 21.
[2] Apãm Napâ*t* (Yt. VIII, 34) or Tistrya (Yt. VIII, 1).

To this Vayu do we sacrifice, this Vayu do we
invoke, for this house, for the master of this house,
and for the man here who is offering libations and
giving gifts. To this excellent God do we sacrifice,
that he may accept our meat and our prayers, and
grant us in return to crush our enemies at one
stroke.

2 [1]. To him did the Maker, Ahura Mazda, offer
up a sacrifice in the Airyana Vaêgah [1], on a golden
throne, under golden beams [2] and a golden canopy,
with bundles of baresma and offerings of full-boiling
[milk] [3].

3. He begged of him a boon, saying : 'Grant me
this, O Vayu! who dost work highly [4], that I may
smite the creation of Angra Mainyu, and that nobody
may smite this creation of the Good Spirit!'

4. Vayu, who works highly, granted him that
boon, as the Maker, Ahura Mazda, did pursue it.

5. We sacrifice to the holy Vayu : we sacrifice to
Vayu, who works highly.

To this part of thee do we sacrifice, O Vayu! that
belongs to Spenta Mainyu [5].

For his brightness and glory, I will offer unto him
a sacrifice worth being heard, namely, unto the awful
Vayu, who works highly. We offer up a sacrifice unto the awful Vayu, who works highly, with
the libations, with the Haoma and meat, with the
baresma, with the wisdom of the tongue, with the

---

[1] Cf. Yt. V, 17.   [2] Fraspât, Persian فرسب.
[3] Cf. p. 169, note 5.   [4] See p. 10, note 4.
[5] As Vayu, the atmosphere, is the place in which the conflict of
the two principles takes place, one part of him belongs to the Evil
Spirit (see Vend. Introd. IV, 17).

holy spells, the words, the deeds, the libations, and the well-spoken words.

Yênhê hâtăm : All those beings of whom Ahura Mazda . . . .

II.

6. I will sacrifice to the Waters and to Him who divides them . . . .

To this Vayu do we sacrifice, this Vayu do we invoke . . . . [1]

7. To him did Haoshyangha, the Paradhâta, offer up a sacrifice on the Taêra of the Hara, bound with iron [2], on a golden throne, under golden beams and a golden canopy, with bundles of baresma and offering of full-boiling [milk].

8. He begged of him a boon, saying : ' Grant me, O Vayu! who dost work highly, that I may smite two-thirds of the Daêvas of Mâzana and of the fiends of Varena [3].'

9. Vayu, who works highly, granted him that boon, as the Maker, Ahura Mazda [4], did pursue it.

We sacrifice to the holy Vayu . . . .
For his brightness and glory, I will offer unto him a sacrifice worth being heard . . . .

III.

10. I will sacrifice to the Waters and to Him who divides them . . . .

To this Vayu do we sacrifice, this Vayu do we invoke . . . .

---

[1] The rest as in clause 1.
[2] Cf. Yt. V, 21, p. 58, note 2.   [3] Cf. Yt. V, 21–23.
[4] Introduced from § 4 into this and all similar clauses, except the one relating to Azi Dahâka (§ 21).

11. To him did Takhma Urupa[1], the well-armed[2], offer up a sacrifice on a golden throne, under golden beams and a golden canopy, with bundles of baresma and offerings of full-boiling [milk].

12. He begged of him a boon, saying: 'Grant me this, O Vayu! who dost work highly, that I may conquer all Daêvas and men, all the Yâtus and Pairikas, and that I may ride Angra Mainyu, turned into the shape of a horse, all around the earth from one end to the other, for thirty years.'

13. Vayu, who works highly, granted him that boon[3], as the Maker, Ahura Mazda, did pursue it.

We sacrifice to the holy Vayu . . . .
For his brightness and glory, I will offer unto him a sacrifice worth being heard . . . .

IV.

14. I will sacrifice to the Waters and to Him who divides them . . . .

To this Vayu do we sacrifice, this Vayu do we invoke . . . .

15. Unto him did the bright Yima, the good shep-

---

[1] Takhma Urupa (in later legend Tahmûrâf) was a brother to Yima. He reigned for thirty years and rode Ahriman, turned into a horse. But at last his wife, deceived by Ahriman, revealed to him the secret of her husband's power, and Tahmûrâf was swallowed up by his horse. But Yima managed to take back his brother's body from the body of Ahriman and recovered thereby the arts and civilisation which had disappeared along with Tahmûrâf (see Minokhired XXVII, 32; Ravâet apud Spiegel, Einleitung in die traditionelle Literatur, pp. 317 seq.; Ormazd et Ahriman, § 137 seq.; cf. above, p. 60, note 1).

[2] Azinava*nt* or zaênahva*nt*: he kept that epithet in later tradition: Zînavend, 'quod cognomen virum significat armis probe instructum' (Hamza Ispahensis, p. 20, tr. Gottwaldt).

[3] As told Yt. XIX, 29.

herd, sacrifice from the height Hukairya, the all-shining and golden, on a golden throne, under golden beams and a golden canopy, with bundles of baresma and offerings of full-boiling [milk].

16. He begged of him a boon, saying : 'Grant me this, O Vayu! who dost work highly, that I may become the most glorious of the men born to behold the sun : that I may make in my reign both animals and men undying, waters and plants undrying, and the food for eating creatures never-failing[1].'

In the reign of the valiant Yima there was neither cold wind nor hot wind, neither old age nor death, nor envy made by the Daêvas[2].

17. Vayu, who works highly, granted him that boon, as the Maker, Ahura Mazda, did pursue it.

We sacrifice to the holy Vayu . . . .

For his brightness and glory, I will offer unto him a sacrifice worth being heard . . . .

V.

18. I will sacrifice to the Waters and to Him who divides them . . . .

To this Vayu do we sacrifice, this Vayu do we invoke . . . .

19. Unto him did the three-mouthed Azi Dahâka offer up a sacrifice in his accursed palace of Kvirinta[3],

---

[1] Cf. Yasna IX, 4–5 (11–20) and Yt. XIX, 31 seq.

[2] This passage is interpolated from Yasna IX, 5 (17–19).

[3] Or, 'his accursed palace of the Stork' (upa kvirintem duzitem). 'Azi Dahâka,' says Hamza (p. 32 in the text, p. 22 in the translation), 'used to live in Babylon (cf. Yt. V, 29), where he had built a palace in the form of a stork; he called it Kuleng Dîs (كلنگ ديس), the fortress of the Stork; the inhabitants called it Dis Het (ديس حت).' Kuleng Dîs was in Zend Kvirinta daêza and Dis Het is nothing else than Duzita. One may doubt

on a golden throne, under golden beams and a golden canopy, with bundles of baresma and offerings of full-boiling [milk].

20. He begged of him a boon, saying: 'Grant me this, O Vayu! who dost work highly, that I may make all the seven Karshvares of the earth empty of men[1].'

21. In vain did he sacrifice, in vain did he beg, in vain did he invoke, in vain did he give gifts, in vain did he bring libations; Vayu did not grant him that boon.

For his brightness and glory, I will offer unto him a sacrifice worth being heard . . . .

VI.

22. I will sacrifice to the Waters and to Him who divides them . . . .

To this Vayu do we sacrifice, this Vayu do we invoke . . . .

23. Unto him did Thraêtaona, the heir of the valiant Âthwya clan, offer up a sacrifice in the four-cornered Varena, on a golden throne, under golden beams and a golden canopy, with bundles of baresma and offerings of full-boiling [milk].

24. He begged of him a boon, saying: 'Grant me this, O Vayu! who dost work highly, that I may overcome Azi Dahâka, the three-mouthed, the three-headed, the six-eyed, who has a thousand senses, that most powerful, fiendish Drug, that

---

whether Kvirinta is the name of a place or the Zend form of Kuleng, a stork: in any case it was a palace in Bawri (Babylon). In the Shâh Nâmah it is called Dizukht (duz-ukhta for duz-ita; see Études Iraniennes, II, 211).

[1] Cf. Yt. V, 30 seq.

demon baleful to the world, the strongest Drug that
Angra Mainyu created against the material world, to
destroy the world of the good principle; and that I
may deliver his two wives, Savanghavâk and Erenavâk, who are the fairest of body amongst women, and
the most wonderful creatures in the world[1].'

25. Vayu, who works highly, granted him that
boon, as the Maker, Ahura Mazda, did pursue it.

We sacrifice to the holy Vayu . . . .

For his brightness and glory, I will offer unto him a sacrifice
worth being heard . . . .

VII.

26. I will sacrifice to the Waters and to Him who
divides them . . . .

To this Vayu do we sacrifice, this Vayu do we
invoke . . . .

27. To him did the manly-hearted Keresâspa[2]
offer up a sacrifice by the Gudha[3], a channel of the
Rangha, made by Mazda, upon a golden throne, under
golden beams and a golden canopy, with bundles of
baresma and offerings of full-boiling [milk].

28. He begged of him a boon, saying : ' Grant me
this, O Vayu ! who dost work highly, that I may succeed in avenging my brother Urvâkhshaya[4], that I
may smite Hitâspa and yoke him to my chariot.'

The Gandarewa, who lives beneath the waters,

---

[1] Yt. V, 34; IX, 14; XVII, 34.

[2] Cf. Yt. V, 37 seq.

[3] An unknown affluent of the Rangha (Tigris).

[4] Sâma had two sons, Keresâspa, a warrior, and Urvâkhshaya,
a judge and law-giver (Yasna IX, 10 [29 seq.]). We have no further
details about Urvâkhshaya's legend than that he was killed by
'Hitâspa, the golden-crowned' (cf. Yt. XIX, 41), and avenged by
Keresâspa.

is the son of Ahura in the deep, he is the only master of the deep[1].

29. Vayu, who works highly, granted him that boon, as the Maker, Ahura Mazda, did pursue it.

We sacrifice to the holy Vayu . . . .

For his brightness and glory, I will offer unto him a sacrifice worth being heard . . . .

VIII.

30. I will sacrifice to the Waters and to Him who divides them . . . .

To this Vayu do we sacrifice, this Vayu do we invoke . . . .

31. To him did Aurvasâra[2], the lord of the country, offer up a sacrifice, towards the White Forest[3], by the White Forest, on the border of the White Forest, on a golden throne, under golden beams and a golden canopy, with bundles of baresma and offerings of full-boiling [milk].

32. He begged of him a boon, saying : 'Grant me this, O Vayu! who dost work highly, that the gallant Husravah, he who unites the Aryan nations into one kingdom[4], may not smite us ; that I may flee from king Husravah[5] ; . . . .

---

[1] A disconnected allusion to the struggle of Keresâspa with the Gandarewa (Yt. V, 38, text and notes ; XIX, 41). On the words 'the son of Ahura . . . .' cf. Ormazd et Ahriman, p. 215, note 1.

[2] No other mention is made of Aurvasâra in the Avesta, unless he is alluded to in Yt. V, 50. He does not appear to have been known to Firdausi.

[3] Spaêtinis razûra is called 'the chief of forests' (Bund. XXIV, 16). According to the Bahman Yast (III, 9), it was the seat of the last and decisive battle between Argâsp and Gûstâsp.

[4] Cf. Yt. V, 49 ; IX, 21.   [5] Cf. Yt. V, 50.

'That king Husravah and all the Aryans in the Forest may smite him [1].'

33. Vayu, who works highly, granted him that boon, as the Maker, Ahura Mazda, did pursue it.

We sacrifice to the holy Vayu . . . .
For his brightness and glory, I will offer unto him a sacrifice worth being heard . . . .

IX.

34. I will sacrifice to the Waters and to Him who divides them . . . .

To this Vayu do we sacrifice, this Vayu do we invoke . . . .

35. To him did Hutaosa, she of the many brothers [2], of the Naotara house [3], offer up a sacrifice, on a golden throne, under golden beams and a golden canopy, with bundles of baresma and offerings of boiling milk.

36. She begged of him a boon, saying: 'Grant me this, O Vayu! who dost work highly, that I may be dear and loved and well-received in the house of king Vîstâspa.'

37. Vayu, who works highly, granted her that boon, as the Maker, Ahura Mazda, did pursue it.

We sacrifice to the holy Vayu . . . .
For his brightness and glory, I will offer unto him a sacrifice worth being heard . . . .

X.

38. I will sacrifice to the Waters and to Him who divides them . . . .

---

[1] This line looks as if it should belong to a counter-prayer by Husravah, which was heard by Vayu, as appears from Yt. V, 50.
[2] See Yt. IX, 26.　　　　[3] See p. 77, note 1.

To this Vayu do we sacrifice, this Vayu do we
invoke . . . .

39. To him did[1] the maids, whom no man had
known, offer up a sacrifice on a golden throne, under
golden beams and a golden canopy, with bundles of
baresma and offerings of boiling milk.

40. They begged of him a boon, saying: 'Grant
us this, O Vayu! who dost work highly, that we
may find a husband, young and beautiful of body,
who will treat us well, all life long, and give us offspring; a wise, learned, ready-tongued husband.'

41. Vayu, who works highly, granted them that
boon, as the Maker, Ahura Mazda, did pursue it.

We sacrifice to the holy Vayu . . . .
For his brightness and glory, I will offer unto him a sacrifice
worth being heard . . . .

XI.

42. I will sacrifice to the Waters and to Him who
divides them . . . .

To this Vayu do we sacrifice, this Vayu do we
invoke . . . .

We sacrifice to that Vayu that belongs to the
Good Spirit[2], the bright and glorious Vayu.

43. My name is Vayu, O holy Zarathustra! My
name is Vayu, because I go through (vyêmi) the
two worlds[3], the one which the Good Spirit has

---

[1] It may be doubted whether the allusion here is to a legend of
marriage en masse, following the marriage of Hutaosa with Vîstâspa, or whether the aorist is used with an indicative meaning:
'To him do the maids who have known no man . . . . They beg
of him a boon, saying . . . .' Cf. Yt. XVI, 17.

[2] Cf. § 5, note 5.

[3] An attempt to an etymological explanation of the name Vayu.
Cf. § 53.

made and the one which the Evil Spirit has made.

My name is the Overtaker (apaêta), O holy Zarathustra! My name is the Overtaker, because I can overtake the creatures of both worlds, the one that the Good Spirit has made and the one that the Evil Spirit has made.

44. My name is the All-smiting, O holy Zarathustra! My name is the All-smiting, because I can smite the creatures of both worlds, the one that the Good Spirit has made and the one that the Evil Spirit has made.

My name is the Worker of Good, O holy Zarathustra! My name is the Worker of Good, because I work the good of the Maker, Ahura Mazda, and of the Amesha-Spentas[1].

45. My name is He that goes forwards.
My name is He that goes backwards.
My name is He that bends backwards.
My name is He that hurls away.
My name is He that hurls down.
My name is He that destroys.
My name is He that takes away.
My name is He that finds out.
My name is He that finds out the Glory (*Hvarenô*).

46. My name is the Valiant; my name is the Most Valiant.

My name is the Strong; my name is the Strongest.
My name is the Firm; my name is the Firmest.
My name is the Stout; my name is the Stoutest.
My name is He that crosses over easily.
My name is He that goes along hurling away.

---

[1] He is their agent and instrument.

My name is He that crushes at one stroke.

My name is . . . .[1]

My name is He that works against the Daêvas.

My name is . . . .[2]

47. My name is He that prevails over malice; my name is He that destroys malice.

My name is He that unites; my name is He that re-unites; my name is He that separates.

My name is the Burning; my name is the Quick of intelligence[3].

My name is Deliverance; my name is Welfare[4].

My name is the Burrow[5]; my name is He who destroys the burrows[5]; my name is He who spits upon the burrows[5].

48. My name is Sharpness of spear; my name is He of the sharp spear.

My name is Length of spear; my name is He of the long spear.

My name is Piercingness of spear; my name is He of the piercing spear.

My name is the Glorious; my name is the Over-glorious.

49[6]. Invoke these names of mine, O holy Zarathustra! in the midst of the havocking hordes, in the midst of the columns moving forwards, in the strife of the conflicting nations.

---

[1] Âiniva (?).   [2] Keredharisa (?).

[3] Doubtful; baoka, cf. زور.

[4] Reading sudhis.

[5] Geredha is the burrow of an Ahrimanian creature (see Vend. III, 10 [33]; VII, 24 [61]): Vayu, in that half of him that belongs to the Evil Spirit, is the seat (the burrow) of Ahriman; but with his better half, he struggles against the fiend and destroys him.

[6] Cf. Yt. I, 11, 16.

50. Invoke these names of mine, O holy Zarathustra! when the all-powerful tyrant of a country falls upon thee, rushes upon thee, deals wounds upon thee, or hurls his chariot against thee, to rob thee[1] of thy wealth, to rob thee of thy health.

51. Invoke these names of mine, O holy Zarathustra! when the unholy Ashemaogha falls upon thee, rushes upon thee, deals wounds upon thee, or hurls his chariot against thee, to rob thee of thy strength, to rob thee of thy wealth, to rob thee of thy health.

52. Invoke these names of mine, O holy Zarathustra! when a man stands in bonds, when a man is being thrown into bonds, or when a man is being dragged in bonds: thus the prisoners flee from the hands of those who carry them, they flee away out of the prison[2].

53. O thou Vayu! who strikest fear upon all men and horses, who in all creatures workest against the Daêvas, both into the lowest places and into those a thousand times deep dost thou enter with equal power[3].

54. 'With what manner of sacrifice shall I worship thee? With what manner of sacrifice shall I forward and worship thee? With what manner of sacrifice will be achieved thy adoration, O great Vayu! thou who art high-up girded, firm, swift-moving, high-footed, wide-breasted, wide-thighed, with untrembling eyes, as powerful in sovereignty as any absolute sovereign in the world?'

---

[1] Literally, coveting.
[2] The translation of this clause is doubtful; the text is corrupt.
[3] Cf. § 42.

55. 'Take thou a baresma, O holy Zarathu*s*tra! turn it upwards or downwards, according as it is full day or dawning; upwards during the day, downwards at the dawn[1].

56. ' If thou makest me worshipped with a sacrifice, then I shall say unto thee with my own voice things of health, made by Mazda and full of glory, so that Angra Mainyu may never do harm unto thee, nor the Yâtus, nor those addicted to the works of the Yâtu, whether Daêvas or men.'

57. We sacrifice unto thee, O great Vayu! we sacrifice unto thee, O strong Vayu!

We sacrifice unto Vayu, the greatest of the great; we sacrifice unto Vayu, the strongest of the strong.

We sacrifice unto Vayu, of the golden helm.

We sacrifice unto Vayu, of the golden crown.

We sacrifice unto Vayu, of the golden necklace.

We sacrifice unto Vayu, of the golden chariot.

We sacrifice unto Vayu, of the golden wheel.

We sacrifice unto Vayu, of the golden weapons.

We sacrifice unto Vayu, of the golden garment.

We sacrifice unto Vayu, of the golden shoe.

We sacrifice unto Vayu, of the golden girdle.

We sacrifice unto the holy Vayu ; we sacrifice unto Vayu, who works highly.

To this part of thee do we sacrifice, O Vayu! that belongs to the Good Spirit.

For his brightness and glory, I will offer unto him a sacrifice worth being heard, namely, unto the awful Vayu, who works highly . . . .

58. Yathâ ahû vairyô.: The will of the Lord is the law of holiness . . . .

I bless the sacrifice and invocation unto, and the

---

[1] Études Iraniennes, II, 110.

strength and vigour of Râma *Hv*âstra, and Vayu, who works highly, more powerful to afflict than all the other creatures : this part of thee that belongs to the Good Spirit.

Ashem Vohû : Holiness is the best of all good . . . .

[Give] unto that man brightness and glory, ... give him the bright, all-happy, blissful abode of the holy Ones.

XVI. DÎN YA*S*T.

Dîn (Daêna) presides over the 24th day of the month (Sîrôzah 24) and gives it her name; she is invoked in company with *K*ista, and in fact this Ya*s*t, though it bears the name of Daêna, is consecrated to *K*ista (§§ 2, 7). These two Genii are, however, very closely connected in their nature, as Daêna is the impersonation of the Zoroastrian Law or Religion, and *K*ista is religious knowledge, the knowledge of what leads to bliss (far*g*ânak, nirvâ*na*g*ñ*âna; the same as *K*isti).

The description of *K*ista is rather pallid, and does not rise above abstractions (see, however, Mihir Ya*s*t, § 126). She was not worshipped by the old epic heroes as Anâhita was, but by Zarathu*s*tra and his wife, because she must have been, from her very name and nature, a goddess of Zoroastrian origin and growth.

---

o. May Ahura Mazda be rejoiced ! . . . .

Ashem Vohû : Holiness is the best of all good . . . .

I confess myself a worshipper of Mazda, a follower of Zarathu*s*tra, one who hates the Daêvas and obeys the laws of Ahura ;

For sacrifice, prayer, propitiation, and glorification unto [Hâvani], the holy and master of holiness . . . .

To the most right *K*ista, made by Mazda and holy, and to the good Law of the worshippers of Mazda,

Be propitiation from me, for sacrifice, prayer, propitiation, and glorification.

Yathâ ahû vairyô : The will of the Lord is the law of holiness . . . .

I.

1. We sacrifice to the most right *K*ista, made by Mazda and holy : we sacrifice to the good Law of the worshippers of Mazda, the supplier of good

stores, who runs quickly to the goal and frees one best from dangers[1], who brings libations, who is holy, clever, and renowned, speedy to work and quick of work; who goes quickly and cleanses well; the good Law of the worshippers of Mazda;

2. To whom Zarathustra did sacrifice, saying: 'Rise up from thy seat, come forward from the Abode[2], thou most right Kista, made by Mazda and holy. If thou art before me, stay for me; if thou art behind me, overtake me.

3. 'Let everything be as friendly to us as anything can be: may we go smoothly along the roads, find good pathways in the mountains, run easily through the forests, and cross happily the rivers!'

4. For her brightness and glory, I will offer unto her a sacrifice worth being heard, namely, unto the most right Kista, made by Mazda and holy. I will offer up a sacrifice unto the most right Kista, made by Mazda and holy, with the libations, with the Haoma and meat, with the baresma, with the wisdom of the tongue, with the holy spells, with the words and deeds, with the libations, with the well-spoken words.

Yênhê hâtãm: All those beings of whom Ahura Mazda . . . .

II.

5. We sacrifice to the most right Kista, made by Mazda and holy: we sacrifice to the good Law of the worshippers of Mazda . . . .[3]

---

[1] Reading nimarezista; cf. vîmarezistem, Yt. I, 2.
[2] The heavenly abode, the Garôthmân.
[3] The rest as in § 1.

6. To whom Zarathustra did sacrifice for righteousness of thought, for righteousness of speech, for righteousness of deed, and for this boon,

7. That the most right *K*ista, made by Mazda and holy, would give him the swiftness of the feet, the quick hearing of the ears, the strength of the arms, the health of the whole body, the sturdiness of the whole body, and the eye-sight of the Kara fish, that lives beneath the waters, and can measure a rippling of the waters not thicker than a hair, in the Rangha, whose ends lie afar and whose depth is a thousand times the height of a man[1].

For her brightness and glory, I will offer unto her a sacrifice worth being heard . . . .

III.

8. We sacrifice to the most right *K*ista, made by Mazda and holy: we sacrifice to the good Law of the worshippers of Mazda . . . .

9. To whom Zarathustra did sacrifice for righteousness of thought, for righteousness of speech, for righteousness of deed, and for this boon,

10. That the most right *K*ista, made by Mazda and holy, would give him the swiftness of the feet, the quick hearing of the ears, the strength of the arms, the health of the whole body, the sturdiness of the whole body, and the eye-sight of the male horse, that, in the dark of the night, through the rain, the snow, the hail, or the sleet, from as far as nine districts, can perceive a horse's hair, mingled with the earth, and knows whether it is from the head or from the tail[2].

---

[1] Cf. Yt. XIV, 29. [2] Cf. Yt. XIV, 31.

For her brightness and glory, I will offer unto her a sacrifice worth being heard . . . .

IV.

11. We sacrifice to the most right *K*ista, made by Mazda and holy : we sacrifice to the good Law of the worshippers of Mazda . . . .

12. To whom Zarathu*s*tra did sacrifice for righteousness of thought, for righteousness of speech, for righteousness of deed, and for this boon,

13. That the most right *K*ista, made by Mazda and holy, would give him the swiftness of the feet, the quick hearing of the ears, the strength of the arms, the health of the whole body, the sturdiness of the whole body, and the eye-sight of the vulture with a golden collar, that, from as far as nine districts, can perceive a piece of flesh, not thicker than a fist, giving just as much light as a needle gives, as the point of a needle gives[1].

For her brightness and glory, I will offer unto her a sacrifice worth being heard . . . .

V.

14. We sacrifice to the most right *K*ista, made by Mazda and holy : we sacrifice to the good Law of the worshippers of Mazda . . . .

15. To whom the holy Hvôvi[2] did sacrifice with full knowledge, wishing that the holy Zarathu*s*tra would give her his good narcotic[3], that she might

---

[1] Cf. Yt. XIV, 33. [2] Zarathu*s*tra's wife.

[3] Bangha; the so-called Bang of Zoroaster (Vend. XV, 14 [44]; Phl. tr.). What must have been its virtue may be gathered from the legends of Gû*s*tâsp and Ardâ Vîrâf, who are said to have been transported in soul to the heavens, and to have had the higher

think according to the law, speak according to the law, and do according to the law.

For her brightness and glory, I will offer unto her a sacrifice worth being heard . . . .

VI.

16. We sacrifice to the most right *K*ista, made by Mazda and holy: we sacrifice to the good Law of the worshippers of Mazda . . . .

17. To whom the Âthravans, sent afar [1], did sacrifice [2], wishing a good memory to preach the law, and wishing strength for their own body.

For her brightness and glory, I will offer unto her a sacrifice worth being heard . . . .

VII.

18. We sacrifice to the most right *K*ista, made by Mazda and holy: we sacrifice to the good Law of the worshippers of Mazda . . . .

19. To whom the king of the country, the lord of the country does sacrifice, wishing peace for his country, wishing strength for his own body.

For her brightness and glory, I will offer unto her a sacrifice worth being heard . . . .

20. Yathâ ahû vairyô: The will of the Lord is the law of holiness . . . .

I bless the sacrifice and prayer, and the strength

---

mysteries revealed to them, on drinking from a cup prepared by the prophet (Zardu*s*t Nâmah), or from a cup of Gû*s*tâsp-bang (Ardâ Vîrâf, II, 29).

[1] The itinerant priests, the ancestors of the modern dervishes.

[2] Or better, do sacrifice; cf. Yt. XIV, 39.

and vigour of the most right *K*ista, made by Mazda and holy, and of the good Law of the worshippers of Mazda.

Ashem Vohû : Holiness is the best of all good . . . .

[Give] unto that man brightness and glory, ... give him long, long life, give him the bright, all-happy, blissful abode of the holy Ones.

XVII. ASHI YAST.

Ashi Vanguhi or 'the good Ashi[1]' is a feminine impersonation
of piety[2], and she is, at the same time, the source of all the good
and riches that are connected with piety[3]. She is described, therefore, as a goddess of Fortune and Wealth, and is invoked in company with Pârendi, the goddess of Treasures (Sîrôzah 25).

She appears in the latter character in the first part of the Yast
(§§ 1–14); she praises and loves Zarathustra (§§ 15–21). She is
worshipped by Haosyangha (§ 26), Yima (§ 28), Thraêtaona (§ 33),
Haoma (§ 37), Husravah (§ 41), Zarathustra (§ 45), and Vîstâspa
(§ 49)[4]. She rejects the offerings of all sterile people (old men,
courtezans, and children, §§ 53–61).

I.

1. We sacrifice to Ashi Vanguhi, who is shining,
high, tall-formed, well worthy of sacrifice, with a
loud-sounding chariot, strong, welfare-giving, healing,
with fulness of intellect[5], and powerful;

2. The daughter of Ahura Mazda, the sister of
the Amesha-Spentas, who endows all the Sao-

---

[1] In Parsi Ardisvang or Ard (Ardis from Artis, the Persian
form of Ashis); she presides over the 25th day of the month; cf.
Sîrôzah 25.

[2] Ashi is not the feminine adjective of Asha, as the i was
originally short (genitive ashôis, not ashyau); ashi is ar-ti, and
means bhakti, piety (Neriosengh).

[3] The so-called Ashi's remedies (ashôis baêshaza; cf. Yt.
XIII, 32).

[4] This enumeration is the same as in the Gôs Yast (§§ 3, 8, 14,
17, 21, 26, 29).

[5] Perethu-vîra; see Études Iraniennes, II, 183.

shya*nt*s [1] with the enlivening intelligence ; she also brings heavenly wisdom at her wish, and comes to help him who invokes her from near and him who invokes her from afar, and worships her with offerings of libations.

3 [2]. For her brightness and glory, I will offer her a sacrifice worth being heard ; I will offer up unto Ashi Vanguhi a good sacrifice with an offering of libations. We sacrifice unto Ashi Vanguhi with the libations ; with the Haoma and meat, with the baresma, with the wisdom of the tongue, with the holy spells, with the words, with the deeds, with the libations, and with the rightly-spoken words.

Yê*nh*ê hâtãm: All those beings of whom Ahura Mazda . . . .

II.

4. We sacrifice to Ashi Vanguhi, who is shining, high, tall-formed, well worthy of sacrifice, with a loud-sounding chariot, strong, welfare-giving, healing, with fulness of intellect, and powerful.

5. Homage unto Haoma, and unto the Mãthra [3], and unto the holy Zarathu*s*tra!

Homage unto Haoma, because all other drinks are attended with Aêshma [4], the fiend of the wounding spear: but the drinking of Haoma is attended with Asha and with Ashi Vanguhi herself [5].

6. Ashi is fair; Ashi is radiant with joy; she is far-piercing with her rays. Ashi gives good Glory

---

[1] The allies of Saoshya*nt*, who are to be active in the restoration of the world to eternal life (frashô-kereti). Cf. p. 165, note 1. Ashi gives them the 'intelligence of life' (frasha khratu), through which they will be enabled to perform their task.

[2] Cf. Yt. V, 10. [3] The Holy Word.

[4] The Daêva of anger.

[5] As drinking Haoma is an act of religion (cf. Yasna XI, 12 [31] seq.).

unto those men whom thou dost follow, O Ashi!
Full of perfumes is the house in which the good,
powerful Ashi Vanguhi puts her . . . . [1] feet, for long
friendship.

7. Those men whom thou dost attend, O Ashi!
are kings of kingdoms, that are rich in horses, with
large tributes, with snorting horses, sounding chariots,
flashing swords, rich in aliments and in stores of
food [2]; well-scented where the beds are spread and
full of all the other riches that may be wished for.
Happy the man whom thou dost attend! do thou
attend me, thou rich in all sorts of desirable things
and strong!

8. Those men whom thou dost attend, O Ashi Vanguhi! have houses that stand well laid up, rich in
cattle, foremost in Asha, and long-supported. Happy
the man whom thou dost attend! Do thou attend
me, thou rich in all sorts of desirable things and
strong!

9. The men whom thou dost attend, O Ashi Vanguhi! have beds that stand well-spread, well-adorned,
well-made, provided with cushions and with feet
inlaid with gold. Happy the man whom thou dost
attend! Do thou attend me, thou rich in all sorts
of desirable things and strong!

10. The men whom thou dost attend, O Ashi
Vanguhi! have their ladies that sit on their beds,
waiting for them : they lie on the cushions, adorning
themselves, ... [3], with square bored ear-rings and
a necklace of gold : 'When will our lord come?
when shall we enjoy in our bodies the joys of love?'

---

[1] ? Âgairimaitis.   [2] Cf. Yt. V, 130.
[3] ? Ankupasmanau.

Happy the man whom thou dost attend! Do thou attend me, thou rich in all sorts of desirable things and strong!

11. The men whom thou dost attend, O Ashi Vanguhi! have daughters that sit . . . .[1]; thin is their waist, beautiful is their body, long are their fingers; they are as fair of shape as those who look on can wish. Happy the man whom thou dost attend! Do thou attend me, thou rich in all sorts of desirable things and strong!

12. The men whom thou dost attend, O Ashi Vanguhi! have horses swift and loud-neighing; they drive the chariot lightly, they take it to the battle[2], they bear a gallant praiser (of the gods), who has many horses, a solid chariot, a sharp spear, a long spear, and swift arrows, who hits his aim, pursuing after his enemies, and smiting his foes. Happy the man whom thou dost attend! Do thou attend me, thou rich in all sorts of desirable things and strong!

13. The men whom thou dost attend, O Ashi Vanguhi! have large-humped, burden-bearing camels, flying from the ground or fighting with holy fieriness[3]. Happy the man whom thou dost attend! Do thou attend me, thou rich in all sorts of desirable things and strong!

14. The men whom thou dost attend, O Ashi Vanguhi! have hoards of silver and gold brought together from far distant regions; and garments of splendid make. Happy the man whom thou dost attend! Do thou attend me, thou rich in all sorts of desirable things and strong!

---

[1] ? Āgamô-paidhisa.   [2] Doubtful.   [3] Cf. Yt. XIV, 11.

15. Do not turn thy look from me! turn thy mercy towards me, O great Ashi! thou art well-made and of a noble seed [1]; thou art sovereign at thy wish; thou art Glory in a bodily form.

16. Thy father is Ahura Mazda, the greatest of all gods, the best of all gods; thy mother is Ârmaiti Spenta; thy brothers are Sraosha [2], a god of Asha, and Rashnu [3], tall and strong, and Mithra [4], the lord of wide pastures, who has ten thousand spies and a thousand ears; thy sister is the Law of the worshippers of Mazda.

17. Praised of the gods, unoffended by the righteous [5], the great Ashi Vanguhi stood up on her chariot, thus speaking: ' Who art thou who dost invoke me, whose voice is to my ear the sweetest of all that invoked me most?'

18. And he [6] said aloud: ' I am Spitama Zarathustra, who, first of mortals, recited the praise of the excellent Asha [7] and offered up sacrifice unto Ahura Mazda and the Amesha-Spentas; in whose birth and growth the waters and the plants rejoiced; in whose birth and growth the waters and the plants grew; in whose birth and growth all the creatures of the good creation cried out, Hail [8]!

19. ' In whose birth and growth Angra Mainyu rushed away from this wide, round earth, whose ends lie afar, and he, the evil-doing Angra Mainyu, who is all death, said: " All the gods together

---

[1] Born from the gods; cf. Yt. XXII, 9.
[2] See Yt. XI. [3] See Yt. XII.
[4] See Yt. X.
[5] Or, ' doing no harm to the righteous.'
[6] Zarathustra. [7] The Ahuna Vairya.
[8] Cf. Yt. XIII, 93.

have not been able to smite me down in spite of myself, and Zarathu*s*tra alone can reach me in spite of myself.

20. '"He smites me with the Ahuna Vairya, as strong a weapon as a stone big as a house[1]; he burns me with Asha-Vahi*s*ta, as if it were melting brass[2]. He makes it better for me that I should leave this earth, he, Spitama Zarathu*s*tra, the only one who can daunt me."'

21. And the great Ashi Vanguhi exclaimed: 'Come nearer unto me, thou pure, holy Spitama! lean against my chariot!'

Spitama Zarathu*s*tra came nearer unto her, he leant against her chariot.

22. And she caressed him with the left arm and the right, with the right arm and the left, thus speaking: ' Thou art beautiful, O Zarathu*s*tra! thou art well-shapen, O Spitama! strong are thy legs and long are thy arms : Glory is given to thy body and long cheerfulness[3] to thy soul, as sure as I proclaim it unto thee.'

III.

23[4]. We sacrifice to Ashi Vanguhi, who is shining, high, tall-formed, well worthy of sacrifice, with a loud-sounding chariot, strong, welfare-giving, healing, with fulness of intellect and powerful.

24[5]. To her did Haoshyangha, the Paradhâta, offer up a sacrifice, upon the enclosure of the Hara, the beautiful height, made by Mazda.

25. He begged of her a boon, saying : 'Grant

---

[1] Cf. Vend. XIX, 4 (13).
[2] Cf. Yt. III.
[3] Bliss after death.
[4] As § 1.
[5] For §§ 24–26, cf. Yt. IX, 3–6.

me this, O great Ashi Vanguhi! that I may overcome all the Daêvas of Mâzana; that I may never
fear and bow through terror before the Daêvas, but
that all the Daêvas may fear and bow in spite of
themselves before me, that they may fear and flee
down to darkness.'

26. The great Ashi Vanguhi ran and came to his
side: Haoshyangha, the Paradhâta, obtained that
boon.

For her brightness and glory, I will offer her a sacrifice . . . .

IV.

27. We sacrifice to Ashi Vanguhi, who is shining, high . . . .
and powerful.

28 [1]. To her did Yima Khshaêta, the good
shepherd, offer up a sacrifice from the height
Hukairya.

29. He begged of her a boon, saying: 'Grant me
this, O great Ashi Vanguhi! that I may bring fatness
and flocks down to the world created by Mazda; that
I may bring immortality down to the world created
by Mazda;

30. 'That I may take away both hunger and
thirst, from the world created by Mazda; that I
may take away both old age and death, from the
world created by Mazda; that I may take away both
hot wind and cold wind, from the world created by
Mazda, for a thousand years.'

31. The great Ashi Vanguhi ran and came to his
side: Yima Khshaêta, the good shepherd, obtained
that boon.

For her brightness and glory, I will offer her a sacrifice . . . .

---

[1] For §§ 28-31, cf. Yt. IX, 8-11.

V.

32. We sacrifice to Ashi Vanguhi, who is shining, high . . . . and powerful.

33 [1]. To her did Thraêtaona, the heir of the valiant Âthwya clan, offer up a sacrifice in the four-cornered Varena.

34. He begged of her a boon, saying : 'Grant me this, O great Ashi Vanguhi! that I may overcome A*z*i Dahâka, the three-mouthed, the three-headed, the six-eyed, who has a thousand senses, that most powerful, fiendish Dru*g*, that demon, baleful to the world, the strongest Dru*g* that Angra Mainyu created against the material world, to destroy the world of the good principle ; and that I may deliver his two wives, Savanghavâ*k* and Erenavâ*k*, who are the fairest of body amongst women, and the most wonderful creatures in the world.'

35. The great Ashi Vanguhi ran and came to his side. Thraêtaona, the heir of the valiant Âthwya clan, obtained that boon.

For her brightness and glory, I will offer her a sacrifice . . . .

VI.

36. We sacrifice to Ashi Vanguhi, who is shining, high . . . . and powerful.

37 [2]. To her did Haoma offer up a sacrifice, Haoma, the enlivening, the healing, the beautiful, the lordly, with golden eyes, upon the highest height of the Haraiti Bareza.

---

[1] Cf. Yt. V, 34 ; IX, 14 ; XV, 24.
[2] For §§ 37–39, cf. Yt. IX, 17–19.

38. He begged of her a boon, saying : 'Grant me this, O great Ashi Vanguhi! that I may bind the Turanian murderer, Franghrasyan, that I may drag him bound, that I may bring him bound unto king Husravah, that king Husravah may kill him, behind the *K*aê*k*asta lake, the deep lake of salt waters, to avenge the murder of his father Syâvarshâna, a man, and of Aghraêratha, a semi-man.'

39. The great Ashi Vanguhi ran and came to his side. Haoma, the enlivening, the healing, the beautiful, the lordly, with golden eyes, obtained that boon.

For her brightness and glory, I will offer her a sacrifice . . . .

VII.

40. We sacrifice to Ashi Vanguhi, who is shining, high . . . . and powerful.

41 [1]. To her did the gallant Husravah, he who united the Aryan nations into one kingdom, offer up a sacrifice, behind the *K*aê*k*asta lake, the deep lake of salt waters.

42. He begged of her a boon, saying : 'Grant me this, O great Ashi Vanguhi! that I may kill the Turanian murderer, Franghrasyan, behind the *K*aê*k*asta lake, the deep lake of salt waters, to avenge the murder of my father Syâvarshâna, a man, and of ·Aghraêratha, a semi-man.'

43. The great Ashi Vanguhi ran and came to his side. The gallant Husravah, he who united the Aryan nations into one kingdom, obtained that boon.

For her brightness and glory, I will offer her a sacrifice worth being heard . . . .

---

[1] For §§ 41–43, cf. Yt. IX, 21–23.

VIII.

44. We sacrifice to Ashi Vanguhi, who is shining, high . . . . and powerful.

45 [1]. To her did the holy Zarathustra offer up a sacrifice in the Airyana Vaêgah, by the good river Dâitya, with the Haoma and meat, with the baresma, with the wisdom of the tongue, with the holy spells, with the speech, with the deeds, with the libations, and with the rightly-spoken words.

46. He begged of her a boon, saying: 'Grant me this, O great Ashi Vanguhi! that I may bring the good and noble Hutaosa to think according to the law, to speak according to the law, to do according to the law, that she may spread my law and make it known, that she may bestow beautiful praises upon my deeds.'

47. The great Ashi Vanguhi ran and came to his side: the holy Zarathustra obtained that boon.

For her brightness and glory, I will offer her a sacrifice worth being heard . . . .

IX.

48. We sacrifice to Ashi Vanguhi, who is shining, high . . . . and powerful.

49. To her did the tall Kavi Vîstâspa offer up a sacrifice behind the waters of the river Dâitya.

50. He begged of her a boon, saying: 'Grant me this, O great Ashi Vanguhi! that I may put to flight Asta-aurvant, the son of Vîspô-thaurvô-asti, the all-afflicting, of the brazen helmet, of the brazen armour, of the thick neck, behind whom seven

---

[1] For §§ 45-47, cf. Yt. IX, 25-27.

hundred camels . . . . ; that I may put to flight the
Hvyaona murderer, Aregat-aspa; that I may put to
flight Darsinika, the worshipper of the Daêvas;

51. 'And that I may smite Tãthravant of the bad
law; that I may smite Spingauruska, the worshipper
of the Daêvas; and that I may bring unto the good
law the nations of the Varedhakas and of the
Hvyaonas; and that I may smite of the Hvyaona
nations their fifties and their hundreds, their hundreds and their thousands, their thousands and their
tens of thousands, their tens of thousands and their
myriads of myriads.'

52. The great Ashi Vanguhi ran and came to his
side : the tall Kavi Vîstâspa obtained that boon.

For her brightness and glory, I will offer her a sacrifice worth
being heard . . . .

X.

53. We sacrifice to Ashi Vanguhi, who is shining, high . . . .
and powerful.

54. And the great Ashi Vanguhi said : ' None of
those libations will be accepted by me, which are
sent to me either by a man whose seed is dried out[1],
or by the courtezan who produces untimely issues[2],
or by young boys, or by girls who have known no
man[3].

'When the Turanians and the swift-horsed Naotaras[4], clapping their hands, ran after me,

---

[1] See Vend. III, 20 [63], note.
[2] By procuring abortion.
[3] She refuses the offerings of all barren beings.
[4] Cf. Yt. V, 98. The following clauses allude to some myth of
Ashi Vanguhi connected with the conflict between the Turanians
and the Naotaras (either Tusa and Vistauru; cf. p. 71, note 7, or
more likely Vîstâspa himself, to whom the preceding chapter

55. 'I hid myself under the foot of a bull walking under his burden; then young boys, and girls who had known no man, discovered me, even while the Turanians and the swift-horsed Naotaras, clapping their hands, were running after me.

56. 'Even I hid myself under the throat of a ram of hundredfold energy : then again young boys, and girls who had known no man, discovered me, even while the Turanians and the swift-horsed Naotaras, clapping their hands, were running after me.'

57. The first wailing of the great Ashi Vanguhi is her wailing about the courtezan who destroys her fruit : 'Stand thou not near her, sit thou not on her bed!'—'What shall I do? Shall I go back to the heavens? Shall I sink into the earth?'

58. The second wailing of the great Ashi Vanguhi is her wailing about the courtezan who brings forth a child conceived of a stranger and presents it to her husband : 'What shall I do? Shall I go back to the heavens? Shall I sink into the earth?'

59. This is the third wailing of the great Ashi Vanguhi : 'This is the worst deed that men and tyrants do, namely, when they deprive maids, that have been barren for a long time, of marrying and bringing forth children. What shall I do? Shall I go back to the heavens? Shall I sink into the earth?'

60. Ahura Mazda answered : 'O fair and wise Ashi, go not back to the heavens, sink not into the

---

[§§ 48–52] and the last but one clause of the Yast refer). She tried to flee in the way practised by Ulysses in the Cyclops' cavern; both parties were pursuing the animal that bore her, though they knew not what it bore, till children discovered her.

earth! Stay here and walk inside the fine kingly palace.'

61. I shall worship thee with such a sacrifice, I shall worship and forward thee with such a sacrifice as Vîstâspa offered unto thee, behind the river Dâitya[1]. The Zoatar lifted up a loud voice, with baresma before him. With that sort of sacrifice shall I worship thee? With that sort of sacrifice shall I worship and forward thee, O fair and wise Ashi?

For her brightness and glory, I will offer her a sacrifice worth being heard . . . .

62. Yathâ ahû vairyô: The will of the Lord is the law of holiness . . . .

I bless the sacrifice and prayer, and the strength and vigour of Ashi Vanguhi; of the good Kisti; of the good Erethe; of the good Rasâstât; of the Glory and Weal, made by Mazda[2].

Ashem Vohû: Holiness is the best of all good . . . .

[Give] unto that man brightness and glory, give him health of body, ... give him the bright, all-happy, blissful abode of the holy Ones.

---

[1] Cf. §§ 49 seq.   [2] Cf. Sîrôzah, § 25.

XVIII. ÂSTÂD YAST.

Arstât is Truthfulness: she is invoked in company with the Genius of Truth, Rashnu Razista (Sîrôzah, § 18), on the day Rashn. On the day especially dedicated to her, the 26th day of the month, she is invoked in company with Mount Ushi-darena, which accounts for the singular fact that her Yast is wholly devoted to the Hvarenô, and thus is hardly distinguishable from the Zamyâd Yast, as Mount Ushi-darena is the actual seat of the Hvarenô (Yt. I, 31, text and note; cf. Yt. XIX, 66). Whence comes this particular connection of Arstât with Mount Ushi-darena is uncertain, unless it alludes to the fact that the possession of the Hvarenô can be secured only through truthfulness: as soon as Yima 'began to find delight in words of falsehood and untruth,' the Hvarenô flew away from him (Yt. XIX, 34).

0. May Ahura Mazda be rejoiced ! . . . .
Ashem Vohû : Holiness is the best of all good . . . .
I confess myself a worshipper of Mazda, a follower of Zarathustra, one who hates the Daêvas and obeys the laws of Ahura ;
For sacrifice, prayer, propitiation, and glorification unto [Hâvani], the holy and master of holiness . . . .

Unto the Glory of the Aryans, made by Mazda,

Be propitiation, with sacrifice, prayer, propitiation, and glorification.

Yathâ ahû vairyô ; The will of the Lord is the law of holiness . . . .

1. Ahura Mazda spake unto Spitama Zarathustra, saying : ' I made the Aryan Glory, rich in food, rich in flocks, rich in wealth [1], rich in Glory ; provided with full store of intelligence, with full store of money, to withstand Need, and to withstand enemies.

---

[1] As it gives food, flocks, and wealth to those who get possessed of it.

2. 'It destroys Angra Mainyu, who is all death :
it destroys Aêshma, the fiend of the wounding spear [1];
it destroys the yellow Bûshyãsta [2] ; it destroys the
contagion [3] of Aêkha [4] ; it destroys the fiend of death,
Apaosha [5] ; it destroys the non-Aryan nations.

3. 'And I made the great Ashi Vanguhi; she
comes in, amid the family; she comes in, inside the
fine royal palace [6].

4. 'Let Ashi, with fulness of welfare, follow the
man who gladdens the faithful with his gifts [7] ! she
comes in, inside his family; she comes in, inside his
fine royal palace.

'With all sorts of flocks, with all victory, with all
intelligence, with all Glory, the great Ashi Vanguhi
puts one foot [8] inside his family; she comes in, inside
his fine royal palace.

5. 'Horses multiply a thousandfold, flocks multiply a thousandfold ; and so does his virtuous offspring, (as) the bright, glorious star Tistrya moves
on equally [9], and so does the strong wind made by
Mazda, and so does the Glory of the Aryas.

6. 'And they bring increase on the tops of all
mountains, down the depths of all vales ; they bring
increase to all the growing plants [10], the fair, the
golden-hued. And they bring (away) [11] the contagion

---

[1] See Vendîdâd, Introd. IV, 22.

[2] Ibid. Introd. IV, 24.   [3] Doubtful.

[4] ? A daêva or a disease.   [5] See Yt. VIII, 22.

[6] See Yt. XVII.

[7] Who gives alms to the poor Mazdayasnians.

[8] Even one foot (?), when she stays not there 'for long friendship' (Yt. XVII, 6).

[9] So that the rain falls in due time (Yt. VIII, 11).

[10] Cf. Yt. VIII, 29.   [11] Cf. § 2.

of Aêkha, they bring (away) the fiend of death, Apaosha.

7. 'Hail to the bright and glorious star Tistrya! Hail to the strong wind, made by Mazda! Hail to the Glory of the Aryas!

'Yathâ ahû vairyô: The will of the Lord is the law of holiness . . . .

'Ashem Vohû: Holiness is the best of all good . . . .

8. 'We worship the Ahuna Vairya.

'We worship Asha-Vahista, the fairest Amesha Spenta.

'We worship the rightly-spoken Words[1], fiend-smiting and healing.

'We worship the healing, well-spoken Words, the fiend-smiting.

'We worship the Mãthra Spenta and the Law of Mazda, and (piety) that delights in Haoma[2].

'We worship the Glory of the Aryas.

'Yênhê hâtãm: All those beings of whom Ahura Mazda . . . .

9. 'Yathâ ahû vairyô: The will of the Lord is the law of holiness . . . .

'I bless the sacrifice and prayer, and the strength and vigour of the Glory of the Aryas, made by Mazda.

'Ashem Vohû: Holiness is the best of all good . . . .

'[Give] unto that man[3] brightness and glory, ... give him the bright, all-happy, blissful abode of the holy Ones.'

---

[1] Arshukhdha vakô, the words conformable to the rites.

[2] Haomakinem; see Études Iraniennes, II, 148.

[3] Who shall have sacrificed to the Aryan Glory.

XIX. ZAMYÂD YAST.

This Yast, inscribed to the Genius of the Earth, is devoted to a description of the mountains and the kingly Glory (kavaêm *Hv*arenô), which are invoked, together with the Earth, in the corresponding formula of the Sîrôzah (§ 28) : there is no Yast devoted to the Earth itself.

The mountains are simply enumerated (§§ 1–8). The rest of the Yast is devoted to the praise of the *Hv*arenô, or, more precisely, to that of those who possessed it, whose powers or feats are described. The list begins with Ahura Mazda (§ 10), and closes with Saoshya*nt* (§ 89) ; that is to say, it begins with the beginning of the world, and closes with its end. It includes the Amesha-Spe*n*tas (§ 15), Haoshyangha (§ 26), Takhma Urupa (§ 28), Yima (§ 31), Mithra (§ 35), Thraêtaona (§ 36), Keresâspa (§ 38), the kings of the Kaianyan dynasty (§§ 66–72), Kavi Husravah (§ 74), Zarathustra (§ 79), Vîstâspa (§ 84). The unsuccessful efforts of Franghrasyan to take possession of it are described at length (§§ 56–64).

This Yast would serve as a short history of the Iranian monarchy, an abridged Shâh Nâmah.

0. May Ahura Mazda be rejoiced ! ....

Ashem Vohû : Holiness is the best of all good ....

I confess myself a worshipper of Mazda, a follower of Zarathustra, one who hates the Daêvas and obeys the laws of Ahura ;

For sacrifice, prayer, propitiation, and glorification unto [Hâvani], the holy and master of holiness ....

Unto Mount Ushi-darena, made by Mazda, the seat of holy happiness ; unto the kingly Glory, made by Mazda ; unto that Glory that cannot be forcibly seized, made by Mazda [1],

---

[1] Sîrôzah I, 28.

Be propitiation, with sacrifice, prayer, propitiation, and glorification.

Yathâ ahû vairyô: The will of the Lord is the law of holiness . . . .

I.

1. The first mountain that rose up out of the earth, O Spitama Zarathustra! was the Haraiti Barez [1]. That mountain stretches all along the shores of the land washed by waters [2] towards the east.

The second mountain was Mount Zeredhô, outside [3] Mount Manusha [4]: this mountain too stretches all along the shores of the land washed by waters towards the east.

2. From there grew up Mount Ushi-dhau Ushi-darena [5], Mount Erezifya [6], and Mount Fraorepa.

The sixth was Mount Erezura [7].

The seventh was Mount Bumya [8].

The eighth was Mount Raoidhita [9].

---

[1] The same as the Hara Berezaiti, the later Albôrz; see p. 58, note 3.

[2] The Caspian sea.

[3] Doubtful: pârentarem aredhô; possibly beyond.

[4] According to the Bundahis, Manusha is another name of Mount Zeredhô (XII, 2). It is the mountain on which Mânûskîhar was born (ibid. 10).

[5] 'The mountain that gives understanding, that preserves understanding,' the later Mount Ôsdâstâr; see p. 33, note 1.

[6] See p. 65, note 2.

[7] Mount Arzûr 'is a summit at the gate of hell' (Bundahis XII, 8; cf. Vend. III, 7 (23); XIX, 140).

[8] The Arzûr Bûm of Bundahis XII, 2, which 'is in the direction of Arûm' (Asia Minor, Bundahis XII, 16).

[9] The Rôyisn-ômand mountain of Bundahis XII, 27; its name

The ninth was Mount Mazi*si*s*v*au.
The tenth was Mount A*n*tare-danghu.
The eleventh was Mount Erezisha.
The twelfth was Mount Vâiti-gaêsa¹.

3. And Mount Âdarana, Mount Bayana, Mount
I*s*kata Upairi-saêna², with the . . . .³ snows;
the two Hama*n*kuna mountains, the eight Vasna
mountains, the eight powerful Frâva*n*ku, the four
Vidhvana summits;

4. Mount Aêzakha, Mount Maênakha, Mount
Vâkhedrakaê, Mount Asaya, Mount Tudhaskaê,
Mount I*s*avaê, Mount Draoshi*s*v*a*u, Mount Sâi-
riv*a*u, Mount Nanghu*s*m*a*u, Mount Kakahyu,
Mount A*n*tare-Kangha⁴;

5. Mount Si*k*idava⁵, Mount Ahuna, Mount
Raêmana, Mount Asha-stembana, Mount Uru-
nyô-vâidhkaê, Mount Âsnava*nt*⁶, Mount Usha-
oma, Mount U*s*ta-*h*v*a*renah, Mount Syâmaka⁷,
Mount Vafray*a*u, Mount Vourusha;

---

means 'the mountain on which vegetation has grown' (ibid. tr.
West).

¹ The Bâdghês mountain near Herât, بادغيس.

² Or 'Mount I*s*kata ("rugged"), belonging to the Upairi-saêna
ridge.' The Upairi-saêna ridge or Aparsên ridge is 'the mountain of Persia, and its beginning is in Seistân and its end in
Susiana' (Bund. XII, 9).

³ ? Kãsô-tafedhra; possibly the name of a mountain; Mount
Kãsô-tafedhra Vafra.

⁴ See p. 67, note 4.

⁵ 'Si*k*idâv, a mountain among those which are in Kangde*z*'
(Bund. XII, 2, tr. West).

⁶ See p. 7, note 5.

⁷ The Mount Siyâk-ômand ('the black mountain') and Mount
Vafar-ômand ('the snowy mountain') of Bundahi*s* XII, 22,
which are said to have grown out of the Apârsên ridge and to
extend towards China.

6. Amongst which stand Mount *G*atara, Mount Adhutav*a*u, Mount Spitavarena, Mount Spe*n*tô-dâta[1], Mount Kadrva-aspa[2], Mount Kaoirisa[3], Mount Taêra[4], Mount Barô-srayana, Mount Ba-rana, Mount Frâpay*a*u, Mount Udrya, and Mount Raêva*nt*[5], and all those heights to which men have given the name of mount,

7. To the number of two thousand mountains, and two hundred and forty and four[6], O Spitama Zarathustra!

8. For its brightness and glory, I will offer it a sacrifice worth being heard, namely, unto the awful kingly Glory. Unto the awful kingly Glory we offer up the libations, the Haoma and meat, the baresma, the wisdom of the tongue, the holy spells, the speech, the deeds, the libations, and the rightly-spoken words[7].

Yê*n*hê hâtãm: All those beings of whom Ahura Mazda[7] . . . .

II.

9. We sacrifice unto the awful kingly Glory, made by Mazda; most conquering, highly working, that possesses health, wisdom, and happiness, and is more powerful to destroy than all other creatures;

---

[1] The Spendyâd mountain, near Mount Rêvand (Bundahi*s* XII, 23).

[2] The Kôndrâsp mountain, by the town of Tûs (in Khorasan, Bund. XII, 24).

[3] The Kôîrâs mountain in Îrân-Vê*g* (Bund. XII, 25).

[4] Cf. Yt. XV, 7, and p. 58, note 2.

[5] See p. 8, notes 1 and 2.

[6] 'The other mountains have grown out of Albûrz, in number 2244 mountains' (Bund. XII, 2).

[7] See notes to Yt. III, 17 (p. 47).

10. That belongs to Ahura Mazda, as (through it)
Ahura Mazda made the creatures, many and good,
many and fair, many and wonderful, many and prosperous, many and bright;

11 [1]. So that they may restore the world, which
will (thenceforth) never grow old and never die,
never decaying and never rotting, ever living and
ever increasing, and master of its wish, when the
dead will rise, when life and immortality will come,
and the world will be restored at its wish;

12. When the creation will grow deathless,—the
prosperous creation of the Good Spirit,—and the
Drug shall perish, though she may rush on every
side to kill the holy beings; she and her hundredfold brood shall perish, as it is the will of the
Lord [2].

13. For its brightness and glory, I will offer it a sacrifice . . . .

III.

14. We sacrifice unto the awful kingly Glory, made by
Mazda . . . . [3]

15 [4]. That belongs to the Amesha-Spentas, the
bright ones, whose looks perform their wish, tall,
quickly coming to do, strong, lordly, who are undecaying and holy;

16. Who are all seven of one thought, who are all
seven of one speech, who are all seven of one deed;
whose thought is the same, whose speech is the
same, whose deed is the same, whose father and
commander is the same, namely, the Maker, Ahura
Mazda.

---

[1] §§ 11–12 = §§ 19–20, 23–24, 89–90.   [2] Doubtful.
[3] As above, § 9.   [4] §§ 15–17 = Yt. XIII, 82–84.

17. Who see one another's soul thinking of good thoughts, thinking of good words, thinking of good deeds, thinking of Garô-nmâna, and whose ways are shining as they go down to the libations;

18. Who are the makers and governors, the shapers and overseers, the keepers and preservers of these creations of Ahura Mazda.

19[1]. It is they who shall restore the world, which will (thenceforth) never grow old and never die, never decaying and never rotting, ever living and ever increasing, and master of its wish, when the dead will rise, when life and immortality will come, and the world will be restored at its wish;

20. When the creation will grow deathless,—the prosperous creation of the Good Spirit,—and the Drug shall perish, though she may rush on every side to kill the holy beings; she and her hundred-fold brood shall perish, as it is the will of the Lord.

For its brightness and glory, I will offer it a sacrifice . . . .

IV.

21. We sacrifice unto the awful kingly Glory, made by Mazda . . . .

22. That belongs to the gods in the heavens and to those in the material world, and to the blessed ones, born or not yet born, who are to perform the restoration of the world[2].

23[3]. It is they who shall restore the world, which will (thenceforth) never grow old and never die, never decaying and never rotting, ever living and

---

[1] §§ 19–20=§§ 11–12.

[2] The Saoshya*nt*s; see p. 165, note 1.

[3] §§ 23–24=§§ 19–20.

ever increasing, and master of its wish, when the
dead will rise, when life and immortality will come,
and the world will be restored at its wish ;

24. When the creation will grow deathless,—the
prosperous creation of the Good Spirit,—and the
Dru*g* shall perish, though she may rush on every
side to kill the holy beings ; she and her hundredfold brood shall perish, as it is the will of the Lord.

For its brightness and glory, I will offer it a sacrifice . . . .

V.

25. We sacrifice unto the awful kingly Glory, made by
Mazda . . . .

26. That clave unto Haoshyangha, the Paradhâta,
for a long time[1], when he ruled over the seven
Karshvares of the earth, over the Daêvas and men,
over the Yâtus and the Pairikas, over the oppressors,
the blind, and the deaf· he who smote two-thirds of
the Daêvas of Mâzana and of the Varenya fiends[2].

For its brightness and glory, I will offer it a sacrifice . . . .

VI.

27. We sacrifice unto the awful kingly Glory, made by
Mazda . . . .

28. That clave unto Takhma Urupa, the well-
armed, while he ruled over the seven Karshvares of
the earth, over the Daêvas and men, the Yâtus and
Pairikas, the oppressors, the blind, and the deaf;

29. When he conquered all Daêvas and men, all
the Yâtus and Pairikas, and rode Angra Mainyu,

---

[1] For forty years, according to the Bundahi*s* (XXXIV, 4); for
thirty years, according to Firdausi.

[2] See Yt. V, 22.

turned into the shape of a horse, all around the earth from one end to the other, for thirty years [1].

For its brightness and glory, I will offer it a sacrifice . . . .

VII.

30. We sacrifice unto the awful kingly Glory, made by Mazda . . . .

31. That clave unto the bright Yima, the good shepherd, for a long time [2], while he ruled over the seven Karshvares of the earth, over the Daêvas and men, the Yâtus and Pairikas, the oppressors, the blind, and the deaf;

32. He who took from the Daêvas both riches and welfare, both fatness and flocks, both weal and Glory [3];

In whose reign both aliments [4] were never failing for feeding creatures, flocks and men were undying, waters and plants were undrying;

33. In whose reign there was neither cold wind nor hot wind, neither old age nor death, nor envy made by the Daêvas [5], in the times before his lie, before he began to have delight in words of falsehood and untruth.

34. But when he began to find delight in words of falsehood and untruth [6], the Glory was seen to flee away from him in the shape of a bird. When his Glory had disappeared, then the great [7] Yima

---

[1] Cf. Yt. XV, 12, and notes.

[2] For six hundred and sixteen years and six months (Bundahis XXXIV, 4).

[3] See Yt. V, 26, text and note.

[4] Food and drink.　　　　　　[5] Cf. Yt. XV, 16.

[6] He pretended to be a god (Firdausi).

[7] Doubtful: fraêsta.

Khshaêta the good shepherd, trembled and was in sorrow before his foes[1]; he was confounded, and laid him down on the ground.

35. The first time[2] when the Glory departed from the bright Yima, the Glory went from Yima, the son of Vîvangha*nt*, in the shape of a Vâraghna bird[3]. Then Mithra seized that Glory, Mithra, the lord of wide pastures, whose ear is quick to hear, who has a thousand senses. We sacrifice unto Mithra, the lord of all countries, whom Ahura Mazda has created the most glorious of all the gods in the heavens.

36. The second time when the Glory departed from the bright Yima, the Glory went from Yima, the son of Vîvangha*nt*, in the shape of a Vâraghna bird.

Then Thraêtaona seized that Glory, he, the heir of the valiant Âthwya clan, who was the most victorious of all victorious men next to Zarathu*s*tra;

37. Who smote A*z*i Dahâka, the three-mouthed, the three-headed, the six-eyed, who had a thousand senses, that most powerful, fiendish Dru*g*, that demon baleful to the world, the strongest Dru*g* that Angra Mainyu created against the material world, to destroy the world of the good principle[4].

---

[1] A*z*i Dahâka and his followers.

[2] The Glory is described as departing three times, because it is threefold, according as it belongs to the king considered as a priest, a warrior, or a husbandman. In that threefold character it is identical with Âdar Frobâ, Âdar Gushasp, and Âdar Bûrzîn Mihr (p. 7, notes).

[3] A raven, one of the incarnations of the Genius of Victory (Yt. XIV, 18–21; cf. ibid. § 35).

[4] Cf. Yt. V, 34.

38. The third time when the Glory departed from the bright Yima, that Glory went from Yima, the son of Vîvanghant, in the shape of a Vâraghna bird.

Then the manly-hearted Keresâspa [1] seized that Glory; he who was the sturdiest of the men of strength, next to Zarathustra, for his manly courage.

39. For Manly Courage clave unto him. We worship Manly Courage, firm of foot, unsleeping, quick to rise, and fully awake, that clave unto Keresâspa;

40. Who killed the snake Srvara, the horse-devouring, men-devouring, yellow, poisonous snake, over which yellow poison flowed a thumb's breadth thick. Upon him Keresâspa was cooking his food in a brass vessel: at the time of noon, the fiend felt the heat, and stood upon his feet: he rushed from under the brass vessel and upset the boiling water: the manly-hearted Keresâspa fell back affrighted [2];

41. Who killed the golden-heeled Gandarewa, that was rushing with open jaws, eager to destroy the living world of the good principle [3];

Who killed the brood of Pathana, all the nine [4];

[1] See V, 37 (pp. 62–63, and notes); XIII, 136; XV, 27.

[2] Cf. Yasna IX, 11 (34–39). This tale belongs to the wide-spread cyclus of the island-whale (a whale whose back is mistaken by sailors for an island; they land upon it, cook their food there, and the monster, awaked by the heat, flies off and carries them away: see Arabian Nights, Seventy-first Night; Babâ Bathrâ, 5).

[3] See Yt. V, 38.

[4] Known in the Minokhired (XXVII, 50) as 'the wolf Kapôd' (perhaps 'the blue wolf,' as Mr. West suggests), 'which they also call Pehan.' Those nine sons of Pathana were nine highwaymen (the very word Pathana seems to have that meaning): their defeat is told by Keresâspa in a Pahlavi Rivâyat as follows: 'I have slain the highwaymen who were so big in body that, when they were

and the brood of Nivika, and the brood of Dâsta-
yana;

Who killed the golden-crowned Hitâspa[1], and
Vareshava, the son of Dâna[2], and Pitaona, attended
by many Pairikas[3];

42. Who killed Arezô-shamana, him of the manly
courage, who was strong, well-beloved[4], hail, energe-
tically rushing, fully awake, never falling back....[5];

43. Who killed Snâvidhaka, him who killed with
his nails, the stone-handed: thus did he exclaim to
all around: ' I am an infant still, I am not yet of
age: if I ever grow of age, I shall make the earth a
wheel, I shall make the heavens a chariot;

44. ' I shall bring down the Good Spirit from the
shining Garô-nmâna; I shall make the Evil Spirit
rush up from the dreary Hell. They will carry my

---

walking, people considered in this way, that "below them are the
stars and moon, and below them moves the sun at dawn, and the
water of the sea reaches up to their knees." And I reached up to
their legs, and they were smitten on the legs by me; they fell, and
the hills on the earth were shattered by them' (West, Pahlavi
Texts, II, 376). Keresâspa's Fravashi, accordingly, is invoked
against thieves (Yt. XIII, 136). Perhaps the assimilation of the
wolf Kapôd with Pehan is merely a guess of the author of the
Minokhired.

[1] The murderer of Keresâspa's brother, Urvâkhshaya (Yt.
XV, 28).

[2] Doubtful: dânayana. Vâresha is the Pahlavi name of a
bird of prey (Bund. XIV, 30), which might induce us to identify
Vareshava with the gigantic bird Kamak, 'which overshadowed
the earth and kept off the rain till the rivers dried up' (West, l.l.
378), and whose destruction was one of the feats of Keresâspa.

[3] Like the Pairika Knãthaiti, who clave to Keresâspa (Vend. I,
10 [36]).

[4] Doubtful: frâzustem.

[5] The rest of the sentence is obscure, and the text seems to be
corrupt.

chariot, both the Good Spirit and the Evil One, unless the manly-hearted Keresâspa kill me.'

The manly-hearted Keresâspa killed him, his life went away, his spirit vanished [1].

For its brightness and glory, I will offer it a sacrifice . . . .

VIII.

45. We sacrifice unto the awful Glory, that cannot be forcibly seized [2], made by Mazda . . . .

46. For which the Good Spirit and the Evil One did struggle with one another [3]: for that Glory that cannot be forcibly seized [2] they flung each of them their darts most swift.

The Good Spirit flung a dart, and so did Vohu-Manô, and Asha-Vahista and Âtar, the son of Ahura Mazda.

The Evil Spirit flung a dart, and so did Akem-Manô [4], and Aêshma of the wounding spear, and Azi Dahâka and Spityura, he who sawed Yima in twain [5].

---

[1] Snâvidhaka reminds one vividly of the Titanic Otus and Ephialtes (Odyssea XI, 308):

    'Such were they youths! Had they to manhood grown,
    Almighty Jove had trembled on his throne:
    But ere the harvest of the beard began
    To bristle on the chin, and promise man,
    His shafts Apollo aim'd.' (Pope.)

[2] The sacerdotal Glory; see p. 11, note 6, cf. § 53.

[3] When it had departed from Yima.

[4] Bad Thought, the demoniac counterpart of Vohu-Manô (Vend. Introd. IV, 34).

[5] Spityura was a brother of Yima's (Bund. XXXI, 3: 'Spîtûr was he who, with Dahâk, cut up Yim,' ibid. 5, tr. West). Nothing more is known of him, though he appears to have played a great part in the original Yima legend, and to have stood to his brother in the same relation as Barmâyûn and Katâyûn to Feridûn, or

47. Then forward came Âtar [1], the son of Ahura Mazda, thinking thus in his heart: 'I want to seize that Glory that cannot be forcibly seized.'

But Azi Dahâka, the three-mouthed, he of the evil law, rushed on his back, thinking of extinguishing it:

48. 'Here give it up to me [2], O Âtar, son of Ahura Mazda: if thou seizest that Glory that cannot be forcibly seized, I shall rush upon thee, so that thou mayest never more blaze on the earth made by Ahura and protect the world of the good principle.'

And Âtar took back his hands, as the instinct of life prevailed, so much had Azi affrighted him.

49. Then Azi, the three-mouthed, he of the evil law, rushed forward, thinking thus in his heart: 'I want to seize that Glory that cannot be forcibly seized.'

But Âtar, the son of Ahura Mazda, advanced behind him, speaking in these words:

50. 'There give it up to me [2], thou three-mouthed Azi Dahâka. If thou seizest that Glory that cannot be forcibly seized, then I will enter thy hinder part, I will blaze up in thy jaws, so that thou mayest never more rush upon the earth made by Mazda and destroy the world of the good principle.'

Then Azi took back his hands, as the instinct of life prevailed, so much had Âtar affrighted him.

51. That Glory swells up and goes to the sea

Shagâd to Rustam. Firdausi does not mention him, and makes Dahâk himself saw Gemshîd.

[1] Âdar Frobâ (the Glory of the Priest) is meant here: 'when they sawed Yim, Âdar Frobâ saved his Glory from the hand of Dahâk' (Bund. XVII, 5; Études Iraniennes, II, 70, 84).

[2] Doubtful.

Vouru-Kasha. The swift-horsed Son of the Waters [1] seizes it at once: this is the wish of the Son of the Waters, the swift-horsed: 'I want to seize that Glory that cannot be forcibly seized, down to the bottom of the sea Vouru-Kasha, in the bottom of the deep rivers.'

52. We sacrifice unto the Son of the Waters, the swift-horsed, the tall and shining lord, the lord of females; the male god, who helps one at his appeal; who made man, who shaped man [2], a god who lives beneath waters, and whose ear is the quickest to hear when he is worshipped.

53. 'And whosoever of you, O men,'—thus said Ahura Mazda,—'O holy Zarathustra! shall seize that Glory that cannot be forcibly seized, he has the gifts [3] of an Âthravan [4]; whosoever shall long for the illumination of knowledge, he has the gifts of an Âthravan; whosoever shall long for fulness of knowledge, he has the gifts of an Âthravan;

54. 'And Riches will cleave unto him, giving him full welfare, holding a shield before him, powerful, rich of cattle and garments; and Victory will cleave unto him, day after day; and likewise Strength, that smites more than a year. Attended by that Victory, he will conquer the havocking hordes; attended by that Victory, he will conquer all those who hate him.'

For its brightness and glory, I will offer it a sacrifice . . . .

---

[1] Apãm Napâ*t*; see p. 6, note 1.

[2] An allusion to old myths on the igneous origin of life (Ormazd et Ahriman, § 78).

[3] Doubtful.

[4] As that Glory is the one that belongs to the Âthravan.

IX.

55. We sacrifice unto the awful Glory, that cannot be forcibly seized, made by Mazda . . . .

56. Which the Turanian ruffian Frangrasyan tried to seize in the sea Vouru-Kasha. He stripped himself naked, wishing to seize that Glory that belongs to the Aryan nations, born and unborn, and to the holy Zarathustra[1]. But the Glory escaped, the Glory fled away, the Glory changed its seat, and an arm of the sea Vouru-Kasha was produced, namely, that lake that is called Lake Husravah[2].

57[3]. Then the most crafty Turanian Frangrasyan rushed out of the sea Vouru-Kasha, O Spitama Zarathustra! thinking evil thoughts: ' . . . .[4] I have not been able to conquer the Glory that belongs to the Aryan nations, born and unborn, and to the holy Zarathustra.

58. ' Then I will defile all corn and liquors[5], as to greatness, goodness, and fairness.'

—'Ahura Mazda will come against thee, ever eager to create new creatures[6].'

Then the most crafty Turanian Frangrasyan rushed down into the sea Vouru-Kasha, O Spitama Zarathustra!

---

[1] See Études Iraniennes, II, 227; cf. § 82.

[2] 'Lake Husru is within fifty leagues (parasang) of Lake Kêkast' (Lake Urumiah, Bund. XXII, 8, tr. West).

[3] Cf. §§ 60, 63.

[4] Itha itha yathana ahmâi.

[5] Tarshuka khshudraka, translated dhânyâni madhûnika (Sansk. tr. to Âfrîgân Gâhambâr, § 12). Afrâsyâb was charged with having laid Iran waste by filling up or conducting away rivers (Hamzah Ispahensis, p. 34; cf. Bund. XXI, 6).

[6] This looks like an answer to Afrâsyâb's threats.

59. A second time he stripped himself naked, wishing to seize that Glory that belongs to the Aryan nations, born and unborn, and to the holy Zarathustra. But the Glory escaped, the Glory fled away, the Glory changed its seat, and an arm of the sea Vouru-Kasha was produced, namely, that lake that is called Lake Vanghazdau[1].

60[2]. Then the most crafty Turanian Frangrasyan rushed out of the sea Vouru-Kasha, O Spitama Zarathustra! thinking evil thoughts: '. . . .[3] I have not been able to conquer the Glory that belongs to the Aryan nations, born and unborn, and to the holy Zarathustra.

61. 'Then I will defile all corn and liquors, as to greatness, goodness, and fairness.'

—'Ahura Mazda will come against thee, ever eager to create new creatures.'

Then the most crafty Turanian Frangrasyan rushed down into the sea Vouru-Kasha.

62. A third time he stripped himself naked, wishing to seize the Glory that belongs to the Aryan nations, born and unborn, and to the holy Zarathustra. But the Glory escaped, the Glory fled away, the Glory changed its seat, and an arm was produced in the sea Vouru-Kasha, namely, the water that is called Awz-dânva.

63[4]. Then the most crafty Turanian Frangrasyan rushed out of the sea Vouru-Kasha, O Spitama Zarathustra! thinking evil thoughts: '. . . .[5] I have

---

[1] The situation of that lake is not stated. [2] Cf. §§ 57, 63.

[3] Itha itha yathana ahmâi avatha itha yathana ahmâi.

[4] Cf. §§ 57, 60.

[5] Itha itha yathana ahmâi avatha itha yathana ahmâi âvoya itha yathana ahmâi.

not been able to conquer the Glory that belongs to
the Aryan nations, born and unborn, and to the
holy Zarathustra!'

64. He was not able to seize the Glory that
belongs to the Aryan nations, born and unborn, and
to the holy Zarathustra.

For its brightness and glory, I will offer it a sacrifice ....

X.

65. We sacrifice unto the awful Glory that cannot be forcibly
seized, made by Mazda ....

66. That cleaves unto him [1] who grows up there,
where lies Lake Kāsava [2], along with the Haêtu-
mant [3] river; there where stands Mount Ushidhau [4],
surrounded by waters, that run from the mountain.

67. It [5] runs unto him, it flows and swells unto
him, bringing good pastures and fine horses, bringing
plenty, full of glory; with beauty and weal; powerful
and friendly, rich of pastures, prolific and golden. It
runs unto him, it flows and swells unto him, bright
and glorious, making the white .... [6] grow, smiting
away all plagues.

68. And there comes with him a horse's strength,
there comes with him a camel's strength, there

---

[1] That is to say, to any one who .... The Kavis or Kings
of Iran are meant: Lake Kāsava was supposed to be 'the home of
the Kayân race' (Bund. XXI, 7). The Kavis are enumerated in
the following clauses (§§ 71 seq.).

[2] The present Zarah or Hamûn sea in Seistan.

[3] The Helmend ('Ετύμανδρος; cf. Vend. I, 14).

[4] The seat of the Hvarenô; see p. 33, note 1, p. 287, note 5,
and Introduction to Yt. XVIII.

[5] The water of the rivers in which the Glory lies, and in the
midst of which the Kavi has been nourished.

[6] ? Varemis.

comes with him a man's strength, there comes with him the kingly Glory: and there is in him, O holy Zarathustra! so much of kingly Glory as might extinguish at once all the non-Aryan nations.

69. And then (through it) living creatures may keep away[1] hunger and death, living creatures (may keep away) cold and heat[1]. Such is the kingly Glory, the keeper of the Aryan nations and of the five kinds of animals[2], made to help the faithful and the Law of the worshippers of Mazda.

For its brightness and glory, I will offer it a sacrifice . . . .

XI.

70. We sacrifice unto the awful kingly Glory, made by Mazda . . . .

71. That clave unto Kavi Kavâta, and unto Kavi Aipivôhu, and unto Kavi Usadha, and unto Kavi Arshan, and unto Kavi Pisina, and unto Kavi Byârshan, and unto Kavi Syâvarshan[3];

72. So that they were all of them brave, all of them strong, all of them healthful, all of them wise, all of them happy in their wishes, all of them powerful kings.

For its brightness and glory, I will offer it a sacrifice . . . .

XII.

73. We sacrifice unto the awful kingly Glory, made by Mazda . . . .

74[4]. That clave unto Kavi Husravah for the well-shapen Strength, for the Victory made by Ahura, for the crushing Ascendant; for the righteousness of the law, for the innocence of the law, for the

---

[1] Doubtful. [2] See p. 182, note 2. [3] See Yt. XIII, § 132.
[4] §§ 74-76 = Yt. XIII, 133-135.

unconquerable power of the law ; for the extermination of the enemies at one stroke ;

75. And for the vigour of health, for the Glory
made by Mazda, for the health of the body, and for
a good, virtuous offspring, wise, chief in assemblies,
bright, and clear-eyed, that frees [their father] from
the pangs [of hell], of good intellect; and for that
part in the blessed world that falls to wisdom and
to those who do not follow impiety ;

76. And for a dominion full of splendour, for a
long, long life, and for all boons and remedies ;

77. So that king Husravah [had the lead] all
along the long race, and he could not pass through
the forest, he[1], the murderer, who was fiercely striving
against him on horseback ; the lord Kavi Husravah
prevailed over all; he put in bonds Frangrasyan
and Keresavazda[2], to avenge the murder of his
father Syâvarshâna, a man, and of Aghraêratha, a
semi-man[3].

For its brightness and glory, I will offer it a sacrifice . . . .

XIII.

78. We sacrifice unto the awful kingly Glory, made by
Mazda . . . .

79. That clave unto the holy Zarathustra, so that
he thought according to the Law, spake according

---

[1] Aurvasâra; see Yt. XV, 32; cf. Yt. V, 50 (where the words
all along the long race have been omitted in the translation).
The words have the lead here have been supplied from Yt. V,
50: the text here has two words, tãm keresem, of which both
the reading and the meaning are doubtful.

[2] Keresavazda, the Karsîvaz of Firdausi, the brother of
Afrâsyâb and the murderer of Syâvarshâna: he was put to death
by Husravah in company with his brother (Études Iraniennes,
II, 227).

[3] See p. 114, note 7.

to the Law, and did according to the Law; so that
he was the holiest in holiness in all the living world,
the best-ruling in exercising rule, the brightest in
brightness, the most glorious in glory, the most
victorious in victory.

80. At his sight the Daêvas rushed away; at his
sight the (demoniac) malices were extinguished; at
his sight the Gainis [1] drew back their ways from the
mortals and, lamenting [2] and wailing, laid violent
hands on the Daêvas.

81. And that one prayer, the Ahuna Vairya, which
the holy Zarathustra sang and repeated four times,
with a song that waxed louder and louder, drove
back all the Daêvas beneath the earth, and took off
from them sacrifice and prayer [3].

82. It was it, the Glory of Zarathustra, that the
Turanian ruffian Frangrasyan tried to seize to rule
over all the Karshvares; round about the seven
Karshvares did that ruffian Frangrasyan rush, trying
to seize the Glory of Zarathustra [4]. But that Glory
escaped to hidden inlets of the sea [5]; and there those
two [6] made my will [7] roll on [8]; they entered my will,
as it was my wish, Ahura Mazda's, and as it was the
wish of the Law of Mazda.

For its brightness and glory, I will offer it a sacrifice . . . .

---

[1] See Vend. XX, 10.
[2] Doubtful. Perhaps: and lamenting and wailing the
Daêvas left off injuring.
[3] Cf. Yt. XIII, 90.
[4] See above, §§ 56–64.   [5] Cf. §§ 56, 59, 62.
[6] Zarathustra and Vîstâspa (?); cf. §§ 84–87.
[7] Meaning my law.   [8] Cf. Yt. XIII, 89, note 5.

XIV.

83. We sacrifice unto the awful kingly Glory, made by Mazda . . . .

84. That clave unto king Vîstâspa, so that he thought according to the Law, spake according to the Law, and did according to the Law; so that he professed that Law, destroying his foes and causing the Daêvas to retire.

85[1]. Who, driving the Dru*g* before him[2], sought wide room for the holy religion; who, driving the Dru*g* before him, made wide room for the holy religion; who made himself the arm and support of this law of Ahura, of this law of Zarathu*s*tra;

86. Who took her, standing bound, from the hands of the Hunus, and established her to sit in the middle [of the world], high ruling, never falling back, holy, nourished with plenty of cattle and pastures, blessed with plenty of cattle and pastures.

87. The valiant king Vîstâspa conquered all enemies, Tâthrava*nt* of the evil law, Peshana, the worshipper of the Daêvas, and the fiendish wicked Are*g*a*t*-aspa and the other wicked *Hv*yaonas[3].

For its brightness and glory, I will offer it a sacrifice . . . .

XV.

88. We sacrifice unto the awful kingly Glory, made by Mazda . . . .

89[4]. That will cleave unto the victorious Sao-shya*nt* and his helpers[5], when he shall restore the

---

[1] §§ 85–86 = Yt. XIII, 99–100.
[2] Or 'with his spear pushed forwards;' see p. 205, note 1.
[3] Cf. Yt. V, 109.　　　　　[4] §§ 89–90 = §§ 11–12.
[5] See p. 117, note 6.

world, which will (thenceforth) never grow old and
never die, never decaying and never rotting, ever
living and ever increasing, and master of its wish,
when the dead will rise, when life and immortality
will come, and the world will be restored at its
wish;

90. When the creation will grow deathless,—the
prosperous creation of the Good Spirit,—and the
Dru*g* shall perish, though she may rush on every
side to kill the holy beings; she and her hundredfold brood shall perish, as it is the will of the Lord.

For its brightness and glory, I will offer it a sacrifice . . . .

XVI.

91. We sacrifice unto the awful kingly Glory, made by
Mazda . . . .

92. When Astva*t*-ereta [1] shall rise up from Lake
Kāsava [2], a friend of Ahura Mazda, a son of Vîspa-
taurvairi [3], knowing the victorious knowledge.

It was that Glory that Thraêtaona bore with him
when A*z*i Dahâka was killed [4];

93. That Frangrasyan, the Turanian, bore when
Drv*a*u [5] was killed, when the Bull was killed [6];

That king Husravah bore when Frangrasyan, the
Turanian, was killed [7];

---

[1] Saoshya*nt*; cf. Yt. XIII, 129.
[2] Cf. § 66 and V*e*nd. XIX, 5 (18).
[3] See Yt. XIII, 142.   [4] Cf. § 36.   [5] Or 'the demon.'
[6] This line is in contradiction with what we know of the Frangrasyan legend, unless the text is corrupt and the name of Frangrasyan
has been introduced here by mistake (for Keresâspa?). Yet it
may allude to brighter sides, unknown to us, of the Turanian hero:
the Bull (*gaus*) may be his brother Aghraêratha, the Bull-man
(Gôpatishâh); see p. 114, note 7.
[7] See § 77.

That king Vîstâspa bore, when he victoriously maintained Holiness against the host of the fiends and took off the Dru*g* from the world of the good principle[1].

94. He[2], with the eye of intelligence[3], shall look down upon all the creatures of the Paê*s*is[4], her of the evil seed : he shall look upon the whole living world with the eye of plenty, and his look shall deliver to immortality the whole of the living creatures.

95. And there shall his friends[5] come forward, the friends of Astva*t*-ereta, who are fiend-smiting, well-thinking, well-speaking, well-doing, following the good law, and whose tongues have never uttered a word of falsehood.

Before them shall Aêshma of the wounding spear, who has no Glory, bow and flee ; he shall smite the most wicked Dru*g*, her of the evil seed, born of darkness.

96. Akem-Manô[6] smites, but Vohu-Manô shall smite him ; the Word of falsehood smites, but the Word of truth shall smite it. Haurvatâ*t* and Ame-retâ*t*[7] shall smite both hunger and thirst : Haurvatâ*t* and Ameretâ*t* shall smite the evil hunger and the evil thirst. The evil-doing Angra Mainyu bows and flees, becoming powerless.

For its brightness and glory, I will offer it a sacrifice . . . .

97. Yathâ ahû vairyô : The will of the Lord is the law of holiness . . . .

---

[1] Cf. § 84.   [2] Saoshya*nt*.   [3] Cf. Yt. I, 28.
[4] A name of the Dru*g*.   [5] See p. 220, note 1.
[6] See p. 297, note 4.
[7] The Genii of the waters and of the plants (cf. Vend. Introd. IV, 34).

I bless the sacrifice and prayer, and the strength and vigour of Mount Ushi-darena, made by Mazda, the seat of holy happiness; of the kingly Glory, made by Mazda; of the Glory that cannot be forcibly seized, made by Mazda [1].

Ashem Vohû: Holiness is the best of all good . . . .

[Give] unto that man [2] brightness and glory, ... give him the bright, all-happy, blissful abode of the holy Ones.

---

[1] Cf. § o.   [2] Who sacrifices to the kingly Glory.

XX. VANANT YAST.

This Yast ought to follow immediately after the Tîr Yast, as it is derived from the same Sîrôzah formula; the one in which Tistrya is invoked along with Vanant and Haptôiringa (Sîrôzah, § 13). It is a mere supplement to that Yast. On Vanant, see p. 97, note 6.

o. May Ahura Mazda be rejoiced! . . . .
Ashem Vohû: Holiness is the best of all good . . . .
I confess myself a worshipper of Mazda, a follower of Zarathustra, one who hates the Daêvas and obeys the laws of Ahura;
For sacrifice, prayer, propitiation, and glorification unto [Hâvani], the holy and master of holiness . . . .

Unto the star Vanant, made by Mazda,
Be propitiation, with sacrifice, prayer, propitiation, and glorification.

Yathâ ahû vairyô: The will of the Lord is the law of holiness . . . .

1. We sacrifice unto the star Vanant, made by Mazda, the holy and master of holiness.

I will sacrifice unto Vanant, strong, invoked by his own name[1], healing, in order to withstand the accursed and most foul Khrafstras[2] of the most abominable Angra Mainyu.

2. Yathâ ahû vairyô: The will of the Lord is the law of holiness . . . .

I bless the sacrifice and prayer, and the strength and vigour of the star Vanant, made by Mazda.

Ashem Vohû: Holiness is the best of all good . . . .
[Give] unto that man[3] brightness and glory, ... give him the bright, all-happy, blissful abode of the holy Ones.

---

[1] See p. 13, note 2.
[2] The reptiles and other Ahrimanian creatures (Vendîdâd, Introd. V, 11) which are destroyed by the rain (Bund. VII, 7).
[3] Who sacrifices to Vanant.

XXI AND XXII. YAST FRAGMENTS.

These two Yasts or Yast fragments are known among the Parsis as the Hâdhôkht Nask, though their context does not correspond to any part of the description of that Nask as given in the Dînkart (West, Pahlavi Texts, I, 224, note 8). A Pahlavi translation of these Yasts has been edited by Haug and West (The Book of Ardâ Vîrâf, p. 269 seq.).

XXI. YAST FRAGMENT.

Yast XXI is a eulogy of the Ashem Vohû prayer, the value of which rises higher and higher, according as the circumstances under which it is being recited are of greater importance.

1. Zarathustra asked Ahura Mazda: 'O Ahura Mazda, most beneficent Spirit, Maker of the material world, thou Holy One!

'What is the only word in which is contained the glorification of all good things, of all the things that are the offspring of the good principle?'

2. Ahura Mazda answered: 'It is the praise of Holiness [1], O Spitama Zarathustra!

3. 'He who recites the praise of Holiness [1], in the fulness of faith and with a devoted heart, praises me, Ahura Mazda; he praises the waters, he praises the earth, he praises the cattle, he praises the plants, he praises all good things made by Mazda, all the things that are the offspring of the good principle.

4. 'For the reciting of that word of truth, O Zarathustra! the pronouncing of that formula, the Ahuna Vairya, increases strength and victory in one's soul and piety.

---

[1] Asha: the Ashem Vohû.

5. 'For that only recital of the praise of Holiness is worth a hundred khshnaothras of the beings of Holiness[1], when delivered while going to sleep, a thousand when delivered after eating, ten thousand when delivered during cohabitation, or any number when delivered in departing this life.'

6. 'What is the one recital of the praise of Holiness that is worth ten others in greatness, goodness, and fairness?'

7. Ahura Mazda answered: 'It is that one, O holy Zarathu*s*tra! that a man delivers when eating the gifts of Haurvatâ*t* and Ameretâ*t*[2], at the same time professing good thoughts, good words, and good deeds, and rejecting evil thoughts, evil words, and evil deeds.'

8. 'What is the one recital of the praise of Holiness that is worth a hundred others in greatness, goodness, and fairness?'

9. Ahura Mazda answered: 'It is that one, O holy Zarathu*s*tra! that a man delivers while drinking of the Haoma strained for the sacrifice, at the same time professing good thoughts, good words, and good deeds, and rejecting evil thoughts, evil words, and evil deeds.'

10. 'What is the one recital of the praise of Holiness that is worth a thousand others in greatness, goodness, and fairness?'

11. Ahura Mazda answered: 'It is that one, O holy Zarathu*s*tra! that a man delivers when starting

---

[1] A hundred times the formula: 'Be propitiation (khshnaothra) unto N. . . . , the holy and master of holiness' (cf. p. 1, note 2).

[2] Eating or drinking (see Vendîdâd, Introd. IV, 33).

up from his bed or going to sleep again, at the same time professing good thoughts, good words, and good deeds, and rejecting evil thoughts, evil words, and evil deeds.'

12. 'What is the one recital of the praise of Holiness that is worth ten thousand others in greatness, goodness, and fairness?'

13. Ahura Mazda answered: 'It is that one, O holy Zarathustra! that a man delivers when waking up and rising from sleep, at the same time professing good thoughts, good words, and good deeds, and rejecting evil thoughts, evil words, and evil deeds.'

14. 'What is the one recital of the praise of Holiness that is worth this Karshvare of ours, *Hv*aniratha [1], with its cattle and its chariots, without its men, in greatness, goodness, and fairness?'

15. Ahura Mazda answered: 'It is that one, O holy Zarathustra! that a man delivers in the last moments of his life, at the same time professing good thoughts, good words, and good deeds, and rejecting evil thoughts, evil words, and evil deeds.'

16. 'What is the one recital of the praise of Holiness that is worth all that is between the earth and the heavens, and this earth, and that luminous space, and all the good things made by Mazda, that are the offspring of the good principle in greatness, goodness, and fairness?'

17. Ahura Mazda answered: 'It is that one, O holy Zarathustra! that a man delivers to renounce evil thoughts, evil words, and evil deeds [2].'

---

[1] See p. 123, note 5.
[2] In a conversion, or in the recital of the penitential prayers.

YAST XXII.

This Yast is a description of the fate that attends the soul of the righteous (§§ 1-18) and the soul of. the wicked (§§ 19-37) after death. They spend the first three nights (the sadis or sidôs ; cf. Commentaire du Vendîdâd, XIII, 55) amongst the highest enjoyments or pains ; they are then met by their own conscience in the shape of a beautiful heavenly maiden (or a fiendish old woman [1]), and are brought in four steps up to heaven or down to hell, through the three paradises of Good-Thought, Good-Word, and Good-Deed, or the three hells of Evil-Thought, Evil-Word, and Evil-Deed : there they are praised and glorified by Ahura, or rebuked and insulted by Angra Mainyu, and fed with ambrosia or poison.

Similar developments are to be found in Yast XXIV, 53-65 ; Ardâ Vîrâf XVII ; Minokhired II, 123-194.

I.

1. Zarathustra asked Ahura Mazda : 'O Ahura Mazda, most beneficent Spirit, Maker of the material world, thou Holy One!

'When one of the faithful departs this life, where does his soul abide on that night?'

Ahura Mazda answered :

2. 'It takes its seat near the head, singing the Ustavaiti Gâtha [2] and proclaiming happiness : "Happy is he, happy the man, whoever he be, to whom Ahura Mazda gives the full accomplishment of his wishes!" On that night his soul tastes [3] as much of pleasure as the whole of the living world can taste.'

---

[1] See p. 319, note 1.

[2] The name of the second Gâtha, which begins with the word usta : the words in the text, ' Happy the man . . . . ,' are its opening line (Yasna XLII, 1).

[3] Literally, sees, perceives.

3. —'On the second night where does his soul abide?'

4. Ahura Mazda answered : 'It takes its seat near the head, singing the Ustavaiti Gâtha and proclaiming happiness : " Happy is he, happy the man, whoever he be, to whom Ahura Mazda gives the full accomplishment of his wishes!" On that night his soul tastes as much of pleasure as the whole of the living world can taste.'

5. —'On the third night where does his soul abide?'

6. Ahura Mazda answered: 'It takes its seat near the head, singing the Ustavaiti Gâtha and proclaiming happiness : " Happy is he, happy the man, whoever he be, to whom Ahura Mazda gives the full accomplishment of his wishes!" On that night his soul tastes as much of pleasure as the whole of the living world can taste.'

7. At the end [1] of the third night, when the dawn appears, it seems to the soul of the faithful one as if it were brought amidst plants and scents : it seems as if a wind were blowing from the region of the south, from the regions of the south, a sweet-scented wind, sweeter-scented than any other wind in the world.

8. And it seems to the soul of the faithful one as if he were inhaling that wind with the nostrils, and he thinks : 'Whence does that wind blow, the sweetest-scented wind I ever inhaled with my nostrils?'

9. And it seems to him as if his own conscience were advancing to him in that wind, in the shape of a maiden fair, bright, white-armed, strong, tall-

---

[1] Thraosta: in Pahlavi rôisman.

formed, high-standing, thick-breasted, beautiful of body, noble, of a glorious seed[1], of the size of a maid in her fifteenth year, as fair as the fairest things in the world.

10. And the soul of the faithful one addressed her, asking: 'What maid art thou, who art the fairest maid I have ever seen?'

11. And she, being his own conscience, answers him: 'O thou youth of good thoughts, good words, and good deeds, of good religion, I am thy own conscience!

'Everybody did love thee for that greatness, goodness, fairness, sweet-scentedness, victorious strength and freedom from sorrow, in which thou dost appear to me;

12. 'And so thou, O youth of good thoughts, good words, and good deeds, of good religion! didst love me for that greatness, goodness, fairness, sweet-scentedness, victorious strength, and freedom from sorrow, in which I appear to thee.

13. 'When thou wouldst see a man making derision[2] and deeds of idolatry, or rejecting[3] (the poor) and shutting his door[4], then thou wouldst sit singing the Gâthas and worshipping the good waters and Âtar, the son of Ahura Mazda, and rejoicing[5] the faithful that would come from near or from afar.

---

[1] 'That is to say, from the gods' (Pahl. Comm.).

[2] Of holy things.

[3] Doubtful. The Pahlavi commentary has the following gloss: 'He would not give his friends what they begged for.'

[4] To the poor:—Urvarô-straya: urvar babâik kart (Pahl. Comm.): âighshân babâ barâ asrûnast (star, to tie, as in frasta-retem baresma). Cf. Yt. XXIV, 37, 59.

[5] With alms to the poor Mazdayasnians (ashô-dâd).

14. 'I was lovely and thou madest me still lovelier; I was fair and thou madest me still fairer; I was desirable and thou madest me still more desirable; I was sitting in a forward place and thou madest me sit in the foremost place, through this good thought, through this good speech, through this good deed of thine; and so henceforth men worship me for my having long sacrificed unto and conversed with Ahura Mazda.

15. 'The first step that the soul of the faithful man made, placed him in the Good-Thought[1] Paradise;

'The second step that the soul of the faithful man made, placed him in the Good-Word[2] Paradise ;

'The third step that the soul of the faithful man made, placed him in the Good-Deed[3] Paradise;

'The fourth step that the soul of the faithful man made, placed him in the Endless Lights[4].'

16. Then one of the faithful, who had departed before him, asked him, saying: 'How didst thou depart this life, thou holy man? How didst thou come, thou holy man! from the abodes full of cattle and full of the wishes and enjoyments of love? From the material world into the world of the spirit? From the decaying world into the undecaying one? How long did thy felicity last?'

17. And Ahura Mazda answered: 'Ask him not what thou askest him, who has just gone the dreary

---

[1] The so-called Hûmat Paradise (cf. Yt. III, 3).
[2] The so-called Hûkht Paradise.
[3] The so-called Hvarsht Paradise.
[4] The seat of the Garôthmân.

way, full of fear and distress, where the body and the soul part from one another.

18. '[Let him eat] of the food brought to him, of the oil of Zaremaya [1] : this is the food for the youth of good thoughts, of good words, of good deeds, of good religion, after he has departed this life ; this is the food for the holy woman, rich in good thoughts, good words, and good deeds, well-principled and obedient to her husband, after she has departed this life.'

II.

19. Zarathustra asked Ahura Mazda : 'O Ahura Mazda, most beneficent Spirit, Maker of the material world, thou Holy One!

'When one of the wicked perishes, where does his soul abide on that night ? '

20. Ahura Mazda answered : 'It rushes and sits near the skull, singing the Kima [2] Gâtha, O holy Zarathustra!

' " To what land shall I turn, O Ahura Mazda ? To whom shall I go with praying ? "

' On that night his soul tastes as much of suffering as the whole of the living world can taste.'

21. —'On the second night, where does his soul abide ? '

22. Ahura Mazda answered : 'It rushes and sits near the skull, singing the Kima Gâtha, O holy

---

[1] Zaremaya is the spring: the word translated oil (raoghna, Persian روغن) might perhaps be better translated 'butter;' the milk made in the middle of spring was said to be the best (Vis-pêrad I, 2 ; Pahl. Comm.; cf. Dâdistân XXXI, 14).

[2] The Gâtha of lamenting, beginning with the word Kãm (Kãm nemê zãm: 'To what land shall I turn?'); Yasna XLVI (XLV).

Zarathustra! "To what land shall I turn, O Ahura
Mazda? To whom shall I go with praying?"
    'On that night his soul tastes as much of suffering
as the whole of the living world can taste.'
    23. —'On the third night, where does his soul
abide?'
    24. Ahura Mazda answered: 'It rushes and sits
near the skull, singing the Kima Gâtha, O holy
Zarathustra! "To what land shall I turn, O Ahura
Mazda? To whom shall I go with praying?"
    'On that night his soul tastes as much of suffering
as the whole of the living world can taste.'
    25. At the end of the third night, O holy Zara-
thustra! when the dawn appears, it seems to the
soul of the faithless one as if it were brought amidst
snow and stench, and as if a wind were blowing
from the region of the north, from the regions of
the north, a foul-scented wind, the foulest-scented
of all the winds in the world.
    26–32. And it seems to the soul of the wicked man
as if he were inhaling that wind with the nostrils, and
he thinks: 'Whence does that wind blow, the foulest-
scented wind that I ever inhaled with my nostrils[1]?'

---

[1] A development similar to that in §§ 9–14 is to be supplied
here: in the Ardâ Vîrâf and the Minokhired the soul of the wicked
is met by a horrid old woman, who is his own conscience: 'And
in that wind he saw his own religion and deeds, as a profligate
woman, naked, decayed, gaping, bandy-legged, lean-hipped, and
unlimitedly spotted, so that spot was joined to spot, like the most
hideous noxious creatures (khrafstar), most filthy and most
stinking' (cf. § 9).
    Then that wicked soul spoke thus: 'Who art thou? than whom
I never saw any one of the creatures of Aûharmazd and Akharman
uglier, or filthier or more stinking' (cf. § 10).
    To him she spoke thus: 'I am thy bad actions, O youth of
evil thoughts, of evil words, of evil deeds, of evil religion! It

33. The first step that the soul of the wicked man made laid him in the Evil-Thought Hell;

The second step that the soul of the wicked man made laid him in the Evil-Word Hell;

The third step that the soul of the wicked man made laid him in the Evil-Deed Hell;

The fourth step that the soul of the wicked man made laid him in the Endless Darkness.

34. Then one of the wicked who departed before him addressed him, saying : ' How didst thou perish, O wicked man? How didst thou come, O fiend! from the abodes full of cattle and full of the wishes and enjoyments of love? From the material world into the world of the Spirit? From the decaying

---

is on account of thy will and actions that I am hideous and vile, iniquitous and diseased, rotten and foul-smelling, unfortunate and distressed, as appears to thee (cf. §§ 11–12).

' When thou sawest any one who performed the Yazishn and Drôn ceremonies, and praise and prayer and the service of God, and preserved and protected water and fire, cattle and trees, and other good creations, thou practisedst the will of Akharman and the demons, and improper actions. And when thou sawest one who provided hospitable reception, and gave something deservedly in gifts and charity, for the advantage of the good and worthy who came from far, and who were from near, thou wast avaricious, and shuttedst up thy door (cf. § 13).

' And though I have been unholy (that is, I have been considered bad), I am made more unholy through thee ; and though I have been frightful, I am made more frightful through thee ; though I have been tremulous, I am made more tremulous through thee ; though I am settled in the northern region of the demons, I am settled further north through thee ; through these evil thoughts, through these evil words, and through these evil deeds, which thou practisedst. They curse me, a long time, in the long execration and evil communion of the Evil Spirit (cf. § 14).

' Afterwards that soul of the wicked advanced the first footstep on Dûsh-hûmat (the place of evil thoughts), &c.' (The Book of Ardâ Vîrâf, XVII, 12–27, as translated by Haug).

world into the undecaying one ? How long did thy
suffering last ? '

35. Angra Mainyu, the lying one, said : 'Ask
him not what thou askest him, who has just gone
the dreary way, full of fear and distress, where the
body and the soul part from one another.

36. 'Let him eat of the food brought unto him,
of poison and poisonous stench [1]: this is the food,
after he has perished, for the youth of evil thoughts,
evil words, evil deeds, evil religion after he has
perished ; this is the food for the fiendish woman,
rich in evil thoughts, evil words, and evil deeds,
evil religion, ill-principled, and disobedient to her
husband.

37 [2]. 'We worship the Fravashi of the holy man,
whose name is Asmô-*hv*anva*nt* [3]; then I will worship
the Fravashis of the other holy Ones who were
strong of faith [4].

38 [2]. 'We worship the memory of Ahura Mazda,
to keep the Holy Word.

'We worship the understanding of Ahura Mazda,
to study the Holy Word.

'We worship the tongue of Ahura Mazda, to
speak forth the Holy Word.

'We worship the mountain that gives understanding, that preserves understanding ; [we worship

---

[1] Cf. Yasna XXXI, 20 : ' He who would deceive the holy One, to
him afterwards (will be) a long weeping in the dark place, bad
food and words of insult. O wicked! this is the place down which
your own conscience will bring you through your own deeds.'

[2] §§ 37-3 , 39-40, 41-42 are separate fragments.

[3] One of the first disciples of Zoroaster ; cf. Yt. XIII, 96.

[4] Cf. p. 33, note 2.

it] by day and by night, with offerings of libations well-accepted [1].

39 [2]. 'O Maker! how do the souls of the dead, the Fravashis of the holy Ones, manifest [3] themselves [4]?'

40. Ahura Mazda answered: 'They manifest themselves from goodness of spirit and excellence of mind [5].'

41 [6]. Then towards the dawning of the dawn [7], that bird Parôdars [8], that bird Karetô-dãsu [9] hears the voice of the Fire.

---

[1] § 38=Yt. I, 31.

[2] A Pahlavi translation of the following two fragments is found in MS. 33, Paris, Supplément Persan (edited in Études Iraniennes, II).

[3] *K*ithra (Paris MS. p. 255).

[4] 'How do they manifest their assistance?' (Pahl. tr. ibid.); that is to say, when do they assist their relations and countrymen? (see Yt. XIII, 49 seq.)

[5] When men are instinct with good spirit and good thought.

[6] The Pahlavi translation of this fragment has here §§ 14–16 of the Âtash Nyâyis, then §§ 18–19 of Vendîdâd XVIII. Therefore the whole passage is to be restored as follows :

Âtar looks at the hands of all those who pass by : 'What does the friend bring to his friend . . . .?' (Âtash N. 14.)

And if that passer-by brings him wood holily brought, or bundles of baresma holily tied up . . . ., then Âtar . . . . will bless him thus :

May herds of oxen grow for thee . . . . (Âtash N. 15–16).

In the first part of the night, Fire, the son of Ahura Mazda, calls the master of the house for help, saying:

'Up! arise, thou master of the house . . . .' (Vend. XVIII, 18–19).

'Then towards the dawning of the dawn . . . .' (see the text).

[7] Cf. Vend. XVIII, 23.

[8] 'He who has knowledge made,' or 'He who has the knowledge of what is made' (kartak dânishn); his other name Parô-dars is 'He who foresees.'

[9] Here again a large passage is omitted : it can only partly be

42. Here the fiendish Bûshyãsta, the long-handed, rushes from the region of the north, from the regions of the north, speaking thus, lying thus: 'Sleep on, O .men! Sleep on, O sinners! Sleep on and live in sin.'

---

supplied from the Pahlavi translation; the words in brackets refer to Zend texts lost to us:

'Then he flaps his wings and lifts up his voice, saying: " Arise, O men! [and also women, grown-up people, and children, &c. . . . . Put on well your girdle and shirt, wash your hands, put your girdle around your body, go and give food to the cattle and recite aloud the five holy Gâthas of Spitama Zarathustra."]

'Here the fiendish Bûshyãsta . . . .' (see the text). Then the Pahlavi translation has: 'Never care for the three excellent things, good thoughts, good words, good deeds' (cf. Vend. XVIII, 25).

XXIII–XXIV. ÂFRÎN PAIGHAMBAR ZAR-
TÛST AND VÎSTÂSP YAST.

'God taught the Zendávasta to Zartusht—a sublime work . . . .
God said to Zartusht, "Go and before Sháh Gushtásp read this
book, that he may come into the faith . . . . keep all my counsel
and repeat it word by word to Sháh Gushtásp [1]." '

Zartusht, in obedience to God, went to the court of Gushtásp: 'He
came forward and called down a blessing on the Sháh [2].' Then he
read to him the Zandávasta and said : ' Learn its statutes and walk
therein. If your desire is towards its laws, your abode shall be in
the paradise of heaven. But if you turn away from its command-
ments, you shall bring down your crowned head to the dust. Your
God will be displeased with you, and will overthrow your prosperous condition. At the last you shall descend into hell, if you
hear not the counsel of the Almighty [3].'

These lines of the Zartusht-Namah are a summary of the following
two Yasts. The first, entitled ' The blessing of the prophet Zartûst,'
contains the words of blessing addressed by Zarathustra when
appearing before the king. These words seem to have followed
a similar blessing pronounced by Gâmâspa [4], the prime minister of
Vîstâspa [5].

Yast XXIV contains the exhortations of the prophet to the
king to follow and closely adhere to the Law of Mazda. It is a
counterpart to the XIXth Fargard of the Vendîdâd, as Zarathustra
plays here the same part to Vîstâspa as Ahura does there to Zarathustra. It is, therefore, a summary of the Law, of the duties it

---

[1] The Zartusht-Namah, translated by E. B. Eastwick, in Wilson's
Parsi Religion, p. 495.

[2] Ibid. p. 499.   [3] Ibid. p. 501.

[4] See Yt. XXIII, 2; whether Anquetil's statement to that effect
(Zend-Avesta II, 623) rests on independent tradition or only on the
text of our Yast is not clear.

[5] See above, p. 70, note 1.

enforces and of the rewards it promises. This accounts for the strange disconnection apparent in it, which makes it a crux interpretum, as, besides the very corrupt state of the text, the chief difficulty of this Ya*st* arises from the fact that many passages in it are incomplete quotations from the Vendîdâd, or allusions to statements therein[1], which, when supplied, help a good deal to relieve this Ya*st* from its apparent state of utter incoherence.

For this translation I was able to avail myself of a Pahlavi translation, of which a copy was kindly lent to me by Mr. West. That translation is apparently of late date and often manifestly wrong; yet it was very useful to me in several passages, besides its giving a Zend text generally more correct and more correctly divided than the text in Westergaard's edition[2].

Ya*st* XXIII was originally no independent Ya*st*, being nothing ʼore than the beginning of Ya*st* XXIV, detached from it, with ʼe slight alterations and inversions.

XXIII. ÂFRÎN PAIGHAMBAR ZARTÛ*ST*.

1. 'I am a pious man, who speaks words of blessing.'

—'Thou appearest unto me full of Glory.'

And Zarathu*st*ra spake unto king Vî*st*âspa, saying : 'I bless thee, O man! O lord of the country! with the living of a good life, of an exalted life, of a long life. May thy men live long! May thy women live long! May sons be born unto thee of thy own body!

2. 'Mayest thou have a son like *G*âmâspa, and may he bless thee as (*G*âmâspa blessed) Vî*st*âspa (the lord) of the country[3]!

---

[1] For instance, §§ 28, 30, 31, 39, &c.

[2] The various readings in Mr. West's manuscript are indicated by the letter W. in the notes.

[3] See the introduction to this Ya*st* and Yt. XXIV, 3, text and note.

'Mayest thou be most beneficent, like Mazda!

'Mayest thou be fiend-smiting, like Thraêtaona [1]!

'Mayest thou be strong, like Gâmâspa [2]!

'Mayest thou be well-armed, like Takhma-Urupa [3]!

3. 'Mayest thou be glorious, like Yima Khshaêta, the good shepherd!

'Mayest thou be instructed with a thousand senses, like Azi Dahâka, of the evil law [4]!

'Mayest thou be awful and most strong, like Keresâspa [5]!

'Mayest thou be a wise chief of assemblies, like Urvâkhshaya [6]!

'Mayest thou be beautiful of body and without fault, like Syâvarshâna [7]!

4. 'Mayest thou be rich in cattle, like an Âthwya-nide [8]!

'Mayest thou be rich in horses, like Pourus-aspa [9]!

'Mayest thou be holy, like Zarathustra Spitama!

'Mayest thou be able to reach the Rangha, whose shores lie afar, as Vafra Navâza was [10]!

'Mayest thou be beloved by the gods and reverenced by men [11]!

---

[1] Cf. Yt. V, 33.
[2] Cf. Yt. V, 68
[3] Cf. Yt. XV, 11.
[4] Cf. Yt. V, 29.
[5] Cf. Yt. V, 37.
[6] See Yt. XV, 28.
[7] See p. 64, note 1.

[8] One belonging to the Âthwya family, of which Thraêtaona was a member. All of them bore names that show them to have been rich in cattle: Pûr-tôrâ, Sôk-tôrâ, Bôr-tôrâ, &c. ('one with abundant oxen, with useful oxen, with the brown ox, &c.,' Bundahis, tr. West, XXXI, 7, note 8).

[9] Pourus-aspa was the father of Zarathustra. His name means, 'He who possesses many horses,' πολύ-ιππος.

[10] Cf. Yt. V, 61.
[11] Cf. Yt. XXIV, 4.

5. 'May ten sons be born of you [1]! In three of
them mayest thou be an Âthravan! In three of
them mayest thou be a warrior! In three of them
mayest thou be a tiller of the ground [2]! And may
one be like thyself, O Vi*st*âspa!
6. 'Mayest thou be swift-horsed, like the Sun [3]!
'Mayest thou be resplendent, like the moon!
'Mayest thou be hot-burning, like fire!
'Mayest thou have piercing rays, like Mithra!
'Mayest thou be tall-formed and victorious, like
the devout Sraosha [4]!
7. 'Mayest thou follow a law of truth, like
Rashnu [5]!
'Mayest thou be a conqueror of thy foes, like
Verethraghna [6], made by Ahura!
'Mayest thou have fulness of welfare, like Râma
*Hv*âstra [7]!
'Mayest thou be freed from sickness and death,
like king Husravah [8]!
8. 'Then the blessing goes for the bright, all-
happy, blissful abode of the holy Ones [9].
'May it happen unto thee according to my
blessing!
'[10]Let us embrace and propagate the good thoughts,
good words, and good deeds that have been done
and that will be done here and elsewhere, that we
may be in the number of the good.

---

[1] Of Vi*st*âspa and his wife Hutaosa.
[2] Cf. Yt. XXIV, 4.   [3] Cf. Sîrôzah, § 11.
[4] Cf. Yt. XI.   [5] Cf. Yt. XII, Introduction.
[6] Cf. Yt. XIV.   [7] Cf. Yt. XV.
[8] Kai Khosrav went alive to Paradise (Firdausi).
[9] He closes his blessing by wishing him bliss in heaven.
[10] Yasna XXXV, 2 (4–5).

'Yathâ ahû vairyô: The will of the Lord is the law of holiness . . . .

'Ashem Vohû : Holiness is the best of all good . . . .

'[Give] unto that man brightness and glory, ... give him the bright, all-happy, blissful abode of the holy Ones.'

XXIV. VÎSTÂSP YAST.

I.

1. 'I am a pious man, who speaks words of blessing,' thus said Zarathustra to the young king Vîstâspa [1].—'She [2] appears to me full of Glory, O Zarathustra!'—'O young king Vîstâspa! [I bless thee [3]] with the living of a good life, of an exalted life, of a long life. May thy men live long! May thy women live long! May sons be born unto thee of thy own body [4]!

2. 'Mayest thou thyself [5] be holy, like Zarathustra!

'Mayest thou be rich in cattle, like an Âthwya-nide [6]!

'Mayest thou be rich in horses, like Pourus-aspa [7]!

'Mayest thou have a good share of bliss [8], like king Husravah!

'Mayest thou have strength to reach the Rangha, whose way lies afar, as Vafra Navâza did [9].

---

[1] Literally, O young king Vîstâspa! (or, O my son, king Vîstâspa!)

[2] The law of Mazda (Pahl.).

[3] Understood in âfri-vakau (who speaks blessing).

[4] Cf. Yt. XXIII, 1.

[5] Khayeus (=nafsman) belongs to § 2 (W.).

[6] See p. 326, note 8.   [7] See p. 326, note 9.

[8] Immortality (cf. Yt. XXIII, 7). W. has ashem merezô= ahlâyîh patmânîk, amargîg (Pahl.).

[9] Cf. Yt. XXIII, 4.

3. 'May ten sons be born of thy own body [1]! three
as Âthravans [2], three as warriors [3], three as tillers of
the ground [4]! May one of them be like *G*âmâspa [5],
that he may bless thee with great and ever greater
happiness [6]!

4. 'Mayest thou be freed from sickness and death,
like Peshô-tanu [7].

'Mayest thou have piercing rays, like Mithra!

'Mayest thou be warm, like the moon!

'Mayest thou be [8] resplendent, like fire!

'Mayest thou be long-lived, as long-lived as an
old man can be [9]!

5. 'And when thou hast fulfilled a duration of a
thousand years, [mayest thou obtain] the bright, all-
happy, blissful abode of the holy Ones!

'Ashem Vohû: Holiness is the best of all good....

---

[1] Cf. Yt. XXIII, 5.

[2] 'Like Âturpât, the son of Mâhraspand' (Pahl. Comm.).

[3] 'Like Spenddât (Isfendyâr), the son of Gûstâsp' (ibid.).

[4] 'Like Zav' (Uzava; 'Zav .... urbes et castella, quae Afras-
siab deleverat, refici jussis, aperuit fluvios, quos ille operuerat, ...
agros denuo coluit, qui in optimam, qua antehac floruerant,
conditionem redierunt,' Hamzah Ispahensis, p. 24 of the Gottwaldt
translation).

[5] Cf. Yt. XXIII, 2.

[6] W. has the same text as Yt. XXIII, 2: yatha dangh*eu*s Vîstâs-
pâi, which is interpreted âfrîn pata*s* obdûnât *k*igûn *G*âmâsp kart
madam matâpat Gûstâsp.

[7] Peshôtanu was a son of Vîstâspa: Zarathu*s*tra made him drink
of a certain sort of milk, and 'he forgot death.' He is one of the
seven immortals, and reigns in Kangdez (Zartusht-Namah and
Bundah*i*s XXIX, 5).

[8] Bavâhi (W.).

[9] Doubtful. The Pahlavi translation follows Yt. XXIII, 4,
though the text is the same as in Westergaard (only bavâi and
zarnumatô instead of bavâhi, zaranumatô).

II.

6 ¹. 'Give ² him strength and victory! Give him welfare in cattle and bread ³!' thus said Zarathustra to the young king Vîstâspa! 'Give him a great number ⁴ of male children, praisers ⁵ [of God] and chiefs in assemblies, who smite and are not smitten, who smite at one stroke their enemies, who smite at one stroke their foes, ever in joy and ready to help.

7. 'Ye gods of full Glory, ye gods of full healing, let your greatness become manifest!'

8. Zarathustra addressed him, saying: 'O young king Vîstâspa! May their greatness become manifest as it is called for!

'Ye Waters, impart and give your Glory to the man who offers you a sacrifice!

'This is the boon we beg (for thee) of Ashi Vanguhi ⁶, of Râta ⁷, with eyes of love.'

9. Pârendi ⁸, of the light chariot, follows: 'Mayest thou ⁹ become manifest unto him, the young king Vîstâspa!

'May plenty dwell in this house, standing upon high columns and rich in food ¹⁰! Thou wilt never

---

¹ For §§ 6–7, cf. Mâh Nyâyis, 10–11.
² The prayer is addressed to Waters.
³ Hvâthrô-nahîm: âsânîh lahmâk.
⁴ Paourvatâtem: kebad farzand.
⁵ Stâhyanãm: kebad stâyîtâr.
⁶ See Yt. XVI.   ⁷ See Vend. Introd. IV, 30.
⁸ See p. 11, note 5.   ⁹ Pârendi.
¹⁰ Plenty will reign in thy house, if thou wilt be liberal to the priest.

offer and give bad food to a priest : for a priest must be to thee like the brightest [1] offspring of thy own blood.'

10. Zarathustra spake unto him : ' O young king Vîstâspa!

' He who supports the Law of the worshippers of Mazda, as a brother or as a friend, he who treats her friendly in any way, looks to keep off want of food from her [2].'

11. The holy Zarathustra preached that law to Frashaostra [3] and Gâmâspa : ' May ye practise holiness and thrive, O young Frashaostra (and Gâmâspa)!'

12. Thus said Ahura Mazda unto the holy Zarathustra, and thus again did Zarathustra say unto the young king Vîstâspa : ' Have no bad priests or unfriendly priests ; for bad priests or unfriendly priests will bring about much harm, and, though thou wish to sacrifice, it will be to the Amesha-Spentas as if no sacrifice had been offered [4].

' Ashem Vohû : Holiness is the best of all good . . . .

III.

13. ' When I teach thee, that thou mayest do the same to thy son [5], O Vîstâspa! receive thou well that teaching ; that will make thee rich in children and rich in milk ; rich in seed, in fat, in milk [6].

---

[1] Raêvatãm ka (not rashvatãm ka) belongs to § 9 (W.).

[2] W. has, hanairê vaêm aiwi vainat (vaêm=Sansk. vayas?).

[3] See Yt. XIII, 103. Frashaostra and Gâmâspa were brothers.

[4] Cf. Vend. XVIII, 1–13. Perhaps, 'Be not bad to the priests! Be not unfriendly to the priest! For he who is bad to the priest, he who is unfriendly to the priest . . . .'

[5] Doubtful.   [6] Cf. Vend. XXI, 6–7.

14. 'Thus do we announce unto thee, Ahura Mazda, and Sraosha, and Ashi, and the Law of the worshippers of Mazda, with the whole of all her hymns, with the whole of all her deeds, with the whole of her performances; the Law of Mazda, who obtains her wishes, who makes the world grow, who listens to the songs and rejoices the faithful man at his wish; who protects the faithful man, who maintains the faithful man;

15. 'From whom come the knowledge of holiness and the increase in holiness of the world of the holy Principle, and without whom[1] no faithful man[2] can know holiness.

'To thee[3] come every Hâvanan, every Âtare-vakhsha, every Frabaretar, every Âberet, every Âsnâtar, every Rathwiskar, every Sraoshâ-varez[4];

16. 'Every priest, every warrior, every husbandman; every master of a house, every lord of a borough, every lord of a town, every lord of a province;

17. 'Every youth of good thoughts, good words, good deeds, and good religion; every youth who speaks the right words; every one who performs the next-of-kin marriage[5]; every itinerant priest; every mistress of a house; every wandering priest, obedient to the Law.

18. 'To thee come all the performers[6] (of holiness), all the masters of holiness, who, to the

---

[1] Doubtful.

[2] Saoshyantem. W. has srashyantem.   [3] To the Law.

[4] The seven priests engaged in the sacrifice (Vendîdâd, p. 64, note 1).

[5] The hvaêtvôdatha (Vend. Introd. p. xlv, note 7; see West, Pahlavi Texts, II, 389 seq.).

[6] Thâtus: kâr kartâr (Pahl.).

number of three and thirty [1], stand next to Hâvani, being masters of holiness.

19. 'May they be fully protected [2] in thee, O young king Vîstâspa! While thou smitest thy adversaries, thy foes, those who hate thee, a hundred times a hundred for a hundred [3], a thousand times a thousand for a thousand, ten thousand times ten thousand for ten thousand, myriads of myriads for a myriad.

20. 'Proclaim thou that word, as we did proclaim it unto thee!

'O Maker of the good world! Ahura Mazda, I worship thee with a sacrifice, I worship and forward thee with a sacrifice, I worship this creation of Ahura Mazda.'

21 [4]. The young king Vîstâspa asked Zarathustra: 'With what manner of sacrifice shall I worship, with what manner of sacrifice shall I worship and forward this creation of Ahura Mazda?'

22. Zarathustra answered: 'We will make it known unto thee, O young king Vîstâspa!

'Go towards that tree that is beautiful, high-growing, and mighty amongst the high-growing trees, and say thou these words: " Hail to thee! O good, holy tree, made by Mazda! Ashem Vohû!"

23. 'Let the faithful man cut off twigs of baresma, either one, or two, or three: let him bind them and

---

[1] See Yasna I, 10 (33).

[2] Thrâtôtemô belongs to § 19 (W.).

[3] He kills a hundred times a hundred of them, while they kill a hundred of his people.

[4] For this clause and the following two, cf. Vend. XIX, 17 seq., text and notes.

tie them up according to the rites, being bound and unbound according to the rites.

'The smallest twig of Haoma, pounded according to the rules, the smallest twig prepared for sacrifice, gives royalty to the man (who does it).'

Ashem Vohû: Holiness is the best of all good . . . .

IV.

24 [1]. Zarathustra said : ' O young king Vîstâspa!

' Invoke Ahura Mazda, who is full of Glory, Ahura Mazda, and the sovereign Heaven, the boundless Time, and Vayu who works highly.

25. 'Invoke the powerful Wind, made by Mazda, and Fate.

'Repeat thou those words, that the god invoked may give thee the boon wished for; that thou, strong, and belonging to the creation of the good Spirit, mayest smite and take away the Drug and watch with full success those who hate thee; smite down thy foes, and destroy at one stroke thy adversaries, thy enemies, and those who hate thee [2].

26. ' Proclaim thou those prayers : they will cleanse thy body from deeds of lust [3], O young king Vîstâspa!

' I will worship thee, O Fire, son of Ahura Mazda, who art a valiant warrior. He falls upon the fiend Kunda [4], who is drunken without drinking, upon the men of the Drug, the slothful ones [5], the wicked Daêva-worshippers, who live in sin.

---

[1] Cf. Vend. XIX, 13.   [2] Cf. Yt. V, 53.

[3] Paourvô vasta saota : read skyaothna (cf. § 40), as in Vend. XVI, 14 (paourvô-vasna skynothna).

[4] Cf. Vend. XI, 9 and Bundahis XXVIII, 42.

[5] Cf. Vend. XIX, 41 ; better: ' on the Drugaskân ' (the sons of the Drug? see Bund. XXXI, 6).

27. 'He[1] trembles at the way[2] made by Time and open both to the wicked and to the righteous.

'They[3] tremble at the perfume of his soul[4], as a sheep does on which a wolf is falling.

28. 'Reciting the whole collection of the Staota Yêsnya[5] prayers brings one up all the way to the blessed Garô-nmâna, the palace beautifully made. That indeed is the way.

29. 'That man does not follow the way of the Law, O Zarathustra[6]! who commits the Baodhô-(varsta) crime[7] with a damsel and an old woman[8],' said Zarathustra to the young king Vîstâspa.

'Let him[9] praise the Law, O Spitama Zarathustra! and long for it and embrace the whole of the Law, as an excellent horse turns back from the wrong way and goes along the right one, smiting the many Druges[10].

30. 'Go forward with praises, go forward the way of the good Mazdean law and of all those who walk in her ways, men and women.

---

[1] The dead man.

[2] The Kinvat-bridge (Vend. XIX, 29).

[3] The fiends (Vend. XIX, 33).　　[4] The soul of the righteous.

[5] See page 152, note 1.

[6] The Pahlavi has, 'the way of Zarathustra' (lâ Zartûhstîg râs yakhsûnît).

[7] Wilful murder (Vend. p. 84, note 1).

[8] To procure miscarriage (see Vend. XV, 12–14).

[9] The sinner.

[10] 'As a horseman on the back of a good horse, when he has gone the wrong way, perceiving that he has lost his way, turns back his horse from that direction and makes him go the right way; so thou, turn back thy horse to the right way; that is to say, turn him to the way of the Law of Mazda; that is to say, receive the Law' (Pahl. Comm.).

'He who wishes to seize the heavenly reward[1], will seize it by giving gifts to him who holds up (the Law) to us[2] in this world here below[3] ....

31. 'Let him[4] give (the Law) to him who is unfriendly to her, that he may become friendly.

'Wash thy hands with water, not with gômêz[5], and let thy son, who will be born of thy wife[6], do the same.

'Thus thy thought will be powerful to smite him[7], who is not so[8]; thy speech will be powerful to smite him, who is not so; thy deed will be powerful to smite him.

32. '"Hear me! Forgive me[9]!"—We, the Amesha-Spentas, will come and show thee, O Zarathustra! the way to that world[10], to long glory in the spiritual world, to long happiness of the soul in Paradise;

33. 'To bliss and Paradise, to the Garô-nmâna of Ahura Mazda, beautifully made and fully adorned,

---

[1] Bliss, eternal life.

[2] Yô nô .... nidârô anghê: lanman dîn barâ dâshtâr (Pahl.).

[3] Naêdhka vanghê paiti usta vanghô buyât; saoshyâs dîs verethraga. I cannot make anything of these words, nor reconcile them with the Pahlavi translation: 'It is not fair when he wishes weal for his own person; that is to say, when, being satisfied himself, he does not satisfy other people and wishes comfort for himself. (Make the Law of Mazda current, till the time when) the victorious Sôshyôsh will make it current.' The last three Zend words appear to be abridged from a longer passage.

[4] The faithful man.

[5] This is an allusion to the Bareshnûm purification (Vend. VIII, 39). The unclean man washes himself with gômêz first and with water last.

[6] Doubtful.   [7] The sinner.   [8] Friendly to the Law.

[9] He recites the prayer Sraotâ mê, merezdâta mê (Yasna XXXIII, 11).   [10] The world above.

when his soul goes out of his body through the will
of fate, when I, Ahura Mazda, when I, Ahura
Mazda, gently show him his way as he asks for it.

'Ashem Vohû: Holiness is the best of all good . . . .

V.

34. 'They [1] will impart to thee full brightness and
Glory.

'They will give him [2] quick [3] and swift horses,
and good sons.

'He wishes to go to the Law, the young king
Vîstâspa.'

Zarathustra said: 'Let him who is unfriendly to
her become a follower of the Law of Mazda, such
as we proclaim it.

35. 'Proclaim thou ever (unto the poor): "Ever
mayest thou wait here for the refuse that is brought
unto thee, brought by those who have profusion of
wealth [4]!" Thus the Drug will not fall upon thee
and throw thee away; thou wilt wield kingly power
there [5].

36. 'The Law of Mazda will not deliver thee unto
pain [6]. Thou art entreated (for charity) by the
whole of the living world, and she [7] is ever standing
at thy door in the person of thy brethren in the
faith : beggars are ever standing at the door of the
stranger, amongst those who beg for bread.

---

[1] The Amesha-Spentas (see § 46).
[2] To Vîstâspa.   [3] Hathwadhka: Pahl. tîzki.
[4] Cf. Vend. III, 29.
[5] If he practises charity he will be a king even in Garôthmân.
[6] Aspahê, from a-spa (no comfort, anâsânîh tangîh, Pahl.
Comm.).
[7] The Law.

[23]   Z

'Ever will that bread be burning coal upon thy head [1].

'The good, holy Râta [2], made by Mazda, goes and nurses thy bright offspring [3].'

37. Zarathustra addressed Vîstâspa, saying: "O young king Vîstâspa! The Law of Mazda, O my son! will give thy offspring the victorious strength that destroys the fiends.

'Let no thought of Angra Mainyu ever infect thee, so that thou shouldst indulge in evil lusts, make derision and idolatry, and shut (to the poor) the door of thy house [4].

38 [5]. 'Âtar thus blesses the man who brings incense to him, being pleased with him and not angry, and fed as he required: " May herds of oxen grow for thee, and increase of sons! May fate and its decrees bring thee the boons thou wishest for! Therefore do thou invoke and praise (me) excellently in this glorious world! That I may have unceasing food, full of the glory of Mazda [6] and with which I am well pleased."

39. 'O Mazda! take for thyself the words of our praise : of these words I speak and speak again, the strength and victorious vigour, the power of health and healing, the fulness, increase, and growth.

'Bring it together with the words of hymns up to the Garô-nmâna of Ahura Mazda. He will [7] first

---

[1] Hvarishnî dâgh pun rôismanî lak yahvûnât (Pahl. Comm.).
[2] Charity.
[3] If thou art charitable, thy children will thrive.
[4] See Yt. XXII, 13.   [5] Cf. Vend. XVIII, 27.
[6] *Hv*arnamazd*au* (W.).
[7] He who will pronounce all prayers and hymns: the full formula is found in the Âbân Nyâyis, § 8.

enter there.   Therefore do thou pronounce these prayers.

'Ashem Vohû: Holiness is the best of all good . . . .

VI.

40. 'Converse ye with the Amesha-Spe*n*tas,' said Zarathu*s*tra unto the young king Vîstâspa, 'and with the devout Sraosha, and Nairyô-sangha, the tall-formed, and Âtar, the son of Ahura Mazda, and the well-desired kingly Glory.

41. 'Men with lustful deeds address the body[1]; but thou, all the night long, address the heavenly Wisdom[2]; but thou, all night long, call for the Wisdom that will keep thee awake.

'Three times a day raise thyself up and go to take care of the beneficent cattle.

42. 'Of these men may the lordship[3] belong to the wisest of all beings, O Zarathu*s*tra! May their lord belong to the wisest, O Zarathu*s*tra! Let him show them the way of holiness, let him show them at once the way thereto, which the Law of the worshippers of Mazda enters victoriously. Thus the soul of man, in the joy of perfect holiness, walks over the bridge, known afar, the powerful *K*inva*t*-bridge[4], the well-kept, and kept by virtue.

43. 'How the worlds were arranged was said to thee first, O Zarathu*s*tra! Zarathu*s*tra said it again to the young king Vîstâspa; therefore do thou[5] praise him[6] who keeps and maintains the moon and the sun.

---

[1] Cf. § 26.   [2] Cf. Vend. IV, 45; XVIII, 6.
[3] The supervision and care.   [4] See § 27.
[5] Thou Vîstâspa.   [6] Ahura Mazda.

' He who has little friendship for the Law, I have placed him down below to suffer.'

44. Thus said Angra Mainyu, he who has no Glory in him, who is full of death : ' This is an unbeliever, let us throw him down below; this is a liar, or a traitor to his relatives, and like a mad dog who wounds cattle and men ; but the dog who inflicts wounds pays for it as for wilful murder [1].

' The first time he shall smite a faithful man, the first time he shall wound a faithful man, he shall pay for it as for wilful murder.

' Ashem Vohû: Holiness is the best of all good . . . .

VII.

45. ' Mayest thou receive [2], O holy young king Vi*s*tâspa ! (a house) with a hundred . . . . [3], ten thousand large windows, ten thousand small windows, all the year long [4], O holy Vi*s*tâspa ! never growing old, never dying, never decaying, never rotting, giving plenty of meat, plenty of food, plenty of clothes to the other worshippers of Mazda.

46. ' May all boons be bestowed upon thee, as I proclaim it unto thee ! May the Amesha-Spe*n*tas impart to thee their brightness and glory and plenty [5]! May they give him quick and swift horses and good sons, strong, great in all things, powerful to sing the hymns.

---

[1] See Vend. XIII, 31.

[2] In Paradise ; see Vend XVIII, 28, text and note.

[3] Satayâre: that stands a hundred years (?). The Vend. XVIII, 28 has 'with a hundred columns.'

[4] Uninjured by the changes of temperature.

[5] Cf. § 34.

47. 'He wields his power according to the wish of Ahura Mazda, the Good Spirit, and for the destruction of the Evil Spirit, whichever of two men goes quicker to perform a sacrifice (to Ahura); but if he chooses to perform the sacrifice and prayer to us not in the right way, he does not wield the right power, he will not reign [1].

48. 'He will receive bad treatment in the next world, though he has been the sovereign of a country, with good horses to ride and good chariots to drive. Give royalty to that man, O Zarathustra! who gives royalty unto thee with good will [2].

49 [3]. 'Thou shalt keep away the evil by this holy spell: "Of thee [O child!] I will cleanse the birth and growth; of thee [O woman!] I will make the body and the strength pure; I make thee a woman rich in children and rich in milk; a woman rich in seed, in milk, and in offspring. For thee I shall make springs run and flow towards the pastures that will give food to the child."

50. 'Do not deliver me [4] into the hands of the fiend [5]; if the fiend take hold of me, then fever with loss of all joy will dry up the milk of the good Spenta-Ârmaiti [6]. The fiend is powerful to distress, and to dry up the milk of the woman who indulges in lust and of all females.

51. 'The perfume of fire, pleasant to the Maker,

---

[1] In Paradise (Pahl. Comm.).
[2] Doubtful.   [3] Cf. Vend. XXI, 6–7.
[4] The Law.
[5] That is to say, let not impiety prevail.
[6] If impiety prevails, the earth will grow barren (cf. Vend. XVIII, 64).

Ahura Mazda, takes them [1] away from afar; . . . . [2];
and all those that harm the creation of the Good
Spirit are destroyed [3];

52. 'Whom Mithra, and Rashnu Razi*s*ta, and the
Law of the worshippers of Mazda wish to be taken far
away, longing for a man who is eager to perform and
does perform the ceremonies he has been taught; . . . [4]

'Ashem Vohû: Holiness is the best of all good . . . .

VIII[5].

53. 'The words of the Vahi*s*tôi*s*ti [6] Gâtha are to
be sung: "Happy is he, O holy Vî*s*tâspa! happy the
man, whoever he be, to whom Ahura Mazda gives
the full accomplishment of his wishes."

'Where does his soul abide on that night [7]?'

54. Ahura Mazda answered: 'O my son, Frashao-
*s*tra! It takes its seat near the head, singing the
U*s*tavaiti Gâtha and proclaiming happiness: "Happy
is he, happy the man whoever he be!"

'On the first night, his soul sits in Good Words [8];

---

[1] The demons (see Vend. VIII, 80).

[2] Nôi*t* ta*t* paiti vohu manô katha sîsraya aya*k*a. The
Pahlavi Commentary has: 'That is to say, good will happen to
thee through the good will of Âtar (fire).'

[3] Te *k*inashanya (W.;—read tae*k*a nashanya?); âigh harvaspin
bêshîtârân min spînâk mînôi dâmân lvît apêtâk avîn yahvûnît
(Pahl. Comm.).

[4] Yatha ya*t* tê fravao*k*âmi (fravao*k*âma, W.) puthrô bere-
thyâ*t* sairimananãm (sairi mananãm, W.) bakhedhrâi (translated as hakhedhrâi: dôstîh, friendship).

[5] This chapter is borrowed, though slightly altered, from Yt. XXII.

[6] Read u*s*tavaiti (? cf. § 54 and Yt. XXII, 2): the Vahi*s*tôi*s*ti
Gâtha is the fifth and last Gâtha.

[7] On the night of his departing.

[8] Not in the Good-Word Paradise, to which he will go later

on the second night, it sits in Good Deeds; on the third night, it goes along the ways (to Garô-nmâna).

55. 'At the end of the third night, O my son, Frashaostra! when the dawn appears, it seems to the soul of the faithful one as if it were brought amidst plants [and scents : it seems as if a wind were blowing from the region of the south, from the regions of the south]¹, a sweet-scented wind, sweeter-scented than any other wind in the world, and it seems to his soul as if he were inhaling that wind with the nose, and it asks, saying : "Whence does that wind blow, the sweetest-scented wind I ever inhaled with my nose ?"

56. 'And it seems to him as if his own conscience were advancing to him in that wind, in the shape of a maiden fair, bright, white-armed, strong, tall-formed, high-standing, thick-breasted, beautiful of body, noble, of a glorious seed, of the size of a maid in her fifteenth year, as fair as the fairest things in the world.

57. 'And the soul of the faithful one addressed her, asking : "What maid art thou, who art the fairest maid I have ever seen ?"

58. 'And she, being his own conscience, answers him : " O thou youth, of good thoughts, good words, and good deeds, of good religion! I am thy own conscience.

'"Everybody did love thee for that greatness, goodness, fairness, sweet-scentedness, victorious strength, and freedom from sorrow, in which thou

---

(§ 61), but in the thought and delightful remembrance of his good words (cf. Yt. XXII, 2).

¹ Supplied from Yt. XXII, 7.

dost appear to me; [and so thou, O youth of good thoughts, good words, and good deeds, of good religion! didst love me for that greatness, goodness, fairness, sweet-scentedness, victorious strength, and freedom from sorrow, in which I appear to thee.

59. '"When thou wouldst see a man[1]] making derision and deeds of idolatry, or rejecting (the poor) and shutting (his door), then, thou wouldst sit, singing the Gâthas, and worshipping the good waters, and Âtar, the son of Ahura Mazda, and rejoicing the faithful that would come from near or from afar.

60. '"I was lovely, and thou madest me still lovelier; I was fair, and thou madest me still fairer; I was desirable, and thou madest me still more desirable; I was sitting in a forward place, and thou madest me sit in the foremost place, through this good thought, through this good speech, through this good deed of thine; and so henceforth men worship me for my having long sacrificed unto and conversed with Ahura Mazda."

61. 'The first step that the soul of the faithful man made, placed him in the Good-Thought Paradise; the second step that the soul of the faithful man made, placed him in the Good-Word Paradise; the third step that the soul of the faithful man made, placed him in the Good-Deed Paradise; the fourth step that the soul of the faithful man made, placed him in the Endless Light.

62. 'Then one of the faithful, who had departed before him, asked, saying: "How didst thou depart this life, thou holy man? How didst thou come,

---

[1] From Yt. XXII, 12–13.

thou holy man! from the abodes full of cattle and full of the wishes and enjoyments of love? from the material world into the world of the spirit? from the decaying world into the undecaying one? How long did thy felicity last?"'

63. And Ahura Mazda answered: 'Ask him not what thou askest him, who has just gone the dreary way, full of fear and distress, when the body and the soul part from one another.

64. '[Let him eat] of the food brought to him, of the oil of Zaremaya : this is the food for the youth of good thoughts, of good words, of good deeds, of good religion, after he has departed this life; this is the food for the holy woman, rich in good thoughts, good words, and good deeds, well-principled, and obedient to her husband, after she has departed this life.'

65. Spitama Zarathustra said to the young king Vîstâspa : 'To what land shall I turn, O Ahura Mazda? To whom shall I go with praying [1]?'

Ashem Vohû : Holiness is the best of all good . . . .

---

[1] This clause, taken from Yt. XXII, 20, shows that the second part of Yt. XXII (§§ 19–36), describing the fate of the wicked, should be inserted here.

NYÂYIS.

NYÂYIS.

A Nyâyis is properly a begging prayer, as opposed to Sitâyis, a prayer of praise. It is a term particularly applied to five prayers addressed to the Sun, to Mithra, to the Moon, to Waters, and to Fire. Every layman over eight years old is bound to recite the Nyâyis: he recites it standing and girded with his Kôstî.

The Sun Nyâyis is recited three times a day, at the rising of the sun (Gâh Hâvan), at noon (Gâh Rapitvin), and at three o'clock in the afternoon (Gâh Uzîren). The Mithra Nyâyis is recited with the Sun Nyâyis, as Mithra follows the sun in its course (see Yt. X, 13).

The Moon Nyâyis is recited three times a month: first, at the time when it begins to be seen; second, when it is at the full; third, when it is on the wane.

The Waters Nyâyis and the Fire Nyâyis are recited every day, when one finds oneself in the proximity of those elements. The Fire Nyâyis is recited with the Penôm on (see Vend. p. 168, 7).

The first four Nyâyis must be recited especially on the days over which the Izads invoked preside; that is to say, on the Khôrshêd, Mihir, Mâh, and Âbân days (the eleventh, sixteenth, twelfth, and tenth days of the month)[1].

I. KHÔRSHÊD NYÂYIS.

1. [Hail unto the Sun, the swift-horsed! May Ahura Mazda be rejoiced[2]!]

---

[1] Anquetil, Zend-Avesta II, pp. 6, 22, 565–566.
[2] This clause is wanting in most manuscripts.

Hail unto thee, O Ahura Mazda, in the threefold way [1]! [Hail unto thee] before all other creatures! Hail unto you, O Amesha-Spentas, who are all of you of one accord with the Sun!

May this prayer come unto Ahura Mazda! May it come unto the Amesha-Spentas! May it come unto the Fravashis of the holy Ones! May it come unto the Sovereign Vayu of the long Period [2]!

2. [Hail unto the Sun, the swift-horsed!]

May Ahura Mazda be rejoiced! May Angra Mainyu be destroyed! by those who do truly what is the foremost wish (of God).

I recite the 'Praise of Holiness [3].'

3. I praise well-thought, well-spoken, and well-done thoughts, words, and deeds. I embrace all good thoughts, good words, and good deeds; I reject all evil thoughts, evil words, and evil deeds [4].

4. I give sacrifice and prayer unto you, O Amesha-Spentas! even with the fulness of my thoughts, of my words, of my deeds, and of my heart: I give unto you even my own life.

I recite the 'Praise of Holiness [3]:'

'Ashem Vohû: Holiness is the best of all good. Well is it for it, well is it for that holiness which is perfection of holiness [4]!'

5 [5]. Hail to Ahura Mazda!

Hail to the Amesha-Spentas!

Hail to Mithra, the lord of wide pastures!

Hail to the Sun, the swift-horsed!

Hail to the two eyes of Ahura Mazda!

Hail to the Bull!

Hail to Gaya [6]!

---

[1] In thought, speech, and deed (Pers. and Sansk. transl.).

[2] Vayu, as being the same with Fate (Vend. Introd. IV, 17), became identified with Time.

[3] The Ashem Vohû.   [4] See p. 22.

[5] § 5 = Yasna LXVIII (22–23 [LXVII, 58–67]).

[6] Gaya Maretan, the first man.

Hail t. the Fravashi of the holy Spitama Zarathustra!

Hail to the whole of the holy creation that was,
is, or will be!

May I grow in health of body through Vohu-Manô,
Khshathra, and Asha, and come to that luminous
space, to that highest of all high things [1], when the
world, O Spenta Mainyu! has come to an end!

Ashem Vohû: Holiness is the best of all good . . . .

6. We sacrifice unto the bright, undying, shining,
swift-horsed Sun.

We sacrifice unto Mithra, the lord of wide pastures, who is truth-speaking, a chief in assemblies,
with a thousand ears, well-shapen, with ten thousand
eyes, high, with full knowledge, strong, sleepless,
and ever awake [2].

7. We sacrifice unto Mithra, the lord of all countries, whom Ahura Mazda made the most glorious
of all the gods in the world unseen [3].

So may Mithra and Ahura, the two great gods,
come to us for help!

We sacrifice unto the bright, undying, shining,
swift-horsed Sun.

8. We sacrifice unto Tistrya, whose sight is
sound [4].

We sacrifice unto Tistrya; we sacrifice unto the
rains of Tistrya [5].

We sacrifice unto Tistrya, bright and glorious.

We sacrifice unto the star Vanant [6], made by
Mazda.

---

[1] The sun: 'May my soul arrive at the sun-region!' (Pahl. transl.)
[2] Yt. X, 7.   [3] In heaven.   [4] See Yt. VIII, 12, note 7.
[5] See Yt. VIII, 12, note 2.   [6] See Yt. XX.

We sacrifice unto Ti*s*trya, the bright a⌐ glorious star.

We sacrifice unto the sovereign sky.

We sacrifice unto the boundless Time.

We sacrifice unto the sovereign Time of the long Period.

We sacrifice unto the beneficent, well-doing Wind.

We sacrifice unto the most upright *K*ista[1], made by Mazda and holy.

We sacrifice unto the good Law of the worshippers of Mazda.

We sacrifice unto the way of content[2].

We sacrifice unto the golden instrument[3].

We sacrifice unto Mount Saoka*n*ta, made by Mazda[3].

9. We sacrifice unto all the holy gods of the world unseen.

We sacrifice unto all the holy gods of the material world.

We sacrifice unto our own soul.

We sacrifice unto our own Fravashi.

We sacrifice unto the good, strong, beneficent Fravashis of the holy Ones.

We sacrifice unto the bright, undying, shining, swift-horsed Sun.

10. I confess myself a worshipper of Mazda, a follower of Zarathu*s*tra . . . .

---

[1] See Yt. XVI.   [2] Or, of pleasure.

[3] 'On Mount Saoka*n*ta there is a golden tube coming from the root of the earth; the water that is on the surface of the earth goes up through the hole of that tube to the heavens, and being driven by the wind, spreads everywhere, and thus the dew is produced' (Sansk. transl.).

Unto the bright, undying, shining, swift-horsed Sun;

Be propitiation, with sacrifice, prayer, propitiation, and glorification . . . .[1]

Ashem Vohû: Holiness is the best of all good . . . .

[We sacrifice] unto the Ahurian waters[2], the waters of Ahura, with excellent libations, with finest libations, with libations piously strained[3].

Ashem Vohû: Holiness is the best of all good . . . .

[Give] unto that man brightness and glory, give him health of body, ... give him the bright, all-happy, blissful abode of the holy Ones.

II. MIHIR NYÂYIS.

1[4]. Hail unto thee, O Ahura Mazda, in the threefold way! [Hail unto thee] before all other creatures!

Hail unto you, O Amesha-Spentas, who are all of you of one accord with the Sun!

May this prayer come unto Ahura Mazda! May it come unto the Amesha-Spentas! May it come unto the Fravashis of the holy Ones! May it come unto the sovereign Vayu of the long Period!

2. May Ahura Mazda be rejoiced! . . . .

3. I praise well-thought, well-spoken, and well-done thoughts, words, and deeds . . . .

4. I give sacrifice and prayer unto you, O Amesha-Spentas! . . . .

5. Hail to Ahura Mazda! . . . .

May I grow in health of body through Vohu-Manô, Khshathra, and Asha, and come to that luminous space, to that highest of all high things, when the world, O Spenta Mainyu, has come to an end!

6[5]. We sacrifice unto Mi hra, the lord of wide pastures, who is truth-speaking, a chief in assemblies, with a thousand ears, well-shapen, with ten thousand

---

[1] The whole of the Khôrshêd Yast is inserted here.

[2] Rivers considered as Ahura's wives (cf. Ormazd et Ahriman, § 32).

[3] From Yasna LXVIII, 10 (LXVII, 30); cf. p. 34.

[4] §§ 1–5=Khôrshêd Nyâyis, §§ 1–5.

[5] §§ 6–7=Khôrshêd Nyâyis, §§ 6–7.

eyes, high, with full knowledge, strong, sleepless, and ever awake.

7. We sacrifice unto Mithra, the lord of all countries, whom Ahura Mazda made the most glorious of all the heavenly gods.

So may Mithra and Ahura, the two great gods, come to us for help!

We sacrifice unto the undying, shining, swift-horsed Sun.

8 [1]. We sacrifice unto Tistrya, whose sight is sound . . . .

9. We sacrifice unto all the holy gods of the world unseen . . . .

10 [2]. I confess myself a worshipper of Mazda, a follower of Zarathustra . . . .

11 [3]. We sacrifice unto Mithra, the lord of wide pastures, who is truth-speaking, a chief in assemblies, with a thousand ears, well-shapen, with a thousand eyes, high, with full knowledge, strong, sleepless, and ever awake.

We sacrifice unto the Mithra around countries;
We sacrifice unto the Mithra within countries;
We sacrifice unto the Mithra in this country;
We sacrifice unto the Mithra above countries;
We sacrifice unto the Mithra under countries;
We sacrifice unto the Mithra before countries;
We sacrifice unto the Mithra behind countries.

12. We sacrifice unto Mithra and Ahura, the two great, imperishable, holy gods; and unto the stars, and the moon, and the sun, with the trees that yield baresma. We sacrifice unto Mithra, the lord of all countries.

13 [4]. For his brightness and glory, I will offer unto him a sacrifice worth being heard . . . .

---

[1] §§ 8–9 = Khôrshê*d* Nyâyis, §§ 8–9.   [2] Yt. X, o.
[3] §§ 11–12 = Yt. X, 144–145.   [4] §§ 13–15 = Yt. X, 4–6.

We offer up libations unto Mithra . . . .

14. May he come to us for help! May he come to us for ease! . . . .

15. I will offer up libations unto him, the strong Yazata, the powerful Mithra . . . .

Yênhê hâtãm: All those beings of whom Ahura Mazda . . . .

16[1]. Yathâ ahû vairyô: The will of the Lord is the law of holiness . . . .

I bless the sacrifice and prayer, and the strength and vigour of Mithra . . . .

Ashem Vohû: Holiness is the best of all good . . . .

[Give] unto that man brightness and glory, ... give him the bright, all-happy, blissful abode of the holy Ones.

III. MÂH NYÂYIS.

1 [2]. Hail to Ahura Mazda! Hail to the Amesha-Spentas! Hail to the Moon that keeps in it the seed of the Bull! Hail to thee when we look at thee! Hail to thee when thou lookest at us!

2 [3]. Unto the Moon that keeps in it the seed of the Bull; unto the only-created Bull and unto the Bull of many species;

Be propitiation . . . .

3. Hail to Ahura Mazda! . . . .

4. How does the moon wax? How does the moon wane? . . . .

5. We sacrifice unto the Moon that keeps in it the seed of the Bull . . . .

6. And when the light of the moon waxes warmer . . . .

7. I will sacrifice unto the Moon . . . .

8. For its brightness and glory . . . .

9. Yathâ ahû vairyô: The will of the Lord is the law of holiness . . . .

10 [4]. Give us strength and victory! Give us welfare in cattle and in bread! Give us a great number of male children, praisers [of God] and chiefs in assemblies, who smite and are not smitten, who smite at one stroke their enemies, who smite at one stroke their foes, ever in joy and ready to help.

---

[1] Yt. X, 146. [2] § 1 = Mâh Yast, § 1. [3] §§ 2–9 = Mâh Yast.
[4] §§ 10–11; cf. Yt. XXIV, 6–8.

11. Ye gods of full Glory, ye gods of full healing, let your greatness become manifest! let your assistance become manifest as soon as you are called for! and ye, Waters, manifest your Glory, and impart it to the man who offers you a sacrifice.

Ashem Vohû: Holiness is the best of all good . . . .
[Give] unto that man brightness and glory, ... give him the bright, all-happy, blissful abode of the holy Ones.

IV. ÂBÂN NYÂYI*S*.

1. May Ahura Mazda be rejoiced! . . . .
Unto the good Waters, made by Mazda; unto the holy water-spring ARDVI ANÂHITA; unto all waters, made by Mazda; unto all plants, made by Mazda,
Be propitiation[1] . . . .

2[2]. Ahura Mazda spake unto Spitama Zarathu*s*tra, saying: 'Offer up a sacrifice, O Spitama Zarathu*s*tra! unto this spring of mine, Ardvi Sûra Anâhita . . . .

3. 'Who makes the seed of all males pure, who makes the womb of all females pure for bringing forth . . . .

4. 'The large river, known afar, that is as large as the whole of the waters that run along the earth . . . .

5. 'All the shores of the sea Vouru-Kasha are boiling over, all the middle of it is boiling over, when she runs down there . . . .

6. 'From this river of mine alone flow all the waters that spread all over the seven Karshvares;

7. 'I, Ahura Mazda, brought it down with mighty vigour, for the increase of the house, of the borough, of the town, of the country[3].

8. 'He from whom she will hear the staota yêsnya[4]; he from whom she will hear the Ahuna

---

[1] As Âbân Ya*s*t, o.   [2] §§ 2–6 = Âbân Ya*s*t, §§ 1–5.
[3] Cf. Âbân Ya*s*t, § 6.   [4] See above, p. 152, note 1.

vairya[1]; he from whom she will hear the Asha-
vahista[2]; he by whom the good waters will be
made pure; with the words of the holy hymns[3], he
will enter first the Garô-nmâna of Ahura Mazda:
she will give him the boons asked for[4].

9[5]. 'For her brightness and glory, I will offer her
a sacrifice worth being heard; I will offer her a
sacrifice well-performed. Thus mayest thou advise
us when thou art appealed to! Mayest thou be
most fully worshipped.

'We sacrifice unto the holy Ardvi Sûra Anâhita with libations.
We sacrifice unto Ardvi Sûra Anâhita, the holy and master of holiness, with the Haoma and meat, with the baresma, with the
wisdom of the tongue, with the holy spells, with the words, with
the deeds, with the libations, and with the rightly-spoken words.

'Yênhê hâtăm: All those beings of whom Ahura Mazda . . . .

10. 'Yathâ ahû vairyô: The will of the Lord is the law of
holiness . . . .

'I bless the sacrifice and prayer, and the strength and vigour of
the holy water-spring Anâhita.

'[Give] unto that man brightness and glory, ... give him the
bright, all-happy, blissful abode of the holy Ones.'

V. ÂTAS NYÂYIS.

1[6]. Take me out[7], O Ahura! give me perfect piety and
strength . . . .

4[8]. May Ahura Mazda be rejoiced! . . . .

---

[1] The Yathâ ahû vairyô prayer.
[2] The Ashem Vohû prayer.
[3] Cf. Yt. XXII, 2, and Yt. XXIV, 39.
[4] Cf. Âbân Yast, §§ 19, 23, 27, 35, 39, 47, &c.
[5] Cf. Âbân Yast, § 9.
[6] §§ 1–3 = Yasna XXXIII, 12–14.
[7] 'Deliver me from Ahriman' (Pahl. Comm.).
[8] As in Ormazd Yast, o.

Hail unto thee, O Fire, son of Ahura Mazda, thou beneficent and most great Yazata!

[1] Ashem Vohû: Holiness is the best of all good . . . .
I confess myself a worshipper of Mazda . . . .
For sacrifice, prayer, propitiation, and glorification . . . .

Unto Âtar, the son of Ahura Mazda; unto thee Âtar, son of Ahura Mazda!

5 [2]. Unto Âtar, the son of Ahura Mazda; unto the Glory and the Weal, made by Mazda; unto the Glory of the Aryas, made by Mazda; unto the Glory of the Kavis, made by Mazda.

Unto Âtar, the son of Ahura Mazda; unto king Husravah; unto the lake of Husravah; unto Mount Âsnava*nt*, made by Mazda; unto Lake *K*aê*k*asta, made by Mazda; unto the Glory of the Kavis, made by Mazda.

6. Unto Âtar, the son of Ahura Mazda; unto Mount Raêva*nt*, made by Mazda; unto the Glory of the Kavis, made by Mazda.

Unto Âtar, the son of Ahura Mazda.

Unto Âtar, the beneficent, the warrior; the God who is a full source of Glory, the God who is a full source of healing.

Unto Âtar, the son of Ahura Mazda, with all Âtars; unto the God Nairyô-sangha, who dwells in the navel of kings;

Be propitiation, with sacrifice, prayer, propitiation, and glorification.
Yathâ ahû vairyô: The will of the Lord is the law of holiness . . . .

7 [3]. I bless the sacrifice and invocation, and the

---

[1] As in Ormazd Ya*s*t, o.　　[2] Cf. Sîrôzah, § 9.
[3] §§ 7–16 = Yasna LXII, 1–10 (LXI). See the Sanskrit translation in Études Iraniennes, II.

good offering, the beneficent offering, the offering of assistance offered unto thee, O Âtar, son of Ahura Mazda!

Thou art worthy of sacrifice and invocation; mayest thou receive the sacrifice and the invocation in the houses of men.

Well may it be unto the man who ever worships thee with a sacrifice, holding the sacred wood in his hand, the baresma in his hand, the meat in his hand, the mortar [1] in his hand.

8. Mayest thou have the right [2] wood! Mayest thou have the right incense! Mayest thou have the right food! Mayest thou have the right fuel [3]!

Mayest thou be full-grown for protecting (this house)! Mayest thou grow excellent for protecting!

9. Mayest thou burn in this house! Mayest thou ever burn in this house! Mayest thou blaze in this house! Mayest thou increase in this house! Even for a long time, till the powerful restoration of the world, till the time of the good, powerful restoration of the world!

10. Give me, O Âtar, son of Ahura Mazda! lively welfare, lively maintenance, lively living; fulness of welfare, fulness of maintenance, fulness of life;

Knowledge, sagacity; quickness of tongue; (holiness of) soul; a good memory; and then the understanding that goes on growing and the one that is not acquired through learning [4];

---

[1] The mortar for pounding the Haoma.

[2] In quality and quantity.

[3] Upasayêni: what is added to keep up the fire when lighted (Pers. transl.).

[4] The gaoshô-srûta khratu and the âsna khratu (see p. 7, note 1).

And then the manly courage,

11. Firm-footed, unsleeping, (sleeping only) for a third part of the day and of the night, quick to rise up from bed, ever awake;

And a protecting, virtuous offspring, able to rule countries and assemblies of men, well growing up, good, freeing us from the pangs (of hell), endowed with a good intellect, that may increase my house, my borough, my town, my country, my empire.

12. Give me, O Âtar, son of Ahura Mazda! however unworthy I am[1], now and for ever, a seat in the bright, all-happy, blissful abode of the holy Ones.

May I obtain the good reward, a good renown[2], and long cheerfulness for my soul[3]!

13. Âtar, the son of Ahura Mazda, lifts up his voice to all those for whom he cooks their evening meal and their morning meal[4]. From all those he wishes a good offering, a beneficent offering, an offering of assistance, O Spitama!

14. Âtar looks at the hands of all those who pass by: 'What does the friend bring to his friend? What does he who comes and goes bring to him[5] who stays motionless?'

We sacrifice unto Âtar, the valiant warrior[6].

15. And if the passer-by brings him wood holily brought, or bundles of baresma holily tied up, or

---

[1] Yâ mê afrasaunghau anghat: yâ me abhût ayogyatâ (Sansk. transl.).

[2] Here.   [3] Above.

[4] Khshafnîm, sûirîm (Études Iraniennes, II, 161).

[5] Âtar.

[6] 'Bodily he is infirm (armêst, motionless); spiritually he is a warrior' (Pahl. Comm.).

twigs of Hadhânaêpata[1], then Âtar, the son of Ahura Mazda, well pleased with him and not angry, and fed as required, will thus bless him:

16. 'May herds of oxen grow for thee, and increase of sons; may thy mind be master of its vow, may thy soul be master of its vow, and mayest thou live on in the joy of the soul all the nights of thy life.'

This is the blessing which Âtar speaks unto him who brings him dry wood, well-examined by the light of the day, well-cleansed with godly intent [2].

17. Yathâ ahû vairyô: The will of the Lord is the law of holiness . . . .

I bless the sacrifice and prayer, and the strength and vigour of Âtar, the son of Ahura Mazda [3] . . . .

Ashem Vohû: Holiness is the best of all good . . . .

18 [3]. We gladden by our virtue thy mighty Fire, O Ahura! thy most quick and powerful Fire, who shows his assistance [4] to him who has ever comforted him, but delights in taking vengeance with his hands on the man who has harmed him.

---

[1] See Vend. p. 94, note 1.

[2] Cf. Vend. XVIII, 26–27.

[3] From Yasna XXXIV, 4.

[4] 'In the var nîrang' (Pahl. Comm.), that is to say, in the fire ordeal; see above, p. 170, note 3.

INDEX TO THE VENDÎDÂD,

VOLUME IV;

AND TO THE

SÎRÔZAHS, YASTS, AND NYÂYIS,

VOLUME XXIII.

INDEX TO VOLS. IV AND XXIII.

The references in small Roman numerals are to the Introduction to the
Vendîdâd; those preceded by II are to this volume; the others are
to the Vendîdâd.

TRANSLITERATION OF ORIENTAL ALPHABETS ADOPTED FOR THE TRANSLATIONS OF THE SACRED BOOKS OF THE EAST.

CONSONANTS.	MISSIONARY ALPHABET.			Sanskrit.	Zend.	Pehlevi.	Persian.	Arabic.	Hebrew.	Chinese.
	I Class.	II Class.	III Class.							
Gutturales.										
1 Tenuis	k			क					ח	k
2 „ aspirata	kh			ख					ח	kh
3 Media	g			ग					ד	
4 „ aspirata	gh			घ					ד	
5 Gutturo-labialis	q								ק	
6 Nasalis	ḥ (ng)			ङ	(ng) (N)					h, hs
7 Spiritus asper	h			ह	ʽ (hv)				ה	
8 „ lenis	ʼ								א	
9 „ asper faucalis	ʽh								ח	
10 „ lenis faucalis	ʽh								ע	
11 „ asper fricatus		ʽh								
12 „ lenis fricatus		ʽh								
Gutturales modificatae (palatales, &c.)										
13 Tenuis		k		च						k
14 „ aspirata		kh		छ						kh
15 Media		g		ज						
16 „ aspirata		gh		झ						
17 „ Nasalis		ñ		ञ						

Chinese	Hebrew	Arabic	Persian	Pehlevi	Zend	Sanskrit	I Class	II Class	III Class	CONSONANTS *(continued)*
y	·	ي	ي	۹	۹ (init.)	य	y			18 Semivocalis
·	·	·	·	·	·	·				19 Spiritus asper
·	·	·؟	·؟	؟	·؟	·		(ẏ)		20 „ lenis
ᵃ	·	·	ᵓ	ᶜ	ᵃ	·		s		21 „ asper assibilatus
·	·	·	·	·	·	·		z		22 „ lenis assibilatus
										Dentales.
t	⊏	د	د	د	ع	त	t			23 Tenuis
th	⊏	·د	·د	·	ٯٯ	त	th		TH	24 „ aspirata
·	·	·	ٮ	·	·	·	d			25 „ assibilata
·	ᴦ	ٮ	ٮ	ٮ	ٮ	त	dh			26 Media
·	ᴦ	·	·	·	·	·			DH	27 „ aspirata
·	·	·	·	·	·	·				28 „ assibilata
n	ٮ	ٮ	ٮ	ٮ	·	त	n			29 Nasalis
⌐	ٮ	ٮ	ٮ	·	·	छ	l			30 Semivocalis
·	·	·	·	·	·	छ		l	L	31 „ mollis 1
·	·	·	·	·	·	·				32 „ mollis 2
s	·ے	ٯ	(د)	ٯ	з	त	s		S	33 Spiritus asper 1
·	ם	·	(ز)	·	·	·				34 „ asper 2
z	۱	·ز	ز	·ک	ـر	·	z			35 „ lenis
ᵃ, ᵃh	ᶻ	ز	ز	·	·	·			z (ȝ)	36 „ asperrimus 1
·	·	·	·	·	·	·			z (ȝ)	37 „ asperrimus 2

Dentales modificatae (lingualos, &c.)		
38 Tenuis	t	
39 " aspirata	th	
40 Media	d	
41 " aspirata	dh	
42 Nasalis	n	
43 Semivocalis	r	r
44 " fricata	r	
45 " diacritica		
46 Spiritus asper	sh	
47 " lenis	zh	
Labialos.		
48 Tenuis	p	
49 " aspirata	ph	
50 Media	b	
51 " aspirata	bh	
52 Tenuissima	p	
53 Nasalis	m	
54 Semivocalis	w	
55 " aspirata	hw	
56 Spiritus asper	f	
57 " lenis	v	
58 Anusvâra	m	
59 Visarga	h	

VOWELS	MISSIONARY ALPHABET. I Class	II Class	III Class	Sanskrit	Zend	Pehlevi	Persian	Arabic	Hebrew	Chinese
1 Neutralis	o									ă
2 Laryngo-palatalis	ĕ									
3 ,, labialis	ŏ					) fin.				
4 Gutturalis brevis	a	(a)		अ	Ᵹ	Ᵹ init.	ا	ا	‎	a
5 ,, longa	â			आ	Ᵹ	Ᵹ	ل	ل	‎	â
6 Palatalis brevis	i	(i)		इ	⁊	ꝫ	ا	ا	‎	i
7 ,, longa	î			ई	⁊		ری	ری	‎	î
8 Dentalis brevis	ḷi									
9 ,, longa	ḹ									
10 Lingualis brevis	ṛi			ऋ						
11 ,, longa	ṝ			ॠ						
12 Labialis brevis	u	(u)		उ	⁊	ꝫ	ا	ا	‎	u
13 ,, longa	û			ऊ						
14 Gutturo-palatalis brevis	e	(e)		ए	ε(e) ξ(e)		ی	ی	‎	e
15 ,, longa	ê (ai)	(ai)		ऐ	Ᵹ ꝫ					ĕ
16 Diphthongus gutturo-palatalis	âi									âi
17 ,,	ei (ĕi)									ei, ĕi
18 ,,	oi (ŏu)									
19 Gutturo-labialis brevis	o	(o)		ओ		⁊	ی	ی	‎	o
20 ,, longa	ô (au)	(au)		औ	⁊ (au)					
21 Diphthongus gutturo-labialis	âu									âu
22 ,,	eu (ĕu)									
23 ,,	ou (ŏu)									
24 Gutturalis fracta	ä									
25 Palatalis fracta	ï